LINES *on the* LANDSCAPE
CIRCLES *from the* SKY

LINES *on the* LANDSCAPE
CIRCLES *from the* SKY

MONUMENTS OF NEOLITHIC ORKNEY

TREVOR GARNHAM

TEMPUS

First published 2004

Tempus Publishing Ltd
The Mill, Brimscombe Port
Stroud, Gloucestershire GL5 2QG
www.tempus-publishing.com

British Library Cataloguing in Publication Data.
A catalogue record for this book is available from the British Library.

ISBN 0 7524 3114 5

Typesetting and origination by Tempus Publishing.
Printed and bound in Great Britain.

CONTENTS

ACKNOWLEDGEMENTS

First of all I would like to thank Peter Kemmis Betty for his perspicacity in seeing something of value in what was a very raw first manuscript and his support in seeing it through to publication. I am extremely grateful to Caroline Wickham-Jones for her judicious comments on early drafts. Her advice has been crucial in ensuring that there are no glaringly obvious errors of archaeological fact and that the source material is up to date. I must also thank Nick Card for reading the manuscript and pointing me in the direction of several important sources and for many stimulating archaeological conversations at Snellsetter.

The visual quality of this book has been hugely improved by the photomontage work of Harry Paticas. It was astonishing to see the chambered cairn of Bigland Round return to the world as if by magic! The week we spent making the model of a Skara Brae house was not only very enjoyable but also provided important insights into how the real things might have been built. Tim Clarke and Emma Parkin of Tempus have been a great help in guiding me through the production process of the book. Thanks also to David Wilson, without whose help I would not have been able to make use of the Starry Night computer programme. I would like to take this opportunity to thank Bill Ungless, not only for helping me collect material for the model, but also for many enjoyable, stimulating and provocative conversations over many years.

I would like to thank Ann and James for making my time at Woodwick House the perfect complement to days spent out in the Orkney landscape. I am very grateful to Barbara of J.&W. Tait for always finding me a car even after they gave up car hire! Most of all I would like to thank Elsie Seatter for the many occasions that I have stayed at Melsetter House during the long period of this book's gestation. I always feel very privileged when I leave, not only for staying in such a wonderful house, but also for having been the recipient of Elsie's welcoming kindness. I am also extremely grateful to Kingston University for providing financial support for the many journeys undertaken for research. The research committee always showed considerable under-standing of why the Orkney weather made fieldwork and photography difficult, making it necessary to return yet one more time! Except where indicated, all the photographs are by the author.

I would like to thank Margy for typing up the long and messy first drafts and Tim for help with the computer and some of the graphics.

Thanks also to Lorna for her patience and help during the long days drawing this to a close.

I would like to dedicate this book to the memory of Maggie Gorn, 1963–1997.

1

INTRODUCTION:

THE IDEA OF A COSMOS AND ITS SIGNIFICANCE FOR PREHISTORY

The task of transporting livestock and other commodities across the open sea in skin boats, log boats or on rafts is formidable in itself, but what is in retrospect truly astounding is the adventurous pioneering spirit that drove these people northwards. It was not necessary in the sense that land elsewhere was scarce. Nor were they foolhardy, for they seem only to have colonised visible horizons: Orkney is easily visible from Caithness, Fair Isle from Orkney, Shetland from Fair Isle. Away to the north-west and invisible from Shetland, the Faroe Islands were to remain uninhabited for another 4,000 years.[1]

Everything we have gathered about 'primitive' peoples indicates that they saw their world as an all-enveloping cosmos, quite the opposite of our own universe. This is probably true not only for non-western cultures but also for prehistoric people. In contrast to the scientific search for a 'theory of every-thing' and explanations in terms of invisible laws of cause and effect, primitive people construct a mental picture of the world from the sum total of their own direct experience. Visible horizons were not only important for Neolithic peoples navigating the seas but also the mind. *Cosmos* is a Greek word that is not simply an earlier equivalent for what we call the universe. Containing the meanings order and ornament, it specifically refers to 'that which constitutes the sum total of experiences'. From this comes the conception of the cosmos as an all-encompassing world of things and phenomena. The essential character of this early form of cosmos bound every aspect of a people's life into recip-rocal relationships with the forces that give shape to their world. Our own Cartesian, rational world view is diametrically opposed to this, predicated on the dualities of mind and body, spirit and matter, subjective and objective.

Levi-Strauss has shown that 'primitive' thinking has its own form of logic. In his book *The Savage Mind* he describes how 'savage thought' is a system of concepts embedded in images: 'it is concrete and takes the form of a complex web of resemblances, correspondences and metaphoric relationships'.[2] Although many of his ideas are now contested, this fundamental point is confirmed by, for example, Hugh Brody's work amongst modern Inuits and other hunter-gatherers. He shows that the Inuit have no generic term for fish; rather they have a series of specific, concrete terms such as lake trout, salmon, 'arctic char, arctic char that are running upstream, arctic char that are moving down to the sea and arctic char that remain all year in the lake'.[3] Primitive people construct their system from how things appear to the eye and the experience directly rather than through a microscope, telescope or other instrument that expands our powers of observation and understanding at the same time as removing us from the immediate physicality of things.

'We need to distance ourselves from the modern world view,' says Miles Russell, 'if we are to understand prehistory'.[4] This is all very well, but how can we do this? The approach taken in this study is to explore how the idea of a cosmos – considered as a web of inter-relationships – might have impinged upon Neolithic people as they constructed their world, the archaeological remains of which are all we have to guide us. The idea of a cosmos will encourage us to set material things in as broad a context as we can, making 'possible worlds probable through the process of contextualisation', as Ian Hodder has said. Searching for the 'savage mind' in this way might take us as close as we can come to grasping the world view that formed the context for the creation of Neolithic monuments. Because Levi-Strauss' association with the larger claims of structuralism has called his work into question, Ernst Cassirer's investigation into what he called 'mythical thinking' will be outlined here and used as a corrective. Cassirer identified a distinctive form of primitive thinking from his philosophical investigation into the nature of language and this will form the basis of the method employed in this book. Neither an archaeologist nor anthropologist, Cassirer had no axe to grind about the efficacy or legitimacy of applying parallels to prehistory. Cassirer's mythical thinking gives us a fundamental structure of thought offering insights into the relationship between material things and the mind of the maker. The title of this book alludes to how processes of making material artefacts resonated with the form of two distinctive features of the visible cosmos, the sun and the moon. Lines inscribed across the landscape seem aimed at weaving nature's eternal rhythms into reciprocal relationships with Neolithic stone monuments. This study provides some evidence for such a process at work.

The suggestion that Neolithic people thought in a fundamentally different way to us is not universally accepted. Colin Renfrew, for example, is sceptical of such a view in the book *The Ancient Mind* where a number of authors explore the idea. This will be discussed in the final chapter where Cassirer's philosophical case for mythical thinking is presented. Renfrew's scepticism arises, perhaps, because he makes no distinction between the capacity of the evolved human brain and a way of thinking. The evolution of the brain's capacity to that of modern humans some 500,000 years ago does not imply that the character of thinking was, or could be, equivalent. Nor does what Steven Mithen describes in *The Prehistory of Mind* as 'the final step to a full cognitive fluidity' made by *Homo sapiens sapiens* about 100,000-200,000 years ago imply this. Mithen suggests that a significant step associated with the adoption of farming some 18,000–10,000 years ago lies in 'the propensity to develop "social relationships" with plants and animals'.[5] In itself this suggests how the first farmers differed both from their hunter–gather predecessors and also from our modern Cartesian rationalist selves. This is not to deny that they were very practical people who adopted technology to varied habitats, but simply to stress that their way of thinking about the forces at work in the world would have been very unlike our own. So much archaeological and anthropological evidence bears this out. Indeed, Renfrew does not entirely rule out the possibility of mythical thought. That the Inuit offer a drink of water to animals they have killed, or that an African tribe could believe yams move of their own accord and swell by magic, might be sufficient to allow us to accept this as a working hypothesis.[6] Proceeding on this assumption offers the potential for a fresh perspective on how we might understand aspects of the Neolithic.

Of course, any conception of the world or cosmos is not found; it is a particular world view that has been constructed. This raises two key issues that need to be addressed if we wish to apply this notion to the Neolithic. Firstly, how is it possible to reconstruct something of their world view when no evidence survives of how Neolithic people thought about the world except the material remains; and secondly, how to constrain to manageable proportions the idea of a cosmos which, by definition, is all–encompassing? Acknowledging that the hypothesis of a distinctive primitive way of thinking is contentious when applied to archaeology, it is, therefore, proposed to focus this study on the buildings of the Neolithic and to concentrate on a particular culture in a circumscribed region. Examining how the range of structures developed from house to stone circle, for example, not only encourages us to see what relationships might exist between different types of buildings, but also acknowledges the specific character of a cosmos. Emphasising the inter-relationships between buildings, between building and artefact and between building and landscape rather than examining them as separated categories is to see them from within something like the perception of a cosmos. This approach chimes with the principal aspect of savage thought which operates by seeing resemblances or contrasts.

An additional advantage of concentrating on built structures is that archaeological remains can thereby be considered as architecture. This allows techniques of analysis developed for architecture and architectural history to be applied which might offer insights into the organisation of form and space as well as meaning in the use of material. Architectural design is much concerned with embodying meaning in form. Hence meaning can be read from the form, which is the purpose of architectural history. As a branch of history it normally has access to documents – both written and drawn – which provide the basis for interpretation. But not always. We have no written account of why the Greek Doric temple was given its particular form, for example, but we can deduce significant aspects of its meaning from what remains. It develops and elaborates the *megaron* form of an early Greek house; unlike the house it has no hearth but a statue of the god or goddess; its details – triglyphs and metopes – are stone representations of timber construction techniques. In sum or outline then, the Doric temple is a house for the god or goddess appropriately transmuted from timber to stone. Of course, we have access to a wide range of Greek writings which help form a context for interpreting the Doric temple, something we do not have for megalithic monuments.

The first architecture seems to have been aimed at making visible the relationship between the patterns of the everyday, human-life world and the forces, earthly and transcendent, that had bearing upon it. In his pioneering study of the origins of architecture, William Lethaby wrote of the interrelationship between microcosm and macrocosm that lies at the heart of the idea of sacred architecture. Temple architecture he described as:

> a local reduplication of the ... World Temple itself – a sort of model to scale, its forms governed by the science of the time, it was a heaven, an observatory and an almanac. Its foundation was a sacred ceremony, the time carefully chosen by augury, and its relation to the heavens defined by observation. Its place was exactly below the celestial prototype; like that it was sacred, like that it was strong.[7]

Lethaby's image is a striking one and worth holding onto despite the fact that he was writing in 1891 at the very outset of ethnography – he relied heavily upon Frazer, Tylor, Müller and Lang – since when our understanding of early cultures has expanded enormously. Lethaby was making a generalised statement about the monumental sacred architecture of what we now understand to be relatively developed traditions, the temples of Sumeria and the lands bordering the eastern Mediterranean. Gathered together these have been taken as the basis of our western tradition but are in fact somewhat removed from the first architecture. Since the advent of radiocarbon dating, we know that the burial tombs which first appeared along the Atlantic sea façade are just as old, and the stone circles of Britain only a little younger. The tombs and stone circles of our Neolithic ancestors, then, might be considered as our own, or indeed, as the very first architecture. Perhaps because these have been generally considered as archaeological and prehistoric they have rarely been considered in architectural terms.

Architecture might be thought of most uniquely as about making space and, through this medium, particular relationships – most obviously that between inside and outside. The concept of space to be developed here is opposed to the Cartesian system where space is considered as mere extension. Our modern, objective form of measurement consists essentially of putting dimensions to an otherwise undifferentiated field of space. The fundamental measure of space, however, is what is commonly referred to as the 'spatiality' of the body – most simply thought of as things being closer to or further away from us, smaller or larger than us, above or below us etc. As Julian Thomas writes in his book outlining the case for an 'interpretive' archaeology, 'our perception of space relies upon a more fundamental ability to experience relationality'.[8] Moreover, dealing with built structures in this way accords with the idea of an inter-related cosmos, for as we will see, a widespread concept drawn from anthropological studies is that of the body – house – cosmos. In some way, building mediates between humans and the world; buildings embody thought and help people think about their world. The evidence gathered from archaeology will be examined from this point of view, set within an architectural framework and considered from the conviction that the horizon of primitive thought was fundamentally set by myth or religion.

It is generally accepted that the first evidence of mankind's distinctive relationship with the world, beyond the brute facts of his existence evidenced in tools, bones from food, and shelter, is his concern for the remains of the dead. So much surviving evidence has come from burial sites that the tomb has dominated discussion of Neolithic building. Little evidence has survived of the first houses, and stone circles have fallen prey to all kinds of irrational explanations such that, until recently, archaeologists have tended to steer clear of these enigmatic remains. But if we are to accept the hypothesis of a prehistoric cosmos being constructed from a complex web of relationships between things (the world around, artefacts, houses, tombs and ceremonial monuments), then each of these categories of building, and the relationship between them, needs to be considered. The next three chapters will take these in sequence beginning with the house for, despite what has been written above, even the merest shelter has been shown by anthropologists to embody its builder's ideas about the cosmos. Throughout this book any correspondences or patterns of relationship detected between the different forms of construction and between them and artefacts will be considered, but a detailed discussion of the interlocked set will be reserved for the concluding chapter.

The role of artefacts in the context of this form of analysis must not be underestimated. For we know that the primitive mind clings tenaciously to what it has grasped, and all traditional cultures reiterate the same actions and everyday practice. Nevertheless, material culture did slowly evolve and expand. By looking at how one thing might resemble another despite being assigned to a very different category of use, we can detect processes of transformation that offer suggestions of what things might have meant from within the world view of a cosmos. Comparing the house with the chambered cairn, and going on to compare these with the emergence of the stone circle might help us understand better the things themselves as well as processes of transformation or invention. Here, considering the basket and the boat may be as important as the building.

There is no better site to study the first architecture in this way than the Orkney Islands (**colour plates 1** & **2**). Orkney has the best preserved

1 *Callanish stone circle is on the ridge in the background. This famous circle on the island of Lewis is surrounded by several others including Callanish iii seen in the foreground*

Neolithic dwellings in Europe and this presents an unrivalled opportunity to bring the house into an enquiry about its relationship with other forms of construction. Orkney also has a plethora of burial tombs. The cairns on the island of Rousay preserve perhaps the most clearly identifiable relationships between burial cairn and settlement in Britain. The extraordinary ceremonial site embracing the Stones of Stenness, the Ring of Brodgar, and the burial mound of Maes Howe ranks along with Avebury, Callanish and Stonehenge as one of the highest achievements marking the culmination of the Stone Age (**1**). Moreover, excavations at the Stones of Stenness almost uniquely shed light on what took place within such circles. The idea of a cosmos and an architectural setting in which prehistoric man might locate himself in an ultimate reality is nowhere better sensed than at Stenness, where water, stone and the dramatically surrounding landscape are woven into a web of relationships with the remains of mankind's earliest truly monumental structures (**2**).

Although Orkney does not represent the final destination of Neolithic man's journey west and north across Europe to the very ends of the earth, nevertheless it bears evidence of a coming to rest, an identifiable occupation of the landscape, and consolidation of transported skills and knowledge into a distinctive culture. Not only is the surviving evidence for this unsurpassed but the archaeological work on the prehistory of Orkney has been extensive and of the very highest order. It is remarkable how modern archaeologists have been able to piece together the lives of these first farmers from the fragments of evidence unearthed during excavation. Often it is from the most minute pieces, the understanding of which can only be grasped by using the sophisti-

2 *The Stones of Stenness, Orkney. Viewed from the north-east, the distinctive Hills of Hoy are in the background*

cated forensic techniques of analysis now available, that our picture of that dim, distant past becomes clearer. Without wishing to detract from archaeologists' achievement, however, it is hard not to recall the story of the little girl who became the first modern to see prehistoric cave paintings on the walls of Altamira, whilst her archaeologist father searched the floor for Palaeolithic tools. Looking up and around does not come naturally to the archaeologist. Caroline Wickham-Jones writes humorously of archaeologists on holiday in the west of Scotland walking the dog with heads down looking for evidence of lithic scatter, producing a potential imbalance to settlement patterns![9]

Of course, archaeology as a discipline has come a long way since the discovery of Altamira. In particular the development of the processual approach in recent archaeology has greatly refined our understanding of the prehistoric past. By constructing models ('attempting some sort of explanation through generalisation', as Renfrew summarises the processual approach) archaeologists have come to focus more on the social fabric of prehistoric peoples and look for patterns of change in society thereby producing a more subtle understanding of pre-history.[10] More recently attempts have been made to understand the significant part the landscape must have played in the mental life of Neolithic people.

It is also understandable that the widespread practice of attributing mystical or irrational forces to these ancient stones should be countered by archaeology's determination to be scientifically rigorous. However, a reluctance to pass beyond the evidence provided by the material remains alone, carries with it the danger of overlooking significant relationships possibly established between the things themselves – the site and its configuration, the landscape and the heavens – in this set of relationships lies the world of meaning. Thomas puts this at the centre of his book *Time, Culture and Identity*. In a section entitled 'encountering things in the world' he explains how any new phenomena is made sense of by what he calls a 'structure of intelligibility. 'Human beings cope with the phenomena they encounter by slotting them in to the understanding of the world which they have already developed'.[11] We recognise things 'as' something or 'like' something, or 'opposed to' or 'contrasting with' something. This is a product of our engagement with the world of material things as familiar, unfamiliar, of potential use, dangerous etc. He summarises this: 'the world in which we dwell, then, is a world of meaning and significance'.

Meaning refers to the mental world of individuals and groups as they encounter the world of things and phenomena, making sense of things by locating them in a framework of understanding. Meaning is always present in any culture at any time, but its specific character in the Neolithic would probably have been dominated by its concrete form and by patterns of inter-relationship between things of very different categories, as defined from our own point of view. Their cosmos would have been quite unlike our universe. It is taken as axiomatic here, drawn from a life involved in architectural design, that people act and make things in response to thought, whether this be conscious or unconscious, individually willed or collectively and culturally impelled. The principal contention advanced in this study is that we cannot understand material culture without attempting to interpret the mental world of its maker. Bergson wrote that 'each act is the realisation of an intention'. What sets humans apart from other animals is not necessarily consciousness itself but a particular characteristic Timothy Ingold calls 'discursive conscious-ness'. This 'involves the construction of mental images of desired future states, that is, the articulation of prior intentions, as a guide for conduct'. Human beings are rather different from bees or beavers, for example, in that we do not have a biological blueprint informing us how to build. What 'distinguishes the most incompetent architect from the best of bees, is that the architect has built a cell in his head before he constructs it'.[12] Ingold calls this process 'intention-in-action'. By this he means that we do not have completely free will to build anything we might imagine, but that our intentions are circumscribed by what he calls our 'practical consciousness', which is bound up with everyday activity, inherited traditions and customs. The beaver builds now as he did back then, whereas humans have adapted to different climatic conditions and cultural characteristics that take shape and change over time.

Without attempting such an understanding the Neolithic cosmos cannot be reconstructed and the meanings of the material things that made up their culture may not be grasped. Of course, it is true that we will never fully comprehend the reasons why prehistoric people built as they did, but we should be alert to the limitations imposed upon us by the mind-set of post–Enlightenment rationality. Thomas argues that archaeology has been constrained by 'the implicit acceptance of a Cartesian view of the world', in particular the stress on objectivity.[13] Anthropologists have made us aware that non-western communities hold 'a view of the world in which separate analytical entities cannot easily be pulled apart' and that attempting to adopt such a world view may be more appropriate for our understanding of prehistoric people than our own modern, scientific world view. Acknowledging that we have to accept the separate categories 'self; world; thing', he nevertheless insists that 'these categories need to be broken down to some extent in order to arrive at a way of thinking which we might describe as relational'. In this way of thinking, where material remains are considered not as isolated or 'dead' objects but rather as 'a conduit through which flows a rich web of material and signifying practices', we can perhaps come closer to the meaning of things for Neolithic people. As Thomas says; 'The thing is a doorway into a web of relationships'.[14] Accepting our scientific world view as an extraordinarily successful means of establishing verifiable facts, nevertheless we will need to step outside that system of thought, or bring others to bear, if we are to understand the origins of architecture as it was conceived and took its significant place in the cosmos of our first ancestors.

There are several disciplines that we can refer to in our desire to steer a path between the unbridled speculations of the crank and the reticence of the archaeologist; anthropology, ethnology, mythology and the history of religions. From the study of living primitive cultures at a comparable stage of development and in conjunction with the rejection of simplistic notions of evolution and progress, we are in a position to understand their particular mentality and how their engagement with the world about them produced particular cultures. It is important to stress this last point, because it would clearly be misguided to search for a singular structure that underlies all primitive cultures and then apply it to a reading of the Orkney prehistoric remains. But it might be legitimate to assume a set of basic predispositions that allows us to sift through the enormous cultural diversity that primitive peoples have produced for material that seems to have some analogy with what can legitimately be inferred from prehistoric Orkney remains. Something similar has been the approach of Mircea Eliade to myths and religion. Without ever leaving the reader unaware of the historical reality and circumstances of a particular myth or religion, he nevertheless finds in them essential patterns which bear comparison with others often from very different parts of the world. From this a framework, or mythical structure, emerges which he uses to organise, compare and discuss vast quantities of ethnographic and other material. Eliade uses the term 'homology' to describe the process whereby the particular details of a myth are sifted in the pursuit of finding essential correspondences that constitute a mythical structure or theme. This framework can be useful in attempting to interpret evidence of ritual activity where, as in our case, its specific meaning is irretrievable. The nature of this kind of study will be discursive, accumulative, never certain but always suggestive – which may in any case be the best way of dealing with enigmatic prehistoric remains at once so palpable yet forever beyond our grasp. Eliade has been criticised from within the field of archaeology for producing 'cross-cultural generalisations of an extravagant kind'.[15] This objection misses the point of his attempts at synthesis which, to repeat, always do locate a myth in a particular culture and context whilst searching for general principles that might explain the almost universal idea of the 'sacred' which underlies diverse ritual or religious practice.

Of the various disciplines we can bear upon to bridge the gap between archaeological remains and the prehistoric mind, mythology will be that most used here, as myth, amongst many things, is a form of explanation for primitive peoples. We have to acknowledge at the outset that it will be an impossible task to find myths that refer to prehistoric Orkney. Myths only survive where an oral tradition has been written down at a relatively late stage of a culture's development – as in the most well-known case of Homer – or have been recorded by anthropologists studying surviving primitive peoples. By definition prehistory remains mute about its mythical world. A statement made as baldly as this suggests that we are left with three alternatives: the severely empirical approach where very limited, if any, inferences are made beyond the evidence of the material remains; the processual approach seeking changes in the structure of prehistoric society from changes in the material record; or the interpretive approach advocated more recently by Thomas, Richard Bradley and others.

In concluding the study in which he pioneered the use of the processual approach, Bradley writes optimistically of 'the possibility of a more rounded approach to prehistory'.[16] His own recent work on monuments and landscape, Saami myth and ritual is evidence of such a movement. The aim here will be to build upon recent developments in archaeology by a consideration of mythology in particular. A principal contention of this study is that the earliest forms of society lived largely within the horizon of myth, the holy, religion, the sacred, or however one might define the all-encompassing natural or supernatural forces. This would have been the predominant frame of mind that conceived the shape of things. Bradley makes the point that patterns of social structure and change can be inferred from the archaeological record of long periods of occupation. Scholars in other fields have detected similar changes in belief systems amongst earlier peoples. A shift from magic to religion, for example, might be as plausible (and as connected) an explanation as changes in the structure of society to account for the emergence of monuments such as stone circles. The argument proposed here is that the archaeological record can be used in this way to check to what extent a mythical comparison is valid.

With this approach, demanding that we deal with myth at the same time as keeping in mind the inherent difficulties of seeking the meaning in Neolithic architecture for its builders, it seems that we have two possible lines of approach. The first is to follow Eliade, reversing his steps back from the general structure of mythology to discuss particular myths that seem to have some relationship with things noted in the archaeological record. Like Eliade's approach, this would acknowledge no geographical limits as, for example, in his magisterial survey *Patterns in Comparative Religion*. Here myths from all over the world are organised under thematic headings such as 'Sacred Stones', 'Agriculture', 'Earth, Woman, Fertility' etc., many of which would seem to be immediately relevant to Neolithic activity.

An alternative approach has been suggested by Renfrew's pioneering book *Archaeology and Language*. Examining what he calls in the subtitle 'the puzzle of Indo-European origins', he comes to the conclusion that there is no evidence for extensive late Neolithic or Bronze Age migrations and that all the languages which share in the Indo-European root must have dispersed along with the first farmers from a source in Anatolia in south-east Turkey in around 6500 BC.[17] The significance of this for us is that the Celtic language would have arrived much earlier than has been accepted hitherto, reaching Britain and Ireland in about 4500 BC. Because Celtic as a material culture can be traced back to the Hallstatt and La Tène artefacts from North Central Europe this is not evidence, Renfrew argues, for any one particular place being the origin of the Celtic language. The case for a Celtic invasion of Britain in the eighth or seventh century BC is replaced by a concept that he calls 'cumulative Celticity' where each of the Celtic-speaking peoples adopted and adapted aspects of the Hallstatt/La Tène material culture. A common or closely related Celtic language may have been in place for millennia.[18]

The importance of such a reassessment for this study is that Neolithic Britain can now be imagined as populated by a culture (or cultures) that brought with them not only a material nucleus – domesticated animals, seeds, ceramics – but also a language with a common core. Renfrew remarks upon the Sanskrit root *raj*, the Latin *rex* and the Irish *ri* having linguistic resemblance and a common meaning. He also cites a study showing that 'early metrical forms of verse seen in archaic Irish and Vedic Sanskrit, as well as in Homeric Greek, appear to be related'. From this Renfrew suggests that:

> It is inherently likely that our first farmers will have had an oral
> literature, perhaps including lyric verse, as do many peasants in
> different parts of the world.[19]

He makes the point that these migrating groups of settlers were simple societies and that there would have been 'considerable continuity from the time of the first farmers onwards'.[20] It seems reasonable, therefore, to infer that it was not only a material culture and a language with a common Indo-European basis that arrived in Britain with the first farmers, but also a collection of myths. In *Rethinking the Neolithic*, Thomas proposed replacing the economic model of the Neolithic with a conceptual one – the Neolithic as a way of thinking about the world. This notion fits well with what is proposed here. It has been said that language and myth are the oldest of our symbolic expressions since 'both are of prehistoric birth' and 'there are many reasons for regarding them as twin creatures'.[21] Just as languages lost and gained words as peoples spread across Europe, so myths changed. However, an essential core which explained the fundamental ground of the material culture – the earth's fertility, seeds, plants, animals, death – might persist just as there is some recognisable relationship between *raj*, *rex* and *ri*. Equally it seems that if we can talk of 'considerable continuity' from the first farmers in Anatolia to those arriving in Britain then it is reasonable to accept considerable continuity afterwards. Reviewing Renfrew's work on language, Brody notes that 66 nouns have been identified as common to eight scattered Indo-European peoples of which 15 were farming terms.[22] Obviously by the time Celtic myths were written down the social conditions of Britain had changed enormously to become a society dominated by warrior aristocrats. The earliest literature, epic tales of heroes and heroic deeds, reflects this. Nevertheless, as in all mythology, older, archaic strata can be detected that speak of the perennial concerns of the peasant farmer whose dealings with the earth remained much the same as the first Neolithic settlers.

The implications of following Renfrew's argument from language to myth, then, become clear: that we should concentrate our search on the Celtic mythology of Britain and Ireland for myths to compare with the Orkney remains. Timothy Neat has shown in his *Summer Walkers* how folk stories told by Scottish travelling people kept distinctly Celtic motifs alive until well into the twentieth century. He concludes that indigenous peoples such as 'the Highland Stewarts, the Davies, the MacPhees all feel a natural, supranational bond with Ireland, and Ireland is integral to many of their oldest stories'.[23] Moreover, significant influences from Ireland have been detected in the Orkney archaeological record. Such an approach might be pursued exclusively, but here it will be used in conjunction with the material, structure and method of Eliade. Its greatest value may lie in being a method whereby the plethora of material provided by Eliade can be measured against the mythology arising in conjunction with the specific kind of culture from the particular region we are concerned with. This provides checks and balances to the criticism of his work being prone to cross-cultural generalisation. By referring to Eliade in this way we remain secure in using a method for dealing with comparative mythology at the same time as having access to more material to help provide an interpretation. The question of myth and language is considered at greater length in the conclusion. Myths referred to in the course of the study will also provide opportunities to elaborate on the pattern of connection to the past.

One last observation about myths, oral traditions and the possibility of considerable continuity. In his book on rural Ulster researched and written in the 1970s, the folklorist Henry Glassie introduces his reader to particular characters of the district – Ballymenone – who take upon themselves the role of historian. Theirs is a task performed in a purely oral manner. Many of the stories that the historian tells are concerned with the 'troubles', the conflict between north and south; Protestantism and Catholicism. Whether these tales refer to characters whom the teller knew directly, or to people of the previous generation, or to events from hundreds of years before, the mode and manner of delivery is the same; there is no sense of a gulf in time between the moment of telling and the event described, there is a collapse of historical time. This feature of oral history becomes particularly noticeable when they talk about St Patrick, for once again there is a complete collapse of historical time. The coming of St Patrick 1,500 years earlier as described in this oral history is an origin myth. St Patrick came with an entourage – 'tradesmen of all classes' – that founded everything necessary for a life that began in faith and continued to be essentially the same for the speaker. Glassie does not explore in detail the mode by which oral history operates but others have. It has been said that 'one must consider the highly conservative character of Irish learned tradition which, thanks to the assiduousness of the hereditary *filidh* (a bard or prophet), survived far into the Christian period and transmitted innumerable elements of form and content'.[24] This has given scholars some confidence that medieval written accounts of earlier Irish beliefs preserve reasonably accurately a good deal of Celtic material, and Glassie's fieldwork shows how long something like oral tradition might persist.

In oral history the mythical framework absorbs and gives shape to historical events and, in the collapse of historical time, events that took place last year or in the last millennium are recalled in much the same way, absorbed into the mythical world view that shapes the mind of the teller. Thus it is quite conceivable that some essential aspect of myth survives for thousands of years. Joseph Campbell considers that some of Grimm's *Fairy Tales*, for example, retain vestiges of prehistoric myth.[25]

Although not an archaeologist, I have been encouraged to enter this field by the recent strong concentration on theory in archaeology, a development that allows the interested outsider to participate in interpreting the prehistoric past. The ideas of Colin Renfrew, Richard Bradley, Ian Hodder, Colin Richards, Julian Thomas and Christopher Tilley have been most significant in shaping the form of this work. It also relies heavily upon the many archaeologists who have excavated on Orkney, in particular Davidson and Henshall, Anna and Graham Ritchie, and John Hedges. Aubrey Burl's work on interpreting stone circles has also been important. The work of these authors provides the foundation for this study which tries to deal comprehensively and collectively with the full range of Neolithic remains found in one location.

With extensive guidance from these authors, from Cassirer and from Eliade on myth and comparative religion, I hope my own disciplines of architecture and architectural history, allied to a deep-seated love of the landscape indulged with frequent visits to Orkney will suffice, in order to offer a fresh view of Neolithic architecture as it took its place in the cosmos, and as found and constructed by our first ancestors.

This study has taken shape over several years and it is only towards the end of the work that I found Tilley's pioneering study *A Phenomenology of Landscape*. He stresses two aspects – 'the symbolics of landscape perception and the role of social memory in choice of site location' – that echoed and clarified the significance of landscape I had sensed from the location of Orkney Neolithic remains which, until then, I had seen largely through the symbolic framework established by Eliade. The presence of the landscape must have been of immense significance to these pioneer farmers. Orkney has its own distinctive characteristics that would have come to play a part in shaping the inhabited cosmos of these people. It is not easy to judge exactly how this island world of sea and sky would have impinged upon the minds and actions of Neolithic people. Nevertheless it is important to include this in any attempt to understand the material remains within the interpretative framework outlined above where the 'relationality' of things is considered paramount. Failing to do so, as Tilley provocatively says, puts us in the position of 'a mole whose head hardly rises above the site to consider wider sets of relationships'.[26]

Although this study is primarily concerned with reconstructing the cosmos of these first 'architects', it would hope to shed some light on what Campbell has called 'the enduring power of myth'. By this he means a concrete under-standing of the reciprocity between the nature of man, his mind, his being and his doings, and the nature of Nature. Vincent Scully's book *The Earth, the Temple and the Gods* laid to rest the fundamentally formal and aesthetic treatment of Greek temples in architectural history by showing relationships that exist between its location, the god it housed, its orientation and particular aspects of the surrounding landscape. The temple mediated between the macrocosm of supernatural forces and the microcosm of human culture. All artefacts and activities of primitive people play something like this role. This study began as an attempt to understand the origins of architecture, looking at the historically real first houses rather than the mythical primitive hut of archi-tectural theory. In the course of examining the archaeological evidence its focus changed such that, at the end, its useful contribution might be to broaden the context of archaeology in the hope of gaining a little more under-standing of Neolithic remains. Building upon much recent archaeological thinking, it modestly aims to follow Scully's path in drawing upon archaeo-logical evidence to suggest that architecture's original purpose is one of making benevolent, fruitful and meaningful connections between mankind and the earth, seen as the fundamental ground of all existence.

2

HOUSE, FORM AND
MATERIAL CULTURE

> Within the spaces and upon the faces of the built environment lie the
> essential vision and understanding of both space and symbolism as
> expressed by the builders. They lie there latent, but alive, awaiting only
> an awareness of specific context(s) and symbols to speak their truth.[1]

The first Neolithic settlers arrived in Orkney early in the fourth millennium
BC. Perhaps after reaping the harvest somewhere in northern Scotland, they
crossed Pentland Firth looking for sufficient time to prepare for the winter
months ahead.[2] There is evidence of earlier Mesolithic activity in Orkney,
although none yet found of settlement. The absence of large animals to hunt
may have precluded this. The pattern of Mesolithic life, however, was
organised around seasonal movement, and they may have set up camps in
different parts of their territory associated with either hunting, fishing or
collecting plants or eggs.[3] Mesolithic settlement has been found on the north
coast of Caithness and it is quite likely that hunter-gatherers from this region
encompassed Orkney in their territory, exploiting its 500 miles of mostly
sheltered coastline. There is some evidence to suggest that initial occupation
of the north coast took place around Thurso, inland beside the Forss and
Dunbeath Waters and the Rivers Thurso and Wick.[4] For this reason it is likely
that the first Neolithic settlers would have known what Orkney, clearly visible
across Pentland Firth, held in store for them, and that they would have known
it as a place of some potential for their way of life, which mixed fishing and
hunting with animal husbandry and planting (**3**).

How Neolithic farmers first interacted with indigenous hunter-gatherers
remains unclear. Inferring from his work with the modern Inuit, Brody
suggests that Neolithic farmers 'moving into new lands would have relied on
herds and hunting while they established fields ... And hunters in many regions
may well have tried to farm or to make use of domestic animals'.[5] The arrival
of the Neolithic throughout Scotland seems to have been 'broadly contemporaneous and generally complete by 3500 BC and probably before 4000 BC'.[6]

Renfrew devotes a substantial part of *Archaeology and Language* to showing that
large-scale migrations over great distances were unlikely in the Neolithic. Instead
he borrows 'the wave of advance' model from geographers to propose a more

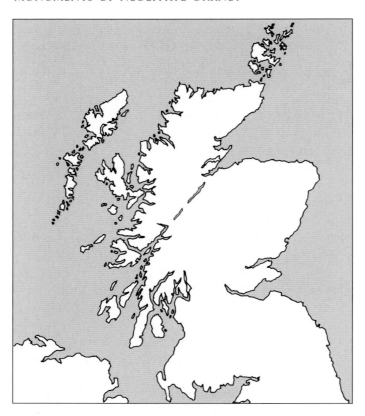

3 *Map of Scotland and Ireland showing the Orkney Isles off the north coast of Scotland*

likely slow, continuous expansion over short distances spreading radially.[7] In this way farming spread throughout Europe with each generation moving no more than 20 to 30 miles away, a process perhaps with pauses and sudden advances. This model allows the replacement of colonisation with the idea of groups moving in without force to areas not occupied by Mesolithic hunter-gatherers. Such a pattern of occupation has been detected in the Clyde region of Scotland where the islands of Argyll, Arran, Bute and Islay became occupied by Neolithic farmers whilst the adjacent Ayrshire coast remained a place of hunter-gatherers. It is thought that these islands became occupied not only to avoid conflict with the indigenous Mesolithic people 'but also because the landscape exploited by both groups was significantly different'.[8] This echoes patterns detected in some of the earliest Neolithic settlements (*c.*6000-5500 BC) on the Atlantic seaboard in Portugal where 'an enclave' established 'a distinct niche' between two groups of hunter-gatherers occupying the Tagus/Sado estuaries and Cantabria.[9] Hunter-gatherers might continue in parallel, but Renfrew argues that when farming reached its capacity the new settlers' range of skills and better nutrition would lead them to outnumber the indigenous people by as many as 50 to 1. Cereals high in carbohydrates would have swelled the birth rate at the same time as diseases inherited from domesticated animals might decimate indigenous populations.[10] It is this slow, continuous process, with backward links being only slowly severed, that led Renfrew to see nearly all of Europe occupied by Indo-European speaking people.

> For if we take the wheat sown in Orkney in the Neolithic around 3000 BC and ask where each year's seed corn had itself been reaped one would trace a line across the map of Europe that would inevitably lead us back to the early Greek Neolithic, and from there back across to western Anatolia.[11]

There is some evidence from Greece and Bulgaria to suggest that the Neolithic 'package' of planting and domesticated animals rapidly transformed the economic base. However, this may not have been the case in north-west Europe where Mesolithic populations were well established. Adoption of corn planting, for example, seems to have been slower than pottery. The evidence from across Europe indicates a continued extensive exploitation of wild resources, which would have acted as a buffer against crop failure. The early Neolithic economy in western Europe has been described as having 'accelerated existing Mesolithic trends'.[12]

Orkney was severed from Scotland in around 11,000 BC when the sea level rose at the end of the last Ice Age. The great ice sheets had worn down the Middle Old Red Sandstone of gently inclined flags to leave an archipelago of some seventy low islands with rounded uplands. The Orcadian poet George Mackay Brown describes them 'like whales basking in the sea'. When the ice retreated Britain was left a largely treeless tundra across which spread a rich diversity of plants and animals. But the Pentland Firth restricted this dispersal, which had left Britain thickly forested, so the first Neolithic settlers probably found Orkney covered only with a scrub vegetation of birch, hazel and willow. Pollen analysis reveals a sharp reduction in this by about 3500 BC, which is evidence of Neolithic man clearing the land for farming, a relatively easy task on the fine-textured soil constituted from the glacial tilth. Recent excavations at Skaill on the east coast of Orkney, however, have questioned this conventional view. Where there is not wind burn from the Atlantic, sheltered enclaves may have supported fairly dense woodland of birch, hazel and willow in addition to some aspen, rowan and pine.[13] Nevertheless, by the time we have archaeological evidence for the first inhabitation of these islands, we can imagine the landscape as not dissimilar to the Orkney we know today. Anna Ritchie suggests that:

> practical daily life can have been little different from the basic Orcadian pattern that survived until recent times. The economic realities of survival for the small farmer-cum-fisherman in a cold and demanding environment were as much a governing factor in the nineteenth century AD as in the thirty-fifth BC.[14]

Six well-preserved settlements from Neolithic Orkney have been known and excavated for some time – Skara Brae, Rinyo, Knap of Howar, the Links of Noltland, Pool, and Barnhouse. Recently three more have been discovered at Crossiecrown, Stonehall and Wideford. The accumulated evidence from the excavations allows us to construct a fairly clear picture of the way of life. Knap of Howar is a settlement of early houses, consequently it encourages a detailed review of how Neolithic settlement might have arrived in Orkney. Skara Brae is from a later period and raises questions about how house types developed. More than anywhere Skara Brae confronts us with an extraordinarily vivid impression of practical, everyday life in the Neolithic. Rinyo on the island of Rousay, although barely visible today, shows not only how the Skara Brae house developed, but also points to a major flaw in accepting primarily practical explanations. Pool on the island of Sanday has yet to be published at the time of writing and will only be touched upon in so far as it clarifies the Skara Brae-type house because it is fundamentally the same. A larger Skara Brae-type settlement at the Links of Noltland on Westray is known only from preliminary reports, which makes it difficult for it to contribute to this discussion. But it will be referred to in examining the puzzle of the origin of the Skara Brae house type. Finally, the settlement at Barnhouse incorporates two new building types amongst a number of Skara Brae-type houses, and hints at an emerging hierarchical society, a question that will be considered at the end of this chapter (**4**).

With much of its furniture and many of its fittings intact, the houses at Skara Brae confront us overwhelmingly with the practical matters of day-to-day life. However, we should be alert to overemphasising the practical as an explanation, for in nearly all pre-modern cultures the house is a significant vehicle of meaning, and the values attached to it are often more symbolic than practical. It will be helpful to broach this contention before we discuss the house and its contents. This will set the house into the context of the idea of a cosmos for, as Eliade informs us 'the house is not an object, a 'machine to live in', it is the universe that man constructs for himself by imitating the paradigmatic creation of the gods, the cosmogony'.[15]

For the primitive (or 'homo religious' as Eliade calls him) the world means something; 'the cosmos lives, ... the world exists because it was created by the gods'. The very life of the natural world itself is proof of its sanctity and it is because man recognises himself as inextricably linked with this life that he acquires the idea that he is a microcosm. Primitive man, in particular, is sensitive to this because his existence is open to the world. He is close to the fundamental cosmic conditions; birth, making his own living, and death. The microcosm-macrocosm is a widespread concept because so many homologies between man and the universe, continues Eliade, 'seem to force themselves upon the mind spontaneously as, for example, the homology between eye and the sun, or of the two eyes to the sun and the moon; ... of breath to the winds,

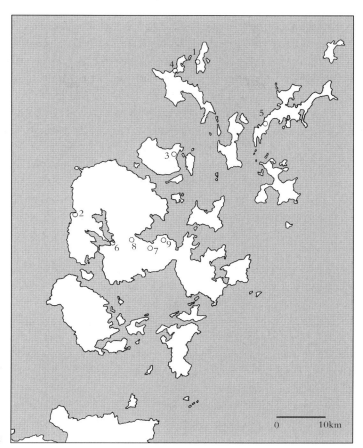

4 *Map of Orkney locating settlements discussed. 1 The Knap of Howar; 2 Skara Brae; 3 Rinyo; 4 Links of Noltland; 5 Pool; 6 Barnhouse; 7 Wideford; 8 Stonehall; 9 Crossiecrown*

of bones to stones, of hair to grass, and so on'.[16] On account of these reciprocal relationships, primitive man desires to dwell at a centre where he may tap into the life force of the cosmos. Once in possession of the microcosm-macrocosm understanding, whereby the body appears to be inscribed with aspects of the world (as in breath for wind), this way of thinking can be reversed with the consequence that the house can 'be regarded as a human body'. This conception has had a long life in traditional building. In 'any culture…the vernacular house … is seen as an organism, an organic structure generally analogous to the human body, and possessing a life force and energy of its own'.[17]

This should not be taken to mean that there is a linear sequence to these thought processes. The body-house concept does not follow the body-cosmos; rather they are intertwined giving us the deeper symbolic structure body – house – cosmos that operates in both directions. For many primitive peoples a fundamental perception of the cosmos, recounted in many origin myths, is the separation between earth and the heavens. This can be bridged or linked by an *axis mundi*; at the cosmic level this might be a sacred tree or mountain, in the house a central pillar or smoke hole, and at the level of body it is the backbone. The creation of a dwelling therefore involves a process of sanctification 'because it constitutes an *imago mundi* and the world is a divine creation'.[18] When primitive man settles he creates a world. But it would be a mistake to presume that the practical simply follows the symbolic for, rather like the body – house – cosmos concept, they are reciprocal and intertwined, as Eliade explains:

> Life is lived on a two-fold plane; it takes its course as human existence and, at the same time, shares in a transhuman life, that of the cosmos or the gods. Probably, in a very distant past, all of man's organs and physiological experiences, as well as all his acts, had a religious meaning.[19]

Unlike anthropologists, however, who can observe the customs of primitive people and relate the curious beliefs that accrue to artefacts and houses, in studying Neolithic cultures we have only the mute remains. So we are forced to approach the Neolithic house by way of the practical, by the concrete evidence of the material remains that we see. But alerted by Eliade's insight into the 'two-fold plane', we can also review the archaeological evidence from a cosmological or symbolic point of view. To do this we can use and develop the symbolic structure implicit in the body – house – cosmos notion and recount any anthropological parallels that seem to speak of a similar world to that evoked by the archaeological evidence from Neolithic Orkney.

Knap of Howar

Radiocarbon dating has established the Knap of Howar houses on Papa Westray to be the oldest in Orkney and the oldest surviving houses still standing in Europe. The Knap of Howar settlement comprises two buildings side by side with the entrances facing the sea (**colour plate 3**). Coastal erosion has brought the shore very close but it seems possible that Papa Westray was joined to Westray by a sandy spit at the time of building. Although such a pair is the exception among known Orkney Neolithic settlements, this is more typical of settlements in fourth-millennium Britain from the little evidence that remains – isolated farmsteads in their own plot of land not unlike latter-day crofts. A series of radiocarbon dates suggests these buildings were occupied between 3700 and 2800 BC.

Both houses at Knap of Howar survive remarkably intact, the dry-stone walling of the larger House 1 (10m by 5m) standing to a height of 1.60m and that of the smaller House 2 (7.5m by 3m) standing to 1.26m. The walls are 1.5m and 1m thick respectively, built of an inner and outer skin of stones about

30cm to 40cm wide with the cavity between filled with midden, the fine remains of weathered domestic rubbish (**5** & **6**). Although quite different in size, the two buildings are similar in organisation, the larger divided into two compartments, the smaller into three distinct areas. Both have traces of stones running parallel with the long walls which probably defined beds, and both had hearths. The buildings are connected by a paved and lintelled passage with door jambs, made from two abutting vertical stones as precisely made as carpentry work, where they enter House 2.

House 1 has a single vertical stone lining at its end of the passage. Both buildings have an entrance lined with similar door jambs (**7**). Archaeologists remain uncertain about how these two connected buildings were used although they can reconstruct extraordinary detail of their inhabitants' lives. Anna Ritchie,

5 Above: *The pair of houses at the Knap of Howar*

6 Right: *Plan of houses at the Knap of Howar. House 1 is on the left.* Redrawn after Ritchie

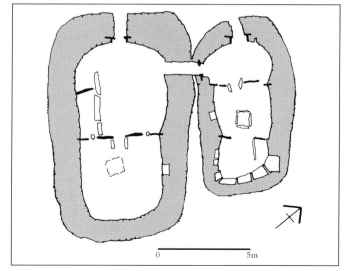

29

who re-excavated the buildings in 1984, says that the larger was built first although the evidence for this is not conclusive.[20] John Hedges noted 'that the seaward entrance to the smaller of the two buildings was quickly blocked up and that it was thereafter entered through the passage from the larger'.[21] The location of the jamb detail to the connecting passage tends to support this interpretation, and perhaps the larger was added as more space became required.

The three distinct compartments of the smaller house each plays a specific role in making an integrated household (**8**). The space nearest the entrance is featureless, although the plan drawn from Ritchie's excavation indicates that an upright slab existed here in the position typically associated with a bed in Neolithic Orkney dwellings. So perhaps there were beds here and they were removed when the passage to the second house was cut. In the central space there was a stone bench or bed along the left-hand wall, storage spaces in the right-hand wall, and a hearth at the centre. Four shallow hollows in the clay floor may have been to hold round-based pots. This seems to have been the working heart of the house. The innermost room is intensively furnished with 'boxes' made of upright flagstones and cupboards or shelves built into the walls (**colour plate 4**). It looks as if it served as a storage space and perhaps retained its function when the second building was added.

The larger house is divided into two compartments by a line of upright slabs and, originally, two timber posts. The outer room was paved and had a stone bench or bed along the south wall. The inner room has one small cupboard or aumbry built into the north wall and also the hearth, beside which was a massive stone quern. This clearly was the main part of the dwelling and, whatever the order of construction, the smaller building probably came to serve as an adjunct, as a workshop-cum-byre. This presupposes a family

7 *The entrance to House 1 Knap of Howar from the interior*

8 *House 2 showing the hearth in the central bay and the storage area at the rear*

arrangement although, of course, other social arrangements exist among peoples studied by anthropologists, such that the separate structures might be for males and females or a separate space for menstruating women. Analysis of later Neolithic houses in Orkney, however, suggests that family occupation was most likely.

Excavation of the surrounding midden revealed a detailed impression of the inhabitants' way of life. Knap of Howar was the homestead of people engaged primarily in a pastoral economy based largely on rearing cattle and sheep. Both would seem to have been of fairly recent domestication, the cattle large like wild aurochs and the sheep a primitive type with poor wool. This seems rather curious, as farming goes back more than 13,000 years to its beginnings in Anatolia, south-east Turkey, and the herding of animals such as goat, gazelle and deer dates from around 11,000 BC in the Levant. At Knap of Howar, a small number of large pigs was also reared. Wheat and barley were grown, perhaps in greater quantity than suggested by the remains as the soil conditions are not conducive to preserving organic material. Three stone grinders about 90mm in diameter were found on the floor of House 2, the working surface ground perfectly flat with a central pitted hollow. Such coarse stone tools are not uncommon from Mesolithic sites and have parallels among food-gathering societies in Africa and Australia where they are used for grinding wild seeds rather than cereals, the pit catching the edge of flat seeds and turning them over. This must have formed a vital part of their tool kit in these northern islands where roots, nuts, berries and fungi were not in such abundance as in temperate

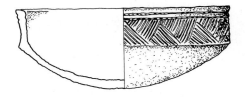 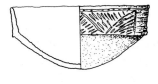

9 *Unstan ware bowls from Unstan chambered cairn (left) and Taversoe Tuick (right).* Redrawn after Davidson & Henshall

Europe.[22] A wide range of fish was caught including species from deep offshore waters. Shellfish provided bait as well as food, and sea birds were caught perhaps for their oil. The pottery used was Unstan Ware (**9** & **colour plate 8**).

The inner walls of both houses were built on the natural subsoil and the outer walls directly on midden from the primary period of occupation. Filling the cavity with midden possibly gave some insulation, eliminated draughts through the dry-stone walling, and reduced damp penetration. Midden continued to accumulate around the walls so the houses became increasingly buried in the earth. This practical advantage probably had its counterpart in a symbolic role that will be discussed when we look at Rinyo and Skara Brae where the curious practice of embedding the house in midden also occurred. The appearance of these houses with their massively thick stone walls buried or half-buried in the earth, is one of enduring permanence very much at odds with the evidence from other parts of Neolithic Britain. It is extremely unlikely, given the nature of the savage mind, that a cultural artefact so novel would simply be invented. It might, therefore, be worth taking a brief look at what is known of Neolithic houses elsewhere to see if any patterns of development or relationship can be detected. This will lead us to a discussion of how models, held onto tenaciously by primitive peoples, can be transformed.

The Neolithic house

The lack of evidence for Neolithic houses in Britain can be attributed largely to their timber construction and the intensity of later agriculture. However, this may not be a wholly adequate explanation. For example, the Danubian longhouses of the early Neolithic Linearbandkeramic (LBK) cultures have left sufficient post-hole evidence to be able to convincingly describe its form and to interpret its possible meaning. These houses were constructed of massive timbers as if representing, or restructuring within the house, the experience of living in the vast forest of central Europe. The 'interior was busy with wood in a way that has always seemed curious', writes Hodder, suggesting that the 'longhouse enculturates the surrounding forest of trees'.[23]

Clear patterns of development have been detected in the house as farming peoples moved westwards across Europe. The evidence from house remains and pottery from across Europe has been interpreted as marking a process of 'greater regional differentiation' as the Neolithic moved westwards.[24] By the time of the Rössen culture on the central stretches of the Rhine the house had become much smaller, approximately 13m by 6 or 7m, as evidenced by the example at Hienheim, not much larger than those at Knap of Howar.[25] The evidence for how the Neolithic expanded into Britain remains inconclusive. Whether first from the Lowlands bordering the North Central European plain or from Brittany is unclear, although perhaps there were parallel and overlapping waves of settlers from both these, or indeed from other regions of the 'Atlantic seaboard'. When the first farmers settled in Britain the house had become a relatively ephemeral construction as indicated by the evidence of post-holes.

The insubstantial nature of the evidence has led Thomas to suggest that people 'lived for most of the time in rather flimsy and temporary dwellings'. This led him to infer that Neolithic farmers were engaged principally in large-scale cattle management pursued by a 'seasonal pattern of fission and fusion, dispersal and aggregation, in which particular segments of communities were engaged in particular tasks at particular times of the year'. In such a Neolithic Britain, argues Thomas, the house may not have been a significant 'structuring structure'.[26]

Such a pattern of farming in relation to dispersed, flimsy dwellings is certainly familiar to anthropologists. Known as 'shifting agriculture', 'swidden', or sometimes also termed 'slash-and-burn', many cultures clear the trees and undergrowth of forested regions, burn the debris, work the land, plant crops, and move on as the earth becomes less fertile, leaving it fallow for animals to graze. Peoples as distant from one another as the Iban of present Sarawak and the Huron of North America practiced such a system, which after 10-20 years led them both to build subsidiary settlements as this form of farming took them deeper into the forest. It eventually reached a point where the distance from the original settlement became so great that a new centre had to be established. The Iban moved outwards at a rate that has been calculated at '50-100 miles per generation'.[27] It is easy to see how this pattern of local movement could develop into the kind of model for widespread dispersal that Renfrew adopts. However, it does not necessarily imply that the Neolithic house was not a structuring structure. The Mongolian nomads' *yurt*, a structure more flimsy than those described by Thomas for example, is known to be organised and inhabited symbolically.[28] We will return to the question of symbolism, but first of all we should consider a modifying factor to the 'wave of advance' theory of colonisation that has a direct and obvious consequence for any discussion of Orkney – movement over water.

A general pattern has emerged of how Europe came to be occupied by the Neolithic package of domesticated animals and plants. Taken up quite quickly in Greece and Bulgaria in around 7000 BC, from here two distinct lines of migration took place westwards, both associated with movement over water. One was up the Danube to the North Central European plain and on to the Rhine and Seine basins that lead to the shores of north-west Europe. The first phase of this expansion shows considerable homogeneity over great distance whereas later regional differences emerged. The other route was along the Mediterranean where Sardinia and Corsica may have been significant 'filters in this process'.[29] Expansion continued westwards to the Iberian peninsular but also up the Rivers Rhône, Loire and Garonne to reach the west coast of France.[30] Alongside the unclear picture from Neolithic settlement evidence can be set the suggestion drawn from patterns of burial that it 'seems reasonable ... to think of two broad traditions – that of the NM (Non-Megalithic) barrows of northern Europe, and of the chambered cairns of western Europe'.[31] A map comparing the area occupied by the LBK culture with the distribution of mega-lithic passage graves supports the likelihood of two broad traditions (11). In his book *The Domestication of Europe*, Hodder has suggested that the long barrows of southern Britain may indicate some relationship to the LBK tradition. Representing a symbolic shift from the long house to the burial tomb, this suggestion fits well with the idea of more dispersed settlement and less permanent dwellings. Although relatively little is known of Neolithic settlement along the east coast of Britain, nevertheless the large 'house' at Balbridie, Aberdeenshire, is similar to one at Flogeln in northern Germany.[32] Perhaps then, there were two broad traditions, one that emanated from the north European plain and spread to southern and eastern Britain, and one from the west European seaboard that came to occupy western Britain and all of Ireland.

There are two or three excavations along this western seaway of Britain that reveal some correspondences with the houses at Knap of Howar. These provide a context or background for how these unique Orkney stone struc-tures might have developed (12). Cunliffe describes the Irish Sea as the 'British Mediterranean' because of its propensity to promote contacts around its borders. It is highly probable that Orkney was populated by people whose ancestors had taken this route. Later in the Neolithic there is evidence of the exchange of artefacts between Ireland and Orkney, but from this earliest period of occupation the strongest evidence comes from North Uist in the Western Isles. At the recently excavated settlement of Eilean Domhnuill on Loch Olabhat, several examples of Unstan Ware were found that are the same type as the bowls from Knap of Howar. Although no dates have been given in the preliminary publication of this excavation, the site continued to be occupied over a long period of time with a succession of houses built one upon the other. The remains are slight and the successive phases of building not easily disentangled, but the house plans remain recognisably similar from the earliest to the later stages of occupation. Ian Armit's simplified plan of the earliest phase of settlement shows it to be remarkably similar to that at Knap of Howar with its distinctive bowed walls (13). Two structures at Eilean Domhnuill sit side by

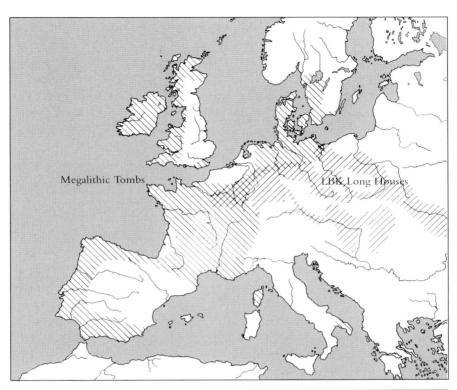

11 *Map of Europe indicating the spread of LBK settlements in relation to the area where megalithic burial cairns are found*

12 *Map of Britain and Ireland locating the houses that show a resemblance to the Knap of Howar.*
1 Knap of Howar; 2 Eilean Domhnuill; 3 Lough Gur A; 4 Haldon

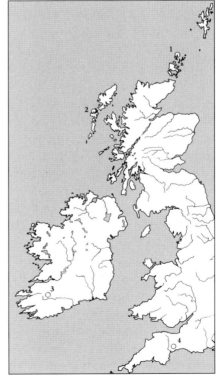

Megalithic Tombs

LBK Long Houses

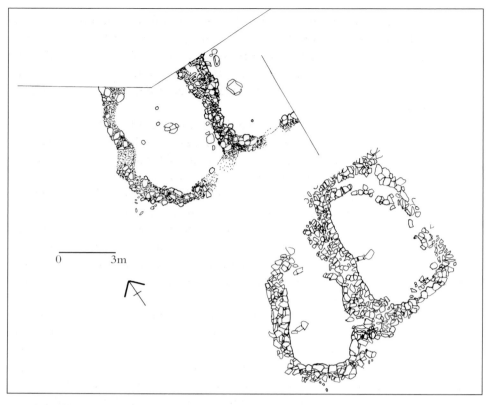

13 *Plans of houses at Eilean Domhnuill, Loch Olabhat, North Uist. Phases 6 and 7 are shown on the left with Phase 1 on the right.* Redrawn after Armit

side in an identical way to those at Knap of Howar and their relative sizes are of the same proportions, although both are slightly smaller. The larger of the two Uist houses measures 6.5m by 3.5m internally, which compares with 7.5m by 3m for the smaller Orkney house. The larger house at Eilean Domhnuill clearly echoes the larger at Knap of Howar with its single constriction at the midpoint of the walls. The smaller is rather ambiguous. The disrupted remains could be interpreted as a smaller version of the same plan, but also as possibly having the third, smaller rear bay of House 2 at Knap of Howar. Short lines of stones within the plan of both houses at Eilean Domhnuill occupy the same position as what are thought to be a screen and post-hole in House 2 at Knap of Howar.[33]

A picture emerges then, of a settlement in the Hebrides that had a distinct kinship with that at Knap of Howar some 200 miles further north-west along the coast of Scotland. One significant difference, however, reminds us of the unique attributes of the Knap of Howar houses – wattlework hurdle fragments were found at Eilean Domhnuill, which led Armit to 'suggest that this was a common structural element'.[34] Taken in conjunction with the numerous post-holes, the evidence points to the houses at Eilean Domhnuill being constructed in a manner more like those found on mainland Britain: a timber frame with infill panels rather than the stone walls of Knap of Howar. The possible issues entailed by this process of transformation will be discussed shortly, but at this point there are advantages to considering a rather different area of similarity.

Remains of Neolithic houses have been discovered at Ballygalley, Co. Antrim, on the very north-east tip of Ireland a mere 12 miles across the sea from Scotland. Although very different from the Knap of Howar houses (but similar in size and with distinctly curved ends) they clarify aspects of the process of settlement. Two points noted from a very early house (3776–3386 BC) by the excavator Derek Simpson are firstly, 'the high incidence of raw materials from non-local sources'. This serves to remind us of how mobile these early settlers were. Secondly, he noted the question of whether a general pattern of early Neolithic settlement might best be described as 'that of dispersed rather than isolated settlement similar to that which prevails in some areas of the west of Ireland today and also preserved in the Scottish system of crofts'.[35] The walls of the Ballygalley house were probably made of vertical abutting split logs with a daub of clay, dung and straw filling the gaps. Of the 50 or so known Irish Neolithic houses 14 were rectangular. Grogan divides these into two 'distinct building traditions', one with vertical plank walls – as at Ballygalley – and the other being 'post and wattle houses that occur only at Lough Gur'.[36]

Although not on the western sea routes of Britain, Lough Gur in the south of Ireland is a site accessible from the upper reaches of the Blackwater river, which drains into the Irish Sea. The best preserved of the remains of several houses discovered, Lough Gur A, has the same characteristic nipping-in at the mid point of the long walls as both House 1 at Knap of Howar and the larger house at Eilean Domhnuill (**14**). At 9.5m by 5.5m it is almost the same size as the larger Knap of Howar house. Of particular interest is its walling system, which suggests how the unique Orkney stone cavity wall might have evolved. The post-holes are paired, between 1m and 1.6m apart, and between the lines of the inner and outer posts was a low stone wall up to 0.5m high. This has been interpreted as a foundation upon which a wall of organic material was built, possibly using straw or rushes but more likely turf sods. (Glassie describes houses with walls of sod still standing in 1970s Ulster.) The paired arrangement of posts suggests that the wall may have been braced through this material. Although no evidence has survived the excavator suggested 'it is probable that the wall facings were wattle'.[37] The plan of a smaller early Neolithic house found at Haldon in Devon has a similar waisted shape and a stone foundation wall like the Lough Gur and Uist houses, but too little is known of this house to incorporate it here.[38]

There is some evidence then, to suggest a connection between houses built at Lough Gur in Southern Ireland, at Eilean Domhnuill in the Western Isles

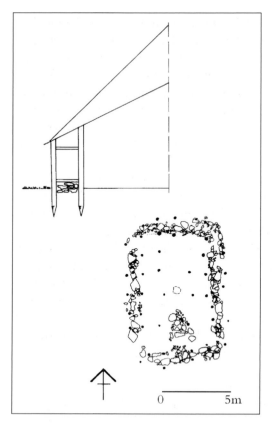

14 *Plan and section of house at Lough Gur A, Ireland. The section of the wall is not to scale and is conjectural.* Redrawn after Grogan

and at the Knap of Howar in Orkney. All three examples are approximately the same size and most significantly all have a very distinctive shape, the long sides nipped closer together at the centre. The three groups of houses have left traces of quite different forms of construction but these differences might in themselves be instructive. The vagaries of surviving evidence at the two former sites might well have masked further similarities. The post-holes immediately either side of the walls at Lough Gur A, for example, could have supported wattle fences to contain the organic material rather than simply for cross-bracing. Similarly, the stone base of the wall at Eilean Domhnuill could have provided a foundation for organic material stuffed between wattle-containing screens.

Building, boat and basket

A major transformation occurs in the Orkney houses through the substitution of stone for the wattle and organic material of the Irish and Hebridean walls. This transformation might be connected to the linking factor of boats that would have been fundamental to these migrations along the Atlantic seaboard.

Evidence has been found for the use of log boats from as early as 7900–6500 BC. A dozen or so have been found bordering the Channel and the east coast of Britain. Some were very sophisticated, such as that from Hasholme on the Humber, which measured 12.78m by 1.4m dug from a single oak log. Reviewing the evidence, however, Cunliffe says that 'the inherent instability of its form' made it 'unsafe around the more turbulent coasts or in the open sea'.[39] Outriggers improve their stability and ocean-going ethnographic parallels are well known, but no evidence for this form of boat has been found on the Atlantic seaboard.

Cunliffe also reviews the Classical literary references to Western Europe where he finds several accounts of hide-covered boats. A poem with its source in the sixth century BC refers to 'skiffs of skin'. Pliny quotes Timaeus from the third century BC describing native Britons making six-day island journeys 'in boats of osier covered with stitched skins'. Caesar himself described 'woven withies covered with hides'. Reviewing all the evidence for sailing on the Irish Sea and off the Hebrides in his book *Britain and the Western Seaways*, E.G. Bowen is 'quite certain that these feats of navigation could never have been accomplished in dug-out canoes: only skin boats would have been capable of attempting such tasks'. Knowing the unpredictable nature of these seas and the North Atlantic weather, Bowen is confident that the boats:

> would be forced to land in narrow sandy coves or, indeed, wherever opportunity allowed. The fact that the skin-boat could be so easily beached and dragged up beyond the tide-line without needing moorings as a wooden ship does was an inestimable boon to these early Western European navigators.[40]

Excavation of the surviving stone houses in Orkney revealed that there was an earlier, primary period of occupation of the site from which no evidence of the form of dwellings remained. However, it is hard to imagine the first settlers simply turning to and building stone houses for there is no evidence for these anywhere in Britain or Ireland during this period. What one can well imagine is that, during the first weeks of occupation, an upturned boat would have provided shelter with one edge perhaps propped up slightly to allow access. Timber huts could be built quite quickly, however, particularly if covered with skins and if material had been prepared on earlier expeditions. Recent excavations at a settlement at Wideford revealed a similar shaped timber structure beneath a Knap of Howar-type house.[41] A point worth noting when making a link between ships and shelter is that the smaller of the two houses at Knap of Howar is the same length (7.5m), as the Neolithic skin boats are believed to have been.[42] Bowen and other maritime archaeologists agree that these Neolithic boats would have been very like the present-day sea-going curraghs of Western Ireland (**15**). Cunliffe illustrates a seventeenth-century sketch of an Irish curragh of something like this length. These light boats, made from the hides of cows sewn together and sealed with pitch and then stretched tightly over a wickerwork frame, would have been extremely seaworthy although extraordinarily lively, and might have been as long as 7.6m and possibly 1.8m wide.[43] With a crew of eight or nine these boats could carry 3 or 4 cattle, or 15 pigs, or 25 sheep or goats. Most likely there would have been some combination of these with their legs tied in a thrown position, as well as essential artefacts and the seed corn, which would have been extremely vulnerable to soaking in these heavily laden open boats.

The Irish curragh is constructed in essentially the same way as the smaller British coracle. Both are made of a frame woven from reeds or saplings covered with hides. The boat's fabrication involves the same technique and material as the basket and in the case of the coracle the same circular form. The circular form makes the coracle notoriously difficult to control on the water and also tends to limit the size of the vessel, for the larger the circle the less stiff the rim. It is easy to imagine a process of development whereby an expanded circle of wickerwork becomes stiffened by pulling closer together two points opposite each other on the circumference. This would have the effect of tensioning the rim with the additional benefit of giving an elongated form that was much easier to handle in the water. With one or two such tensioning members stretched from rim to rim we arrive, of course, at the form of the houses at Knap of Howar. Given the evidence of wickerwork and frame construction by

15 *Curragh of the type used until recently on the loughs and coastal waters of western Ireland. This comparatively small example shows the same distinctive shape as the Knap of Howar houses.* Photograph courtesy of Kay Ungless

their southern counterparts on Uist and in Ireland, we can see how a technology that began in basket-making became expanded to become first the boat, the coracle, the curragh, and then the house (**colour plate 7**).

It is probably best not to think of this simply as an extension of practice but also as an intrinsic aspect of the maker's world of meaning. Basket-making is an extraordinary, quite magical process. In its simplest form, the basket maker begins by making a cross from two or four pieces of wet, pliable willow. Several lengths of willow are then woven over and under and around this cross, producing a spiralling, sunburst form (**colour plate 5**). With the wall staves inserted, the weaver threads the willow in and out almost unconsciously, gradually forming a volume or space (**colour plate 6**). So from a simple process the line becomes a cross that transforms itself into a circle, and from the line grows an enclosed volume. Moreover, the soft, pliable willow magically transforms itself into a hard and rigid vessel when dry. Aldo van Eyck makes a point about the linked meaning of things in his study of the Dogon:

> his cities, villages and houses – even his baskets – were persuaded by means of symbolic form and complex ritual to contain within their measurable confines that which exists beyond and is immeasurable: to represent it symbolically. The artefact – whether small or large, basket or city – was identified with the universe or the power of the deity representing the cosmic order.[44]

Van Eyck, an architect, did his research in conjunction with the anthropologist Paul Parin, who explained how the basket established the source of meaning for the Dogon's artefacts:

> the beautiful woven basket which the Dogon woman uses to carry grain and onions on her head, and as a unit of measure, has a square bottom, and a round rim; the cosmos is represented by the basket inverted: the sun is round and the heaven above is square.[45]

The symbolism is not only carried by the form but also the material, for the Dogon basket is woven from millet straw, a plant drawn forth from the earth by the warmth of the sun. This has a certain resonance with Celtic mythology, where barley and wheat were sometimes referred to as 'spears of Lugh', a solar god. The Dogon transfers the symbolism of the cosmos secured in the basket to the house and granary by a combination of form and materials. Their buildings have a square base and are capped by a circular, pyramidal roof made of millet-straw thatch.

It seems quite possible that a similar transference occurs in the sequence of artefacts that contained, carried and sheltered the Neolithic peoples who came to occupy Orkney. Although we cannot know the fundamental source of this because no remains of Neolithic baskets have survived, nevertheless there may be some significance in the fact that all three; basket, boat and house hitherto were woven. The nineteenth–century architect Gottfried Semper developed a theory of architecture based on four fundamental principles of making: baking (producing bricks and ceramics), weaving (cloth, wickerwork or wattle), cutting and jointing (timber framework) and cutting and piling up (masonry).[46] From this analysis he condensed the essence of architecture to two primary archetypes; the hearth and the partition. The hearth creates a centre around which human life and culture gathers, the partition marks off one world from another, an interior world from the exterior. For Semper, weaving was the fundamental process of making which, in conjunction with framing, establishes inhabitable space.

What is also interesting in relation to the connection advanced here between basket, boat and building is that Semper considered weaving perhaps to have been developed after men or women observed the construction of nests. In his book *The Poetics of Space*, the philosopher Gaston Bachelard attempts to grasp what is the essence of inhabiting for human beings. His source material is poetic images that tend to emphasise the sense of intimacy that comes from certain kinds of interior space:

> images that, in order for us to live them, require us to become very small, as in nests or shells. Indeed, in our houses we have nooks and corners in which we like to curl up comfortably. To curl up belongs to the phenomenology of the verb to inhabit, and only those who have learned to do so can inhabit with intensity.[47]

The Irish writer J.M. Synge, describing a storm at sea in a curragh, wrote: 'Down in this shallow trough of canvas that bent and trembled ... I had a far more intimate feeling of the glory of the power of the waves'.[48] In Bachelard's final chapter, entitled 'The Phenomenology of Roundness', he alights upon Michelet's image 'a bird is almost completely spherical' and Rilke's poem:

> *This round bird-call*
> *Rests in the instant that engenders it.*

The plumped breast of a bird on its nest perhaps evoked this poetic image for Rilke. Drawing these and other threads together, Bachelard declares that 'being is round': 'The round cry of round being makes the sky like a cupola. And in this rounded landscape, everything seems to be in repose. The round being propagates its roundness, together with the calm of all roundness'.[49]

The bird building its nest is, for Bachelard, the model upon which rests human understanding of what the deepest meaning of dwelling can be; the protection of being. Given Semper's view that weaving might have come from the observation of nests, we begin to grasp how the roundness of the basket might have conveyed a profound sense of the containment that seems essential to all life, to birds in their nests, nuts in their shells, snails and shellfish. Perhaps the bowed side walls of the houses at Knap of Howar and the rounded ends are not simply a vestige of the form of the boat and the way it was built but also an allusion to, or a harkening back to, the roundness of the basket and what Bachelard refers to as the fundamental roundness of being. This is reinforced by the ubiquitous circular form of the pot and, along with other manifestations of the Neolithic, has lead Bradley to suggest a 'circular archetype' may have been at work[50]. This idea will be further explored.

The houses at Knap of Howar have great slabs of standing stone built into the coursed stone wall at the point where the wall nips in. This unusual construction has been interpreted as buttresses to the walls, which are considered to be shallow horizontal arches.[51] Although this looks compelling in plan, for this to be effective as an arch in actual construction the wall material needs to be bonded (as in the 'crinkle-crankle' brick garden walls of Suffolk and Norfolk), or the stones need to be coursed so that forces acting upon them are transmitted from one to another. Neither of these conditions occurs at Knap of Howar. The position of these megaliths, however, corresponds to the points where ribs would occur in the construction of wicker-framed boats to stiffen the rim. These tensioning members pulling in the sides would be like the thwarts on the well-known gold model of an Iron Age boat found at Broighter in Northern Ireland.

Much later the ship itself did become used as a symbol of shelter or salvation. Persecuted by the Romans for their belief, the early Christians likened the Church to a ship. Surrounded by a hostile world, it is easy to see how those huddled together in their secret, intimate places of worship could make such a comparison. The Latin word for ship *navis*, became adopted for the main space of the nave, the body of the church. In the Christian tradition the symbolism of the ship of salvation is intertwined with that of the ark, which derives from the Latin *arcere* meaning 'to contain or maintain'.[52] In this historically documented example we see the important process of metaphor at work; the church is a ship, a protective, containing vessel. This helps to suggest the process of the cultural transformation of a model – in our Neolithic case from boat to house, perhaps from basket to boat, as well as from timber house to stone – something the primitive mind does with extreme reluctance, timorous of letting go of the fragile grip on the world given to him by material things.

From wood to stone

From this extended discussion on baskets, boats and building we can see how processes of transformation occur and are embedded in the mental world of meaning. But we are left with the problem of the stone walls at the Knap of Howar houses. There are two interrelated aspects of this problem: firstly, there are no examples of stone dwellings elsewhere in Britain before this time and secondly, where stone was used for building it was always for burial tombs as a material associated with the dead. The Orkney settlers were no exception to this pattern, bringing with them, and gradually adapting, a stone form of passage grave found in Caithness. Given the propensity for primitive peoples to cling onto what they know and make advances by adaptation and analogy, the shift from timber to stone houses (from stone for the dead to stone for the living) represents a remarkable leap which needs to be considered.

We know that the Orkney native scrub included willow and hazel, both usable for wattle walls. Perhaps the climatic conditions did not allow for swift enough regeneration for its continued availability as a building material. It is also quite likely that the inherited tradition would have used hardwoods for the principal structure, particularly important for posts set into the ground. Perhaps the absence of hardwoods in Orkney necessitated a different approach. All of these could have been significant practical factors. Another factor which may be significant is that the double skin stone wall could be seen as analogous to the double skin wall of posts and wattle at the house Lough Gur A. The use of midden may have a symbolic significance as well as a practical application. The excavators considered it likely that the wall infill at Lough Gur A was made of organic material. At Knap of Howar the use of midden represents a very particular kind of organic material, the characteristics of which may help us to understand the process of transformation at work in turning a timber wall into a stone one.

The word midden is derived from Middle English *myddyng*, whose Danish root means 'muckheap'. It specifically refers, in fact, to kitchen waste. So the creation of a kitchen middens was the equivalent of making a compost heap. Indeed, archaeologists are of the opinion that midden played a significant part in the manure used in Neolithic Orkney farming. It clearly would have taken on great significance here, where exhausted soil meant ruination, for it must have been known that land was filling up further north in Shetland prohibiting further migration. In a connected way, perhaps the midden came to be seen as a medium by which the stone, hitherto associated with containing the dead, could be transformed into a material suitable for the living, for sustaining life itself. It is hard to explain this curious custom without considering the symbolism potentially associated with the midden, the peculiar fecundity of this 'earth' made from the discarded waste material that had sprung from the ground. Encasing the stone in the midden may have been an act of expiation for transplanting this material from the realm of death into the everyday world of life. Some such symbolic action would help transform the meaning of the material as well as adding to the idea of house associations with the fecundity of the dark, enclosing earth, peculiarly apposite here where regeneration could no longer take place over the horizon but only within the occupied land.

Archaeologists have remarked upon the practical advantages of this use of midden, giving protection from wind and rain as well as adding stability to the wall. But it has to be said that there are distinct structural disadvantages to building a stone wall with two separate skins in this way. In masonry construction the thicker and more bonded a wall the more stable it becomes. In modern houses, for example, the ubiquitous brick and blockwork cavity walls have their inner and outer leaves tied together to make them laterally stable as a single entity. Filling the cavities at Knap of Howar and Skara Brae with midden might restore some of the walls' stability, but there is no logical reason to build a dry stone wall with a cavity in the first place. The conclusion seems inescapable that the walling system of the Neolithic Orkney houses begins not in a practical response — other than making use of the easily split stone due to a scarcity of timber — but in the transformation of a type brought with the first settlers. Of course they must have been eminently practical people, adapting their lifestyle to varying circumstances. They possessed the skill of stone-working from building burial cairns, and all around them on Orkney they would see a natural model for dry stone walling in the cliffs found on almost every island. The ubiquitous presence of this material form 'containing' the islands and underlying the earth may have both suggested and eased this transition. In conjunction with this practical background, all that may have been required were symbolic acts necessary to make everyday use of this readily available material hitherto only used for the dead. Perhaps packing the wall cavity and encasing the house in midden was an attempt to cover the stone bones of the house with a material analogous to living flesh. As Eliade has shown, it is commonplace amongst primitive peoples to view the house as a kind of body, the homology house — body — cosmos emerging as a powerful and persistent framework in primitive belief systems.

A clear example of a symbolic relationship established between house and cosmos is provided by the Kogi, living descendants of pre-Colombian civilisations. Weaving is a particularly significant activity for the Kogi, carried out in 'the *nuhue*, the world house'. In the beginning 'before life had been defined', says Kogi myth, 'the Mother was the weaver'. Weaving became a symbol of the original order of creation, the weft was thought of as travelling between the cardinal points as the sun traverses the sky, the threads of the warp open to the penetration of the shuttle as female is to male. From this metaphor, the loom became seen as 'a model for the frame of the universe, a basic concept of order, whose trace is seen in the four cardinal points of the sky, the limit of the sun's travel'.[53] The ceremonial house, or *nuhue*, is built around a four-poled frame that both echoes the loom and symbolises the Kogi's conception of the universe.[54] Other layers of meaning are embodied in its construction, but this is sufficient to illustrate Eliade's point that the material artefacts of primitive cultures embody, or develop reciprocal relationships with, the perceived order and rhythms of the cosmos.

The Kogi are descendants from the Tairona, a sophisticated culture destroyed by the Spanish invaders. As one might expect, their cosmology embraced complex notions of the heavens. In Neolithic Orkney we would expect to find a very different world view because the weaving of cloth had not been invented. Also the level of social organisation associated with simple farming people tends to preclude the development of higher religious beliefs. Furthermore, the proliferation of burial tombs suggests that the beliefs of these first settlers were more chthonic than celestial. What we would expect from a culture such as Neolithic Orkney is that an important part of its belief system would be built around the practice of farming – the mystery of new life springing from seed placed in the earth – as the Kogi's is around weaving.

In many cultures, particularly those at a very early stage of development such as Australian aboriginals, human maternity itself is believed to result from the direct insertion of a child, an 'earthling', from the earth to the womb. 'A human mother simply receives children in an embryonic state. She is a container'.[55] In this way 'women became epiphanies of the sacred power of the earth', a mythical background, perhaps, to the carving of female goddess images that characterise the early seed-planting cultures of Europe. One can imagine in these northern islands, where the winter is long and dark, wet and windy, that long periods must have been spent in virtual hibernation. The experience of this hibernation, surrounded by stores to survive the winter, perhaps became identified with that of the seed's repose in the dark earth before bursting forth with new life in the spring. Half buried within the earth with the walls stuffed with midden, by analogy the protective shell of the house draws itself close to the essential nature of seed, a mysterious dormitory of new life, the deep symbolism of which perhaps underlies the ark and all other protective vessels including the house. In some such way the symbolism inherent in the midden, replete with its own regenerative powers, would help transport the belief systems associated with farming – the most significant part of these people's cultural tradition – into the practice of house building with this new material in this new, less reliable environment.

Skara Brae

Skara Brae is like Knap of Howar in that it has double skin stone walls packed and encased with midden, but also unlike it in that it is a compact group of seven or more dwellings. A curious feature of this settlement has been the discovery by archaeologists that a midden heap was created as the first stage of the construction process. Houses from an earlier period of occupation have been discovered beneath surviving houses, from which it is believed the midden material must have been kept nearby and used to sink the later phase of buildings. Such a spread of midden, extending over 1,100m² has been found

16 *Exterior wall of House 4 at Skara Brae with the Bay of Skaill beyond. Half-buried in midden, the original appearance of the houses may have been not unlike this with a shallow pitch turf or thatched roof*

at the Links of Noltland, a similar group of dwellings.[56] It appears that the mound was allowed to consolidate before houses were constructed half-buried in the earth (**16**).

The origin or source of the Skara Brae house type presents a major difficulty in our understanding of Neolithic Orkney. Two or three remarks should be made about this before describing them. At Rinyo, as we will see, Skara Brae-type houses are associated with a passage grave whose plan form echoes the Knap of Howar house. The nearest passage graves to the Knap of Howar – Holm of Papa Westray Centre, Holm of Papa Westray North, and Vere Point – are themselves of a similar type. The simple picture presented as it has been of a burial cairn representing a house for the dead of a particular culture consequently becomes confused at Rinyo. Nothing in the early form of the Skara Brae house suggests an evolution from the Knap of Howar type. Perhaps it represents a mingling of different cultural traditions as the islands became crowded. Sharples refers to anthropological studies by Leach and Bloch to show that two cultures have been known to exist within close proximity.[57] Communities would probably be linked by various social transactions – typically, the exchange of women for marriage.[58] Excavations at Pool, however, revealed distinct layers of occupation with early, roughly circular 2m-diameter houses encased in turf through to 7m-long double-skin stone wall structures.

Another related possibility might be suggested by a modification of the 'wave of advance' model for Neolithic migration. Given the process of diversification that marked the culmination of the Neolithic journey across Europe and the diverse forms of early Neolithic occupation in Britain, it seems

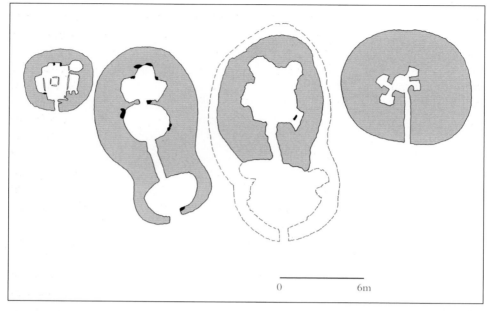

17 *Comparison of the plan of early Skara Brae House 9 (left) with Neolithic houses from Shetland (centre pair). The Bernie house is on the left, the Standing Stones of Yorie are on the right (their later extension is shown with a broken line). Vinquoy Hill chambered cairn is on the far right*

unlikely that one single culture steadily advanced through Britain. It is more likely (and consistent with the evidence) that one culture followed another, implying a kind of 'leap-frog' process. Some Neolithic people may have had to undertake long journeys to find suitable land.[59] This would seem to be a reasonable adjustment to the wave of advance model for the relatively inauspicious landscape of western Scotland. The paucity of evidence in this region makes it difficult to explore this possibility.

However, by far the greatest number of Neolithic dwellings discovered in any region to date are on Shetland, yet none has a resemblance to Knap of Howar. Perhaps the first settlers here had 'leap-frogged' Orkney. A rough typological similarity can be seen, however, between the earliest Skara Brae houses and a number from Shetland (**17**). The most striking similarity is with the Standing Stones of Yorie, before their later extension, and the Bernie house. Both have the characteristic central space with small bays off. The relatively amorphous shape of these examples contrasts with the more strictly geometric early house at Skara Brae, but is very similar to the house plans at the Links of Noltland. The resemblance between the Maes Howe-type passage graves and Skara Brae houses has been noted. Vinquoy Hill, for example, is strikingly similar in plan form and irregularity to the Shetland houses.

Coastal erosion has eaten into Skara Brae such that it is impossible to know exactly how many dwellings constituted the settlement, although seven remain recognisable from the final phase of building. At Rinyo, unaffected by the sea but disturbed by ploughing and never subject to a complete excavation, it is thought that there may have been considerably more houses.[60] The seven houses from the final phase of building at Skara Brae sit either side of a common entrance passage, six of them entered directly from it and the seventh connected by a short branch passage (**18** & **19**). The main passage is entered from an open paved area in which sits another building, Hut 8, which is not considered to be a dwelling as it had none of the distinctive Orkney beds or storage tanks found in other houses (**colour plates 10** & **11**). Stones fractured by heat and an immense number of chert chips lead archaeologists to conclude it to have been a workshop. Incidentally, the fact that this building was not further embedded in midden suggests the difficulty of the explanation that this curious practice was for structural stability.

The passage is low and narrow, generally about 1m wide but in places only 0.7m, and was roofed with flat stone slabs covered with midden. It would have been very dark, the inhabitants having to feel their way along with their stooping bodies filling its width, their shadow cast before them blocking out what little light penetrated, past neighbours' entrances before finding their own door. After the dark passage and the narrow threshold, the house itself would have appeared quite spacious, a large single room completely enclosed by its round-cornered dry stone walls (**20**). These survive in some places more than 2.4m high. Here it would probably have been only a little less dark, light

18 *The entrance to the shared passage that connects all houses at Skara Brae. Hut 8 (the workshop) is on the left*

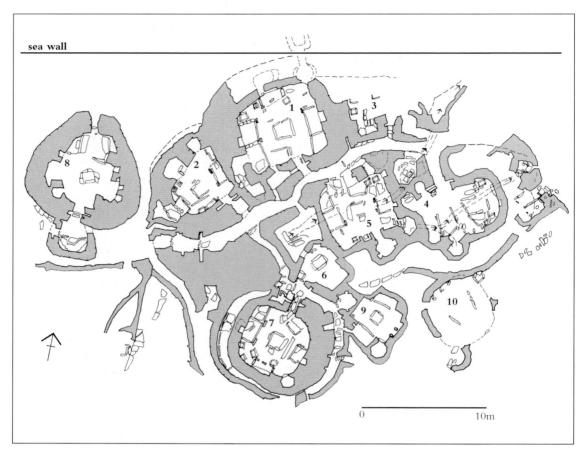

sea wall

8 2 1 3 4 5 6 9 7 10

0   10m

19 *Plan of the settlement of Skara Brae*. Redrawn after HMSO guidebook

20 *Interior view of Skara Brae House 7. Entrance to a small side cell is in the left-hand corner*

coming from the burning hearth and from the smoke hole, if one existed. The walls are of the same construction as the Knap of Howar houses, although thick enough in places for usable recesses to be hollowed out.

The interior of Skara Brae conjures up a vivid image of the Neolithic way of life not only because of its well-preserved enclosing walls but also because so much of the furniture − made from thin slabs of the easily split sandstone − survives. First occupied in around 3100 BC, Skara Brae was abandoned around 2500 BC. The reason why remains inconclusive. Gordon Childe, who supervised the first proper excavation between 1928 and 1930, believed it may have been because of a violent storm such as that in the winter of 1850 which first exposed the settlement to modern eyes. Recently archaeologists have come to consider this less likely than a slow abandonment of the settlement as patterns of social organisation changed. This suggestion has been made in response to the emergence of new forms of monument such as the Stones of Stenness with its adjoining settlement of Barnhouse where a hierarchy of buildings appears for the first time. Because so much detail of everyday occupation is visible, it is hard not simply to describe the everyday domestic life of Neolithic people, for there is nowhere comparable to Skara Brae where this is possible. This approach dominates most accounts of the settlement. All the houses are slightly different but all are arranged in a consistent pattern and the line of development from the early to the later houses is straightforward and clearly seen. This long period when the house form remained basically unchanged led Clarke and Sharples to conclude their account of Skara Brae as follows: 'where the scope for variation in the design is small, as in this case, studies of more recent dwellings suggest that the symbolic function is strongest'.[61]

There are two ways by which the question of symbolism or meaning might be approached. We can follow Parker-Pearson and Richards, who have investigated possible patterns of movement and activity implied by the interior layout of the houses in the conviction that, 'meaning is realised through social practices'.[62] This method applies anthropological theory to our understanding of prehistoric culture, treating the spatial ordering of the house as being both shaped by, and shaper of, symbolic meanings embodied in ritualised practice. An alternative approach would be to treat the house as an object of contemplation or a conveyor of meaning in terms of how it is directly perceived or experienced. In pursuing this approach we will need to remember that, unlike other artefacts, the house is a peculiar cultural object in that it is something to be immersed in rather than to be seen and understood from the outside. Acknowledging that we are not considering an object in the normal sense but rather a spatial entity and a container of human existence, one way by which we might grasp the possible structure of this as understood in experience is to take up and extend Eliade's notion of body − house − cosmos. For the house is not simply an object but, as he said, 'the universe that man constructs for

21 *Looking down on House 1. A quern and grindstone are to the right of the dresser and a stone-lined tank is set into the floor immediately in front of it*

22 *Looking back to the entrance of House 1. The small opening in the right-hand corner is to a side cell. Only entrance doors were lined with thin stone jambs*

23 *Detail of left-hand bed in Skara Brae House 1*

himself'. Before this analysis is broached we need to describe the houses at Skara Brae as they present a picture of practical, everyday life.

Although the surviving houses vary in size from 6.4m by 6.1m to 4.3m by 4m they all conform to a basic type. The two best preserved houses, numbered 1 and 7, are almost identical in their layout and appear to present an ideal configuration from which the others depart perhaps in response to local circumstances (**21**). It seems reasonable, therefore, to describe them in their general characteristics rather than one by one.

Each house is entered by a small doorway measuring no more than 1.2m high (**22** & **colour plate 13**). As at Knap of Howar, these are lined with vertical stones to form jambs. Some also have a stone sill. All have holes associated with the doorway that would have housed some device for securing a door. A stone bar was found in place at House 4. The excavators have suggested that the doors may have been a stone slab, although as none have survived it is perhaps more likely that they were made of a wooden frame or wickerwork covered with skin. In eighteenth-century Orkney houses a straw mat was sometimes used.

On entering the house there is a large single space from where the hearth can be seen straight ahead together with an extraordinary stone structure built into the wall opposite referred to by archaeologists as a 'dresser' because of its resemblance to this traditional piece of furniture (**colour plate 14**). The large, stone-lined hearths are no less than 1m square and would probably have burnt a mixture of heather, bracken, dried animal dung and seaweed, there being very little available wood (almost no charcoal was found in the excavation) and no peat at that time. A large square block of stone beyond the fireplace in House 2 has been interpreted either as a seat, perhaps honorific, or a working surface associated with food preparation at the fire. The stump of a broken stone slab that once stood 46cm high in a similar position in House 2 may have served as a 'fireback' like that at the traditional croft at Kirbister, now a farm museum on Mainland Orkney (**colour plate 15**).

The dresser is presumed to be for storage and possibly where prized objects might have been displayed, as on a modern mantle shelf. The suggestion that its significant form and position in the house might make it an altar has been considered but generally rejected. However, it might be worth reviewing the possibility again for two reasons. All of the houses have a small cell or cells embedded in the thick walls, some of which are very secretive, hidden behind the dresser and only approached through it. In these hidden chambers hoards of beads, pendants and pins have been found, 2,400 in a cell to House 1. Precious things, therefore, may have been hidden away rather than displayed. In House 1, for example, a ceremonial axe head was found in an alcove above one of the bed spaces, a significant object one would have expected to find on the dresser if the mantle shelf analogy were to hold (**23**). So, on the one hand, care must be taken about uncritically making use of modern notions of display.

On the other hand, we should remember that an altar does not have to be a structure upon which sacrifices or offerings are made, but can be like the family altars of Roman houses, for example, where a presiding deity might be represented and honoured. This will be further discussed when the house is discussed as a symbolic 'object'.

Set into the floor beside the dresser each house has two or three boxes made of four pieces of stone, the joints luted with clay to make them water-tight. It is thought limpets might have been soaked in these to soften them for use as bait for fishing. They may presumably have been used simply for storing drinking water or possibly have served for libations, the practical requirement of water storage equally well-served by clay pots. We will see similar tanks within the circle of the Stones of Stenness. A large stone mortar and grinding stone or quern situated beside the dresser at House 1 originally lay near the hearth.

From remains found in the midden we know that barley was the main cereal grown together with some wheat. The general pattern of farming conforms to that seen at Knap of Howar. Cattle and sheep seem to have been the predominant domesticated animals of these largely pastoral people. Evidence of pig, deer and goat has also been found. Neolithic Orcadians may have eaten sea birds, for the bones of a wide range of common birds as well as eggs have been identified at the site. Fishing seems to have provided a major part of their economy on the evidence of remains found in the midden. It is likely that the inhabitants would have supplemented their diet with wild plants, fruits and nuts, although none of this perishable material has survived. One remarkable survival was the outer skin of a puffball, *Boavista nigrescens*. The inner tissue of these particular fungi acts as a blood-clotting agent. The weather on Orkney deteriorated towards the end of the Neolithic reinforcing the emphasis on animal-rearing, and even today Orkney is still rich in grass.

On either side of the hearth are distinctive Neolithic Orkney beds. These are made of stone slabs laid on edge and built up against the surrounding wall. At both inner corners of the best surviving example is a tall pillar of stone on which skins could have been draped to prevent any rain that leaked through the roof from soaking the bedding, probably bracken, heather or chaff and animal skins. Looking not unlike a four-poster bed, similar canopies were observed in nine-teenth-century Hebridean 'Blackhouses', and the traditional Orkney box-bed is similarly enclosed to eliminate draughts. The dimensions of the beds at Skara Brae vary from 2m by 1m to 1.5m by 0.8m, the bed on the right-hand side of the entrance always being the largest. Smaller, similarly constructed enclosures adjoin the beds, and another can also be found to the left of the entrance. Whilst that adjacent to the left-hand bed may be another bed, those on the other side have a raised slate floor which has led archaeologists to interpret them as a storage area for pots. Pottery remains discovered here have been of the Grooved Ware type, pot sizes varying from small thumb-pots to large ones up to 60cm in diameter.

24 *Detail of bed in Skara Brae House 1. The shelves built into the wall and bed-head suggest how full and well-adapted was Neolithic life*

Built into the walls above the beds are small cupboards or shelves. In House 1 there are also shelves built into the end of a bed where it is unusually constructed of dry-stone walling rather than a single slab (**24**). Perhaps other small artefacts were kept in these, in addition to the stone ceremonial axe head found here. Bone pins, pendants and awls have been found as well as ivory stone and shell beads and small stone and bone containers – some of which had traces of red ochre – perhaps for body painting or for decorating clothes.

Above one of the beds, and in several other places at the settlement, stones have been incised with a decorative criss-cross pattern. Although it has been stated that the abstract nature of the design and no clear context makes it unlikely that it had any significant meaning, or that its meaning must be beyond our grasp, it is worth reconsidering this in the light of what has gone before. Alexandra Shepherd has made a detailed study of these designs in the context of European and particularly Irish megalithic art. She considers that the criss-cross patterns may correspond to fissures in the natural rock forma-tions of Orkney frequently found by the shore. She further demonstrates that the decorative patterns are remarkably similar to the lines on a human palm.[63] The criss-cross decoration is found on more than one occasion and in some of the clearest examples it is in conjunction with vertical lines (**25**). Together these form a pattern that might equally be read as a representation of a woven, basket-like wattle material. In the context of the argument advanced here, perhaps this is another aspect of the transformation of a former timber house

25 *Decorative markings found on stone at Skara Brae showing a distinct resemblance to basket weave. Top from Hut 8, bottom from right-hand bed in House 7.* Redrawn after Shepherd

type into stone, the vestigial marks of a wattle wall carved onto the stone wall. Neolithic pots frequently have their rim decorated by a weaving pattern, a clear indication that such a process did take place.

Beside the hearth of one of the houses at Rinyo the remains of a clay oven were found. It survived to a height of 23cm and was circular in form apart from the interior, which was a square with sides of 37cm, with rounded corners. It was built on a stone slab which was hollowed out in correspondence with the plan of the clay walls above. Two other such stones were found at Rinyo, so clearly, ovens formed a not uncommon part of domestic life although no ovens were found at Skara Brae itself. This may indicate that there were no such ovens, or that there were ovens built on clay bases that have been completely destroyed; evidence of building on a blue clay base has been found in several places at Skara Brae. There is also some evidence to suggest that the outside walls of the houses may have been covered with clay. Ovens would have been built up from clay coils in the same way as pots. It would not have taken a big leap of imagination to build up courses of stone to form the house walls in a similar manner.

In his book *The Jealous Potter*, Levi-Strauss recounts many curious myths associated with the production of pots. These give interesting insights into the relationship between cultural artefacts and the cosmos. Some trace the origins of pot-making to an ancestral snake. In widespread myths snakes, with their spineless, shifting form, are used as an image of the chaos from which emerged the cosmos. There are many early Greek representations of the snake as a fertility *daimon*. In this way myths bear comparison with habitual practice, for the clay is formless until rolled into a snake-like coil that is then used to form the base and the walls of the pot. From soft clay (earth) mixed with water (rain/sky), given form and then fired emerges the hard pot. Like basket-weaving, the process transforms the line into the circle and a containing volume, significant for storing and cooking food.

Analysis of the human remains found in Isbister burial cairn has built up a picture of the people who might have inhabited such a settlement. From a staggering number of bones, analysis found there to have been at least 342 individuals, although there may have been more as one cell had been emptied and the contents unrecorded. Renfrew's excavation at Quanterness produced similar quantities. Constantly comparing his excavation of Isbister with Renfrew's, Hedges considers that the whole population of the community was buried here. From this he draws a fairly comprehensive picture of the population structure: '24 of the individuals … died in infancy (0-2 years), 70 as children (2-12 years), 63 as teenagers (13-19), and 185 as adults (20 years or more)'.[64] Only about 5 per cent of the population reached 40, probably none reached 50, and the average life expectancy of what he calls 'an Isbister-type population' was 19 years 11 months, which he compared with the modern expectancy of 67 years for males and 72 for females.[65] Although the bones that could be sexed indicated twice as many males as females, Hedges believed this figure to be distorted by the large number of bones that could not be sexed. There were only slightly more males than females at Quanterness.

From an impressive statistical survey, Hedges shows that such a population structure could produce a stable community, the number of deaths being matched by the possibilities of birth. He outlines what a typical Neolithic Orkney community might have been like. Extrapolating within the range of radiocarbon dates from the buried remains he suggests 'a population of at least 21 people over sixteen generations but with a greater likelihood of it having been 42 people over eight'.[66] Sticking with these figures, then, we can imagine a typical Neolithic community such as may have occupied Skara Brae. Only 2 or 3 would be over 40, most likely to be men because of the prevalence of death in childbirth for women. There would be between 4 and 8 women of childbearing age; at the age of 20 men would outnumber women by three to two and at 30 by two to one. Half the population would be of school age in our terms. From this Hedges draws the inference that, as in the Victorian age, children would be working at everyday unskilled tasks. He also poses the question of how skills and knowledge were transmitted when the average life expectancy was so short. He raises this in relation to the hypothesis advanced by Thom and others of 'astronomer priests' specialising in the gathering and transmission of celestial knowledge. There would not have been a problem with the more everyday knowledge involved in producing pottery, knapping flint for stone tools, basket-making and other domestic tasks, nor any of the multiplicity of skills associated with farming. Among the remains at Isbister, however, were a number that do indicate more esoteric practices, a problem that will be considered in the next chapter.

Yet before leaving Skara Brae some curious aspects of House 7 should be noted. Not only is it separated from the other houses by an independent passage, but also its door can only be closed from the outside. Uniquely for this group of houses, buried remains of two females were discovered beneath one of the beds. Taken together, these have led to the suggestion that it may have played a ritualistic role.

Rinyo

In trying to understand the development and overall appearance of Skara Brae it is helpful to look at Rinyo because there we can see how the early, cruciform, three-celled plan develops step-by-step to the more open, spacious houses of the later period at Skara Brae. Rinyo also provides evidence for how these might have been roofed. Furthermore it offers support for the suggestion that the symbolic may have been of greater significance than the practical to these first stone-house builders. Beneath the level of the final settlement at Skara Brae, House 9 is a well-preserved example of the earlier house (**colour plate 9**).

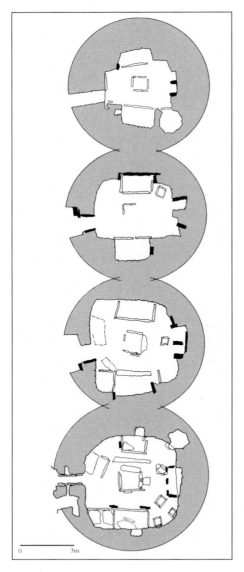

26 *Comparative plans showing the development of the Skara Brae house. From the top; Skara Brae House 9; Rinyo House A; Rinyo House G; Skara Brae House 7.*

Much smaller and incorporating the distinctive dresser, the significant difference is that the beds are built as alcoves set into the side walls. From one of the most complete and decipherable plans produced from the excavation at Rinyo, House A, we see the right-hand bed is completely embedded in the external wall to make a distinct cellular space, but the left-hand bed is half in the wall and half in the main space (**26**). In the most well-preserved plan, House G, the left-hand bed now stands completely within the room marked by its stone slabs on edge, and the right-hand bed pushes half out of the wall, its inside edge made of stone walling. The next step was for both beds to be in the large living space.

At Rinyo, post-holes were found within the most developed house that give us some evidence for reconstructing the interior appearance of these houses. We can be certain that the roof was not corbelled stone (as were the Neolithic huts in Crete and the later 'beehive' houses of Ireland) for this would have left enormous quantities of stone detected in excavation. The stone walls do corbel inwards, however, reducing the area to be roofed. Reconstruction drawings usually simply show rafters bearing directly onto the walls. But the post-holes indicate that this was unlikely and the corbelling would have made the cavity walls unstable in such an arrangement.

Whether the posts at Rinyo were of timber, driftwood collected from the shore or whalebone we cannot be sure. The surviving post-holes at House G at Rinyo form a cluster between the hearth and the dresser (**27**). Five in all are distributed in such an incoherent way that it is impossible to suggest convincingly what form of timber structure would have supported the roof. However, it is hard to imagine such a forest of columns in such a small working area of the house between the hearth, dresser and luted water tanks. Perhaps some were discarded as larger timbers appeared on the shore or perhaps the system of support changed. Given that we can see the house at Rinyo developing over the years, it seems reasonable to assume the structure might also have changed and to look for a logical pattern, or patterns, amongst the cluster of posts in House G.

We get little help from the post-holes found in Neolithic timber-house excavations elsewhere in Britain. This is partly because none has a remotely similar plan configuration and partly because post-hole evidence is incomplete or muddled by incoherent groupings as at Rinyo. However, it is possible to infer two general types of roof structure from the body of evidence which is consistent with the demands of a logical timber roof structure (**28**). In narrow houses such as at Kemp Knowe, Hazleton, and Windmill Hill, there appears to be a line of post-holes down the approximate centre of the plan.[67] These would be to support a ridgepole and the roof would be covered with rafters spanning from ridge to wall. Wider buildings, such as Structure A, Lismore Fields or Llandegai, often seem to have a double row of post-holes, one on either side of the centre line (although sometimes other odd post-holes occur). This suggests a roof structure of rafters bearing on purlins at their approximate mid point and the purlins supported by the timber posts.

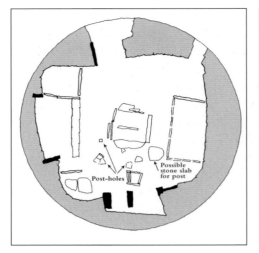

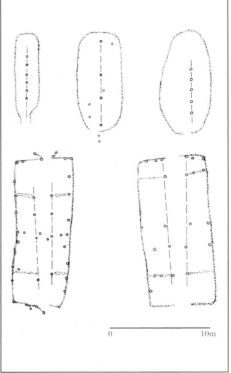

27 *Plan of House G at Rinyo indicating position of post-holes.* Redrawn after Childe and Grant

28 *Plans of Neolithic timber structures. Top from left to right: Kemp Knowe; Hazleton; Windmill Hill. Bottom pair; Structure A, Lismore Fields; and Llandegai.* Redrawn after Darvill

Perhaps the most likely roof structure for the Skara Brae-type house is a compact version of the latter with either two posts on each side of the hearth at the dresser end or, more likely, four posts gathered symmetrically around the hearth (**colour plate 12**). The case for this proposal would take into account a post-hole found at Rinyo House A in an almost exactly symmetrical position to that forward of the left-hand side of the hearth at House G. The evidence of post-holes, although incomplete, indicates that posts stood in similar positions on the entrance side of the hearth. The argument for this form of structure would call upon two further lines of support. Firstly, if we hold in mind the early Skara Brae house, we can imagine that the bed cells were pushed into the side walls because the central space was the largest possible span for a roof made from the small trees indigenous to Orkney. The house type develops by gradually becoming wider, and this may then have involved the introduction of supporting posts. A post-hole is located halfway between the hearth and the edge of a bed half-built into the wall in one of the later houses at Rinyo. Its distance from the wall is exactly the same as that from the wall to the edge of one completely exposed bed on the other side of the house. There are paving stones here on which a post might have stood. In the final phase of the houses at Skara Brae, with both beds entirely in the main space of the house, we could imagine that there might be timber posts adjacent to the corner bed-posts rising to support the roof (**29**). This would be a logical position and also carry a memory of key supporting points in the first, cellular house. The later houses could have been roofed by having four principal roof members rising from the walls at these points to bear upon purlins fixed to the four posts (**30**). Such a primary structure would allow much smaller pieces of wood for rafters, on which would rest the roof covering. This might have been straw thatch as in the Hebridean Blackhouses, or perhaps turf laid over strips of hazel or birch bark used as tiles. Drains lined with hazel bark were found at Rinyo and houses roofed in this way can be seen in the Folk Museums of Oslo and Stockholm, for example. Given the significance of midden, it is interesting

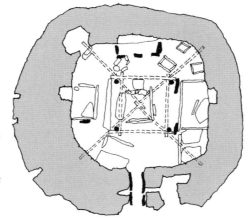

29 *Section drawing showing conjectured reconstruction of roof structure for Skara Brae-type houses. The plan below shows posts with purlins and hip-rafters in a broken line. See caption to* **colour plate** **12** *for outline of arguments for this particular form of structure*

to note that the Blackhouses also had a cavity filled in this way and that the roof drained into it, which seems illogical but some say was done to encourage the growth of algae.[68] This is less likely (algae needs light) than the possibility that the cavity would provide a drainage channel – abutting houses could not simply drain sideways into a neighbouring house. Whether there was a smoke hole or whether smoke percolated out through the thatch as in the Blackhouses we cannot know. The latter practice may have been adopted to reduce the possibility of the roof catching fire, as burning material from friable fuel can be drawn rapidly into the air by the draught from a smoke hole.

The second indicator of such an arrangement of posts is the structure implied by the post-holes found at Knap of Howar. Although the relationship between these two kinds of houses and the two sets of peoples who built them is far from clear, the resemblance between the stalled–chamber burial cairn overlooking Rinyo and the tripartite division of the Knap of Howar house has been noted. This is discussed in more detail in the next chapter, but clearly Rinyo seems to have had some knowledge of, and some significant relation to, the cultural traditions that produced the Knap of Howar houses. Perhaps similar constructional solutions were forced upon peoples in the common condition of these virtually treeless islands.

30 *Model showing primary roof structure of four posts (above) and with purlins and rafters added (below). The rafters at one end are not included in order to show more clearly the pattern of purlins and hip-rafters that made the most convincing roof structure while building the model.* Photograph courtesy of Harry Paticas

One other post-hole position should be touched upon: that in House G at Rinyo, which stands on the central axis between the hearth and the dresser. This could imply a ridge-and-beam structure although, as has been seen, there is no other evidence in Orkney to support this. Intriguingly, its location here does reintroduce us to speculations concerning the body − house − cosmos conception. For the central-pillared house appears throughout the primitive world always linked to and symbolising the 'cosmic tree'. The tree in many different forms and in many cultures symbolised the regenerative force of the cosmos, the 'living cosmos'. Eliade describes migrating peoples who carried their cosmic tree with them and erected it at the centre of the dwelling to recreate the cosmos. There is insufficient evidence at Rinyo to establish whether or not there once was a central post-and-ridge roof structure, or whether a free-standing post stood in this significant position at House G. In this context, it is worth taking a second look at the dresser, for its central supporting post is on the line of axis. In the later houses at Skara Brae this vertical stone is turned face-on to the entrance, significantly increasing its visible presence. Perhaps this extraordinary structure, set into its shallow niche, represented some memory of a central post or other form of cosmic tree, or some related expression of the same idea.

Symbolism or practicality?

There are two other interlinked points that should be considered before leaving Rinyo. Firstly, as it appears today with only a few stumps of stone projecting above the ground but close up against a stone escarpment, we are presented with a striking image of how the sandstone beds and cliffs of Orkney offer a natural model for dry stone walling (**31** & **32**). Secondly, by building up against the live rock-face, Rinyo provides further evidence for a symbolic rather than practical role for midden.

As at Skara Brae the settlement of Rinyo was encased in midden. At first sight the location of the settlement, hard up against a stone outcrop on the landward side of Faraclett Head to its north and looking across a fertile valley to the south, seems to occupy a perfect microclimate. Not happy enough with simply obtaining shelter from the cold north winds, the builders piled up midden against the natural stone face and set their dwellings into this. In at least one instance they used the cliff face in place of an outer section of the house wall. So what erosion and quarrying had done in removing a portion of the hill, the midden replaced. But a major problem stemmed from this, which must have been known to the builders at the outset and, in any case, did not deter them from successive rebuildings in the same location. When it rains water runs out from the rock face. This resulted in an extraordinarily complex and comprehensive drainage system − in some places a V-shaped channel made of slates lined with clay − constructed beneath the dwellings to divert the water

31 *View of Rinyo. Built up against the cliff beyond, all that remains visible is a jumble of stones protruding from the earth*

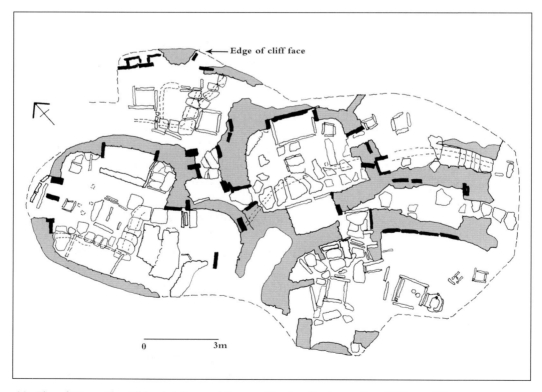

32 *Plan of Rinyo. The cliff face is indicated at the top of the plan.* Redrawn after Childe and Grant

away.[69] Despite this ingenuity, it is hard to imagine the dwellings dry in winter, an impractical outcome of this curious desire to build the dwellings into the earth or midden, when building a metre or so away from the rock face would have alleviated this while still giving wind protection. According to Eliade the construction of a house by primitive man involved an attempt to endow it with something of the life force present in both animate and inanimate nature. Sinking the houses into the earth or midden in this way may have been a vital part of this process. Just as seeds could be safely transmitted to the protective care of the dark earth, perhaps also could human life.

Symbolism works by the recognition and construction of such concrete correspondences as those we have seen Eliade describe, whereby a relationship is perceived between, for example, sacred mountain, tree, central post or smoke hole and the backbone. Symbolism, he explains, is the process whereby people connect fragments of experience into a greater whole; i.e. a thing that becomes a symbol tends to become one with the whole'.[70] In this way the tree, central post and backbone all participate in the symbolic structure described as the *axis mundi*. Eliade's elaboration of what he calls 'the logic of symbols' seems to offer a deeper explanation for the use of midden in this way. We have seen how, before the Orkney houses, stone was not associated with dwelling but rather with burial and death. Consequently there would have been two distinct symbolic systems at work; one to do with death (that incorporated stone amongst other things) and another to do with dwelling (its symbolic structure possibly embracing boats, baskets and weaving.) The use of midden, then, could be a symbolic device to shift the structure of meaning that linked stone with death to another symbolic structure that had in its place associations with life. The hard protective shell of seeds enfolded in the dark earth might have presented itself as an analogy to develop this new symbol within another symbolic structure. In this way the stone of the house would become transferred from one symbolic system to another. In a complex discussion on the Polynesian term *mana*, Eliade identifies this as a positive force that may reside in many different things – a dead man's bones, the head of a family, a little stone amulet etc. – and may manifest itself in various ways. This will be discussed in the concluding chapter. The earth is a particularly powerful and vivid instance of such a force that runs through all life and into which primitive mankind (humans, *humus*) tries to tap with all his activities. Eliade argues that the earth became chthonic with the appearance of agriculture. However, the first understanding of the earth as a conduit of life force was 'indistinct':

> it did not localise sacredness in the earth as such, but jumbled together
> as a whole all the hierophanies in nature as it lay around – earth, stones,
> trees, water, shadows, everything. The primary intuition of the earth as
> a religious 'form' might be formalised thus: 'the cosmos – repository of
> sacred forces'.[71]

With the advent of planting the earth itself became a particular focus of the relationship between sacred forces and fertility:

> Every expression of life is the result of the fertility of the earth; every form is born of it, living, and returns to it the moment its share of life is exhausted; ... earth *produces* living forms.[72]

Yet human life is more of an ongoing process than is suggested by this analogy between seeds in the earth and stone walls in midden, although the symbolism of this may have been utilised, not only for transforming the meaning of stone, but also in relation to the nurturing role of the house. Having earlier described the practical facts of the Neolithic house let us now see what might be ascertained about the symbolism of occupation. In particular we will need to consider how human life is unlike seed in that it does not require a shell but needs space to be shaped around it.

Parker-Pearson and Richards point out the striking homogeneity in the internal organisation of Neolithic Orkney houses. The house is centred on a hearth and incorporates a bi-axial symmetry, always having bed-boxes on both the left- and right-hand side, and the entrance having opposite it a dresser. By inferring patterns of use that interweave with this formal arrangement and drawing upon anthropological research, they construct a reading of the house that offers insights into social patterns of occupation. Their analysis begins by noting that the entrance to Skara Brae houses is frequently offset slightly to the right. In fact, all of the surviving houses have their entrance like this except for House 7. Parker-Pearson and Richards concentrate their discussion upon this house, for its entrance, which is directed slightly to the left of centre, has a set of paving slabs that seem to direct movement to the right.

Following Gordon Childe, who interpreted the larger beds on the right as constituting a male domain and the smaller on the left a female, they elaborate this gendered articulation of space by evidence not only from archaeology but also anthropology and folklore. Richards' excavations at Barnhouse revealed that the hearth had been tended and cleared from the left. There was also some evidence of food preparation in this same area. 'Traditionally, in Orkney', write Parker-Pearson and Richards, 'it has been the woman's duty to tend the fire and prepare the food'.[73] In the Blackhouse of the Western Isles, the left-hand side space was where women prepared food and did their work.

From this they suggest that there would have been a shift in how the space of the Skara Brae house was understood through the experience of moving into it by turning to the right. The initial 'deep space' occupied by the dresser would become supplanted by the left-hand side, the female space, becoming the perceived deep space after this movement had taken place. This analysis is undermined somewhat by their suggestion that moving to the right would have been reinforced by the left-hand side being 'concealed in semi-darkness' and the right-hand side 'illuminated by light coming through the doorway'.[74] As we have seen, all the houses at Skara Brae were in fact entered from a long, winding and narrow passage down which almost no light would have funnelled to the house entrance. The houses would have been evenly lit from the centre, therefore, either by light from the fire or from a smoke hole if one existed.

Parker-Pearson and Richards begin their discussion of possible cosmological structuring principles in Neolithic Orkney houses by noting that 80 per cent of the entrances lie on a north-west/south-east axis. They suggest that this structured set of relationships has its source in cosmology. Quickly setting this line of enquiry aside, however, they replace it with a focus on the hearth, a discussion which is more readily sustained because some entrances at Skara Brae face diametrically opposite others, a consequence of the shared entrance passage. This would cause problems if orientation to cardinal points is deemed to be significant. Because the orientation of the hearth is established in relation to the axis of the house, they are able to demonstrate that its four sides are orientated approximately towards the four significant quarters of the horizons in these northern latitudes; midsummer sunrise and sunset, and midwinter sunrise and sunset.

An alternative way of thinking about this issue of house and cosmos might be to consider the possibility that the house is not given a developed orientation to the world as such but rather that it separates itself from the larger world and establishes a coherent and meaningful world within its own walls. This world within a world, as it were, is Eliade's 'universe that man constructs'. The entrance to Skara Brae is suggestive of such an interpretation, for the long, winding, dark passage can be seen as making a deliberate rupture, a boundary and a threshold between the external world and the interior of the house. There is some anthropological evidence for such an interpretation that comes from a group of West African tribes:

> Usually measuring less than 1m (3ft) high, the doorway opening requires that one stoop down, proceed into the dark interior in this position, then stand up halfway to stride over a small semicircular wall. Such an entrance ...required the act of entering and exiting to be done with a marked change of body position ... Rites of separation and reintegration ... are performed at these doorways.[75]

Stooping to enter the house through a low and narrow doorway is exactly what the occupants were obliged to do at Skara Brae. To conclude this discussion of the Skara Brae house from this point of departure will enable us to see how the notion of body – house – cosmos might be elaborated to suggest how a world within a world is established.

After following the long winding passage and stooping to enter, the occupants arise and directly ahead of them see the dresser beyond the fire. In the conjunction of this return to uprightness and things organised on axis is a

deeply phenomenological experience which here seems to be used to constitute the meaning of the space. Phenomenology has shown that the conception
of space as a volume, an empty void or mere extension measurable in metres
awaiting our action, is not true to the nature of our lived experience. 'The
experience of space is neither innocent nor primal' says Thomas, 'but
inescapably social and cultural'.[76]

In his book *Existence, Space and Architecture*, Norberg Schulz agrees with this
first point but his more considered analysis reveals three 'levels' of spatial
concepts. Not only is there an objective scientific description of space and 'public
space' – his equivalent of Thomas' social and cultural space – but also a 'private
or individual space'.[77] Addressing the problem of architectural design, Norberg
Schulz argues that meaningful space arises only through the integration of an
individual concept of space with a public one. Individual space is not to be
considered as merely private or idiosyncratic, however, but as having some
aspects of a universal structure which makes it possible for meaning to be grasped
and allows cross-cultural comparisons. 'Certain African languages, for instance,'
says Norberg Schulz, 'use the same word for "eye" and "in front of"'.[78] Our
experience is rooted in a context which originates from us, which has been
called the spatiality of the body.[79] The notion of verticality, for example, derives
from the uprightness that follows our action of rising from stooping or sleep.
Without a continuous effort towards this uprightness we would not exist as
distinctively human beings; it is our first motion of constructing order from
chaos. Hence the significance of the *axis mundi*. So after crawling along the dark,
twisting passage, which might be interpreted in this context as an expression of
chaos or disorientation, and after stooping to pass through the narrow entrance,
the body regains its natural, active, upright human position where it confronts
the interior world of the house ordered by an axis and symmetry. Norberg
Schulz developed the concept of 'existential space' to describe mankind's understanding of the structure of space as experienced in relation to a fundamental
need for orientation. 'It stems from a need to grasp vital relations in his environment, to bring meaning and order into a world of events and actions'.[80]

The notion of an axis is derived, according to the tenets of phenomenology,
from our sense of frontality which comes automatically with verticality. We
stand upright and we face the world which gives us a sense of directionality;
an axis is the organisation of things or movement in space that derives from
this. At Skara Brae the most significant things that constitute the life of the
house itself are placed on the axis presented to the returning occupants on
regaining the vertical position. Of first significance is the fire in the hearth,
which establishes the centre of the house by providing life-sustaining warmth,
hardening clay into pots, and transforming raw nature into cooked food.
Beyond, on axis is the dresser that, although we cannot be sure what was
displayed upon it, clearly evokes the idea of storage. Housed in this structure
may have been food gathered from the world or artefacts associated with such

tasks – whether practical or magical. This axis, then, connects and organises all that sustains the life of the house brought in, yet separated, from the outside world beyond the low entrance. Perhaps here again we should look closely at how the dresser is set up, with its central pillar presented in such a way as to give a pronounced sense of frontality to the entrance, this frontality emerging from the stone being both face-on to the entrant and set up vertically. The dresser has a distinct anthropomorphic feel to it, evoked by its facing central pillar and its verticality in addition to the arrangement of stones that can be read as torso, head and outstretched arms set into the shallow recess in which it is housed. Perhaps its form and arrangement served to remind the entering occupants of this active, upright aspect of being that structured the life of the house and in which, thanks to the gathered fruits of activity stored here, the counter-balancing necessity of repose could take place.

The idea of a line structuring the experience of space is the central theme of Hodder's book *The Domestication of Europe*. From the beginning of agriculture, the household becomes 'a production unit' and everything 'wild' becomes transformed into the 'cultured' through what he calls the *domus*. 'The *domus* as defined here', he writes, 'is the concept and practice of nurturing and caring, but at a still more general level, it obtains its dramatic force from the exclusion, control and domination of the wild, the outside'. 'Agri-culture' he defines as 'culturing the wild', which takes place outside and is opposed to the *domus*. He interprets the LBK long houses, with their three rows of posts and division into three sections, as 'adding to the sense of linearity within the house'.[81] The line and graded thresholds into the deepest space of the house are the expression of the fundamental principle inherent in the process of farming, the domestication of plants and animals. Hodder argues that the similarity between megalithic remains found along the Atlantic façade stems not simply from diffusion but 'from a common cultural background' rooted in the *domus*. If Thomas is correct in arguing for the Neolithic to be considered 'an integrated conceptual classificatory system' as well as an economic model, then perhaps the axis at Skara Brae, focusing on material brought in from the 'wild', is a particular example of Hodder's principle.[82] We will see a more elaborate use of lines in relation to the Barnhouse settlement and the Stones of Stenness.

But the genesis of a line is not explicable by the idea of oppositions in itself. As Eliade demonstrated with the body – house – cosmos concept and *axis mundi*, such concepts emerge from the reciprocal relationships sensed between the self and the world. As well as verticality, frontality and directionality, the notion of symmetry is derived from our sense of the spatiality of the body, the experience of our body in space as we go about our existence. Not only do we face the world as a consequence of our upright posture, but we also face others. From this encounter the fundamental nature of our bodily symmetry is inescapable: two ears, two eyes, two arms, two legs, two breasts are arranged symmetrically either side of a central axis comprised of nose, mouth, spine, navel and genitals. Given this, and the pervasiveness of the body – house – cosmos notion amongst primitive people, it is not surprising to see the Skara Brae houses organised symmetrically as well as axially. The dominant components of this are the beds, which are not only disposed symmetrically either side of the line of entry but also arranged on an axis perpendicular to it originating from the central hearth. Thus both life's activity and repose are woven together across the central hearth as the structuring principles of the house. Whereas the axis of activity is presided over by the central pillar of the dresser – an appropriately vertical symbol – a large recumbent slab of stone dominates the beds. If the combination of horizontal stone to contain the bedding material and sleeping occupants and vertical stone to support a protective cover makes for practical good sense, we should not forget Eliade's contention that, for the primitive, the practical is inextricably intertwined with the symbolic. The vertical is often seen as a masculine symbol and the horizontal as a female, a symbolism which is often 'misconstrued as opposition when their complementarity is the fundamental aspect of their relationship'.[83] Perhaps this arrangement of stones symbolised the complementary relationship between male and female just as the bi-axial arrangement of the house around the fire seems to demonstrate the reciprocity between action and repose.

The arrangement of the house using bi-axial symmetry may also incorporate a cosmological principle not unlike that proposed by Parker-Pearson and Richards in relation to the orientation of the hearth, but perhaps drawn from the inter-relationship perceived between body – house – cosmos. The upright body not only gives us symmetrical left and right sides but also a front and back. Eliade described how the backbone became linked with the tree and the mountain in the shared concept of *axis mundi*. In a similar way the four horizontal divisions of the body, front, back, left and right, have a qualitative relationship with the quartering of the earth's surface as it forms the basis of cosmogony; the quarter where the sun is at its highest and strongest, that where it never enters, the quarter where the sun rises and that where it sets. All early societies attributed similar qualitative values to the cardinal points. Of the Roman city, for example, organised strictly around the *cardus* and *decumanus*, it has been said that the Roman citizen always knew whether he was going towards or away from the sun, or following the sun's path.[84] Perhaps in the organisation of the Skara Brae house we see a similar process at work, although with a very different specific meaning. Where the Roman city was open to the world over which it reigned, the Orkney house set itself off from the external world and created its own order within its walls. The structuring principle of the house mirrors that of both the human body and how the world or cosmos itself was perceived to be structured.

The houses at Skara Brae seem to be fundamentally powerful symbols of protection and gathering, echoing that of the pot and the basket. The 'natural human inclination is to "house" that which is most sacred' and the dominant feature of Skara Brae is the dresser that presumably 'housed' something significant and in turn was itself 'housed' in a shallow recess in the wall.[85] This axis, then, might be considered as open yet with diametrically opposed values; at one end the large spacious dresser, storing gathered things essential for life, at the other end the constricted entrance, dark and opening to the world beyond. This axis might be qualitatively linked with north and south, where one is wholly positive, the sun at its strongest, giver of warmth, light and life, and the other associated with darkness and danger. The axis perpendicular to it follows the path of the sun from sunrise to sunset. Thus at the periphery of the house, at these two quarters associated in the outside world with the transition from day to night, are placed the beds, transporting the occupants from activity to sleep. In such a way, Skara Brae constructs a world within a world, centred on the vital life-giving hearth and with its periphery structured by axes that allow the reciprocity between body and cosmos to be embodied within the house itself. It formed the constant unmoving centre of their cosmos as the cycles of cold and warmth, dark and light, winter, spring, summer and autumn revolved endlessly above.

Barnhouse

The settlement at Barnhouse has houses similar to those at Skara Brae and Rinyo and is situated close to both Maes Howe and the Stones of Stenness. Potsherds found at the settlement were 'identical to the Grooved Ware from … (the) Stones of Stenness'.[86] Grooved Ware was found not only at Skara Brae, but also at Rinyo, hence its earlier name of Rinyo/Clacton ware. Grooved Ware has become associated with a particular pair of problems: first, its origin, and second, what it indicates about changing social patterns. A general consensus has emerged that it is most likely to have originated in Ireland or Scotland, possibly in Orkney itself. Ann MacSween uses the settlement at Pool as the basis for a study of Orcadian pottery sequence that sheds light on the bigger picture.

Pool was occupied in the Neolithic between around 4000 and 2000 BC. MacSween identifies three phases of pottery during this period. The earliest phase is represented by round bottomed, mostly undecorated sherds which are recognisably Unstan ware. From Phase 2, baggy vessels were recovered, mostly flat-bottomed and straight-sided averaging 20cm in diameter. Many of these thick walled vessels had incised decoration in the later stages of this phase. Phases 1 and 2 suggested 'gradual stylistic evolution', whereas phase 3 'differs in form, fabric, surface finish, technology and decoration'. In this final phase bucket shaped vessels were most common; 'Decorative scalloped and notched rims appear, and applied decoration including ladder, lattice, trellis and fish-scale motifs is dominant'. In this we find the classic description of Grooved Ware (33). MacSween's observation of 'the presence at Pool of a degree of technological and stylistic continuity between the round-bottomed and flat-bottomed' raises a problem for the traditional dichotomy of round-bottomed/Grooved Ware.[87]

In her discussion of this material, MacSween identifies locations of Grooved Ware and a rough chronology which helps establish the context of Barnhouse. 'This early Grooved Ware', as she describes Pool Phase 2, has a similar form and incised decoration to that found in the later phases of Rinyo and the early phases of Skara Brae. The Pool Phase 3 'is most similar to that from the Links of Noltland', but its relief decoration is also paralleled in the 'early phase pottery' at Barnhouse. Although, as she makes clear, this establishes no definitive claims to the origin of Grooved Ware in Orkney, nevertheless it supports the case for seeing processes of major social change taking place that culminate in the settlement at Barnhouse.

A crucial point made by MacSween concerning 'the general absence of Grooved Ware in tombs' reinforces the suggestion of significant changes abroad at the time of the late Neolithic. This is mirrored in the deposition of other artefacts. Reviewing the curious stone balls found at Skara Brae and elsewhere in Orkney in *Their Use is Wholly Unknown*, Edmonds refers to the related and important point 'that because of the lack of secure associations with graves, these items may have been "family or clan possessions"'. He concludes by suggesting that 'like Grooved Ware, carved stone balls were implicated in reproducing the new forms of authority and obligations which characterised the later Neolithic'.[88] Barnhouse and its surroundings provide the best settlement evidence for this. Thomas says that later in England Grooved Ware was

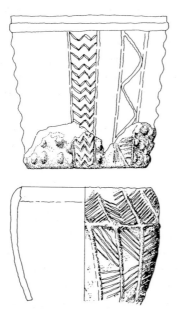

33 *Grooved Ware pots with decoration showing resemblance to basket weave. Top pot from Pool, bottom from Durrington Walls.* Redrawn after Shepherd (top) and Megaw & Simpson (below)

used in parallel with other ceramic traditions. It is linked to henges, which leads him to reiterate Edmonds' interpretation of it being used for 'controlling ritual practice and dominating "lower status big men"'. This Grooved Ware incorporated shells – 'exotic and distant' – for tempering the clay, whereas Peterborough ware found in contemporaneous domestic contexts is decorated with seed impressions – 'near and domesticated'.[89]

The form and construction of one rather different building at Barnhouse shows distinct resemblances to Maes Howe. As we will see in the next chapter, the enormous size of Maes Howe has been interpreted by Renfrew as evidence for an emerging hierarchical society. Written before the discovery of Barnhouse, two unusual and large structures tend to confirm Renfrew's hypothesis described by the excavator Colin Richards as 'a hierarchical spatial structure'.[90]

Because the site has been greatly ploughed down leaving only a few centimetres of wall remaining, the smaller houses surrounding these buildings have been drawn in a partial way and consequently are less specific than Skara Brae or Rinyo (**34** & **colour plate 16**). The general impression given from this is of a site more like Rinyo where the distinctive beds are sometimes embedded in the wall and sometimes free-standing in the living space. Richards has described this pattern as a 'situation of flux' with houses being demolished and rebuilt in a somewhat confusing sequence. The houses 'had a skin of stacked turfs', he continues, which could be interpreted as the skin of the earth as it were, wrapped around the body of the house, fulfilling the role that midden performed at Skara Brae and Knap of Howar.

The two buildings that differ from the familiar house type are monumental and present problems of interpretation. House 2 is a much larger structure than the Skara Brae-type houses and has a much more formal plan arrangement than anything seen in Orkney hitherto (**35** & **colour plate 17**). A resemblance to the plan arrangement of the Maes Howe chamber has been noted. Also the construction technique is very similar incorporating a distinctly faced straight wall to the interior using large, long stones. Maes Howe has four bays made in this way whereas Barnhouse 2 has six. The walls are approximately 2.5m thick and the cavity is filled with clay.

A screen divides into two what otherwise would appear to be a large 7m by 4m central space. Entry is into the right-hand compartment directly in front of which a stone-lined cist containing fragments of bone was found. A large hearth occupied the centre of both compartments formed by the screen, although Richards considers there to have been some re-organisation of the space, including covering the cist and right-hand hearth with a clay floor. He makes much of the experience of entering this arrangement over the buried remains of what might have been ancestors and towards an ancestral fire with the new centre, focused on the left-hand hearth, hidden from immediate view. He suggests that the left-hand compartment may represent a second phase and that instead of six bays there were 'possibly four in a cruciform arrangement'.[91] Such

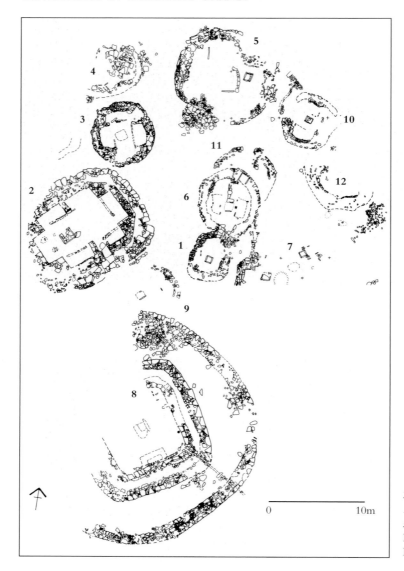

34 *Plan of Barnhouse settlement.* Redrawn after Richards

an arrangement would be similar to the early house at Skara Brae, although markedly more formal. The immediacy of focus found at the Skara Brae house would have been similar in such a first phase of Barnhouse 2.

Richards describes Barnhouse 2 as fusing 'the architecture of the house with the passage grave'.[92] He interprets it as a house because of the presence of hearths, but also because of slots for bed sides as at Skara Brae. If this was a monumental house it reinforces the interpretation of an emerging social hierarchy. But the arrangement of six bed spaces and the paucity of evidence for domestic activity raises questions about such an attribution. Perhaps it was a purely ritual structure akin to the *nuhue* or 'world house' of the Kogi, a meeting place or social house

35 *View of House 2 at Barnhouse. Ploughed down to its foundations, it has been rebuilt 3 or 4 courses high since excavation*

36 *Plan of House 2 at Barnhouse compared with Staneydale, Shetland (left).* Redrawn after Richards with addition of wall line at top right

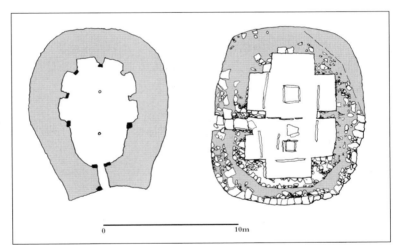

for the elders of the tribe. Whether this was strictly speaking a house or used for some other purpose, nevertheless it would be equally consistent with the interpretation of Barnhouse as a hierarchical settlement.

A large house-like structure in Shetland, called Staneydale Temple, has a similar arrangement of side bays to Barnhouse 2 and featured two central posts. In her survey of *Neolithic Britain and Ireland*, Caroline Malone suggests that this 'might have functioned as a communal or even a ceremonial place'.[93] It has a typological resemblance to Shetland houses with their side bed-bays, which, as here at Barnhouse, has been monumentalised both by its increased size and greater geometrical arrangement in plan (**36**). Even more suggestive is that

75

there are six bed spaces, the same number as at House 2 at Barnhouse. Twenty pieces of Arran pitchstone were discovered at Barnhouse indicating long-range contact between communities. It may be that not only material artefacts were exchanged but also ideas about society and religious beliefs.

Structure 8 is an even more monumental building, which the evidence suggests was not a house because there are no bed spaces or slots found for bed sides (**37** & **38**). However, Richards has described its basic arrangement as 'a large building drawing on certain elements of the house and transforming them into monumental proportions'. Constructed in the familiar thick, stone cavity wall, the interior measures 7m by 7m, 'the largest covered and enclosed space experienced by Neolithic people in Orkney'.[94] It had a large central hearth and holes were found for a Skara Brae-type dresser, with both these features on axis with the entrance. A drainage channel was built into one corner and a complete Grooved Ware pot was found buried in the floor.

An intriguing feature of this building is that the entrance porch, which jutted out from the enclosing walls, was flanked by two standing stones and had a hearth associated with it. To enter the building would involve stepping over this hearth, a distinctly ritualistic movement which could be associated with purification. This entrance, moreover, is aligned with midsummer sunset.[95] All this led Richards to interpret Structure 8 as a 'ritual building'.

The building itself is surrounded by a roughly circular wall. The space between wall and building Richards found to be covered with a clay platform and in this were 'several elaborate hearths, pots and remains of stone boxes'.[96] This suggested cooking and possibly feasting. The concept of 'big men' who develop allegiances by presiding over feasts is well known from anthropology. Richards points out that a clay-sealed floor is also to be found in the ring surrounding Maes Howe. He also shows that the arrangement of hearth and adjacent megaliths at the entrance to this 'feast hall' is very similar to an arrangement found at the Stones of Stenness. The entrance through the encircling wall is located such as to form an axis that links the hearth and the Watch Stone (**39**). Located where Loch Stenness joins Loch Harray, this gigantic standing stone has further significance amongst a web of lines in the vicinity, as will be seen in the next two chapters.

Both House 2 and Structure 8 at Barnhouse, then, show a kinship in being monumentalised adaptations of pre-existing house types and/or passage graves. Richards reads the relationships between these two new forms of structure and Maes Howe, and between these and the Stones of Stenness, as evidence for greater control over ritual activity in the late Neolithic. Such an interpretation reflects the evidence from tombs and stone circles for an emerging hierarchical society, an issue to be explored in more detail in the following two chapters. In concluding this chapter it is worth considering Sharples' hypothesis for why the unique Orcadian pattern of Neolithic villages – Pool, Links of Noltland, Rinyo and Skara Brae – might have developed and the implications this had

37 *Barnhouse Structure 8. Viewed from outside the entrance, note the projecting porch and the unusual presence of a hearth at the threshold*

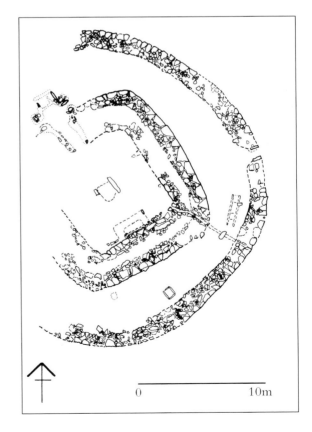

38 *Plan of Barnhouse Structure 8.*
Redrawn after Richards

0   10m

39 *The entrance through the perimeter wall to Barnhouse Structure 8. A line between it and the Watch Stone passes across the hearth at the centre of the building*

for the hierarchical society that seems to have emerged at Barnhouse. Early Neolithic settlements in Orkney were on machair land, he argues, which disintegrates when the surface is broken, hence the importance of midden. But Barnhouse is on rich, relatively heavy land that would not have been easy to farm without drainage.[97] This may have been less of a technical problem – we saw drainage at Rinyo – and more of a social one of sufficient labour being mobilised to open up more difficult, but ultimately more productive land. Sharples wonders whether the 'number of economic and social innovations which enabled the creation of villages' might be because Mesolithic peoples continued to linger on in the Northern Isles. Sheridan and Sharples point out elsewhere that 'what "Neolithic" means for the south of England is far removed from what it means in Orkney, with its semi-domesticated deer population and rich variety of wild and domesticated resources'.[98] Mixing the attributes of hunter-gatherers' more collective form of socio-economic practice with developed farming, at a time when the islands had become densely populated, might have provided the necessary flexibility of mind to develop village communities. From such a position the advantages of a larger social group might naturally prosper, leading to the new form of settlement we see at Barnhouse surrounded by new and larger monuments. As will be seen, such an economic or practical explanation has its complement in the more obviously symbolic sphere of belief system.

3

A HOUSE FOR THE DEAD

My interest in the chambered cairns of Orkney began during a second visit to the islands. Having most of the weekend to kill before there was a ferry to Hoy, I set off on a tour of Mainland. After seeing the Broch of Gurness and Brough of Birsay, I drove on to Skara Brae where the custodian had gone home but sufficient light remained to see. It was one of those wonderful Orkney March days when the full range of island weather swept across the afternoon skies. Returning to my hotel I passed the Ring of Brodgar and stopped at the Stones of Stenness where the sun slipped beneath the clouds low down against the horizon, filling the sky with honeyed light. The sun setting behind the Stones of Stenness lit up the mountains of Hoy like two haloed sugar loaves. A rainbow spread across the sky, slowly veiled by a passing shower, the rain suffused with light.

Next morning I visited the chambered cairns of Wideford Hill, Cuween Hill and Maes Howe. Prompted perhaps by Scully's book *The Earth, The Temple and the Gods*, in which he drew attention to relationships Greek temples established with clefts in the landscape, I noticed that the entry passage to Wideford faced Cuween and a line of sight seemed to pass along the shore to a pair of hills. Crawling into Cuween Hill, pleased to escape the wind-driven sleet and linger in the deep silence of the chamber, I was struck by a resemblance between these cairns and the houses at Skara Brae. The beds here had become independent but connected side chambers not unlike the earlier houses. There was neither hearth nor furniture nor any sign of life's processes — as was only to be expected in a place for the dead. Similarly the most obvious difference, the tall, chimney stack-like vault, seemed to me best explained by a demand that the structure of the cairn should be wholly of stone, a material associated with the dead.

Although these observations were rather naive and probably incorrect, nevertheless the direct, intuitive noticing of a resemblance between house and cairn did seem to suggest that here was the first architecture or, indeed, the impulse to make architecture itself. Strictly speaking, buildings for the dead serve no useful or practical purpose. But some of the evidence of man's earliest occupation of the earth shows his concern for the dead. Modern anthropological studies of more recent 'primitives' indicate that rites associated with death were not only for remembrance but formed part of complex systems of rituals that ordered all aspects of their life, society and culture. We have to presume an extensive pattern of rituals dominating the Orcadian Neolithic but, as everywhere from Brittany northwards, death and burial were the impulses to produce the first non-utilitarian structures.

The immediate source of Orkney passage graves is self-evident: 'The typology of the tombs makes it quite clear that the Orkney islands were colonised from Caithness'. There is some consensus that passage graves origi-nated on the west coast of France or independently at other locations along the Atlantic seaboard. But no conclusive pattern such as we saw with the house emerges to clarify the northward route of these tomb-builders. Reviewing the three possible routes, Henshall dismisses the east coast of Britain because no supporting evidence has been found there. In contrast, passage graves are found all along the west coast of Britain and throughout Ireland, although the bewil-dering array of different types compounds the difficulty of plotting a line of descent for the Orkney cairns. Of the two possible routes, up the west coast to Cape Wrath and along the north coast of Scotland, or through the Great Glen, Henshall favours the latter. 'The Black Isle forming the north shore of the (Cromarty) Firth has many Orkney-Cromarty-type cairns. From here they are found all along the east coast'.[1]

The subsequent discovery of houses on Uist similar to Knap of Howar, north of the entrance to the Great Glen, complicates this picture. The presence of Orkney-Cromarty passage graves in Sutherland adds a further twist. Although Henshall explains how the Sutherland cairns could have arrived from the north-east, but equally they could represent a settlement continuing along the west coast northwards from Uist. It seems quite likely that pioneer groups would strike out in different directions to find suitable available land. The Black Isles, being particularly good farmland, may well have been the springboard for what Henshall describes as 'a spread northwards from an initial settlement in Easter Ross'.[2] Paradoxically, however, the fertile soil might have created small distances between settlements and hence a slow expansion northwards thereafter. In contrast, the north-west passage might have dictated long sea journeys from which the fertile valleys around Thurso would have appeared most welcome. Until we have more radiocarbon dates from Orkney-Cromarty cairns we cannot be certain by which route they first arrived in Caithness.

The origins of monumental stone burial tombs are not fully understood although some general points of interpretation have found a consensus. There was no monumental building in the preceding Mesolithic. The building of stone burial tombs 'seems to have been triggered by the arrival on the Atlantic seaboard of agriculturalists from central and southern Europe'.[3] The idea that farming in itself 'made monuments possible', however, is now rejected.[4] It seems more likely that the Neolithic, interpreted by Thomas as 'an integrated classifi-catory system' – something to think with rather than an economic system – intersected in some way with 'the complex funerary traditions of the preceding Mesolithic'.[5] There are three factors associated with this conjunction that perhaps explain why it has been difficult to nominate a single point of origin for burial cairns. Firstly there were a large number of very productive Mesolithic societies on the Atlantic seaboard from Portugal to Denmark. At many of these, huge shell middens had accumulated and in some, human remains were interred. On the islands of Teviec and Hoedic in Brittany, for example, burials were found in 'slab-lined cists' set into shell middens.[6]

The idea of burial became particularly pronounced in early farming societies for, as Eliade says; 'Agriculture taught man the fundamental oneness of organic life ...; like seed hidden in the earth the dead can hope to return to life in a new form'.[7] In this there may be a significant point of connection with the shell midden, which might have suggested the idea of a burial cairn. The shell 'is a symbol of the moon'; its 'ever-recurring cycle makes the moon the heavenly body above all others concerned with the rhythms of life'.[8] Cunliffe titled his book *At the Ocean's Edge* to suggest a distinctive shared background between the character of people from Brittany to Orkney. The tide's relationship to the waxing and waning of the moon must have seemed of particular significance to them. Time is measured by the moon. Fertility is linked with water and the sea was the principal source of the Mesolithic way of life and continued to be of great importance to farmers on the 'Ocean's Edge'. The diurnal rhythm of night and day corresponding to the rise and fall of the tide, covering and uncovering the shellfish produced by the sea in such great abundance, must have seemed significant to Mesolithic people. Perhaps the idea of such a harvest growing from beneath water struck Neolithic farmers as similar to their own harvest growing from beneath the earth. Bradley describes the curious presence of *Spondylus* shells from the Aegean in LBK burial contexts throughout central Europe, immensely distant from their source.[9] The moon is not only associated with human fertility in the menstrual cycle, but in many cultures it is also known as 'the first of the dead' because it seems to die and be reborn three nights later. In the overlapping symbolism of shell and seed, we might see the fundamental impulse to bury the dead in such a way as to suggest continued life. The end of a relatively short human life – 'like the flower in the field' – because located in the matrix that seemed to embody nature's rhythms of eternal return.

The second point is that the incoming Neolithic technology and food production joined with what Cunliffe describes as 'the strength of the coastal socio-economic system' to promote population growth. This created 'labour on an unprecedented scale' that could be mobilised to create 'spectacular architecture, much of it focused on the glorification of the ancestors'.[10] It is not difficult to see how the early form of the large, long mound at Barnenez, for example, could have developed in this way from the shell midden idea or its inherent symbolism. Moreover, in his early volume on *Ancient France*, Scarre agreed with this, suggesting that the impetus for burial mounds might have 'arisen from the need felt by the early Neolithic communities of north-west France to express social reorganisation'.[11]

The third factor is that the two westward and northward expansions of the Neolithic across Europe – the LBK along the Danube, Rhine and Seine, and the Cardial ware cultures from Iberia and south-west France – met in north-west France. Cunliffe says Brittany became a 'pressure point' and, following Scarre, suggests that it may have been here and for this reason that monumental burial mounds were first constructed. By interring the bones of their ancestors in a monumental stone tomb conspicuously placed in the landscape, a community established its claim to the land on which it had settled. Scarre's early suggestion that burial mounds were built as territorial markers has stood the test of time, although there may have been other factors involved as suggested above.

Three basic types of burial tomb emerged from this period of ferment; simple dolmens, passage graves, and rock-cut tombs. From this relatively simple basis arose an incredibly complex array of burial monuments ranging from long barrows to circular and other-shaped cairns such that it is impossible to trace back the source of the Orkney-Cromarty type. Single, polygonal-chambered cairns were possibly the source of all passage graves and in this we see the essential core of the idea that underlies all variants (collective burial, human remains set apart from but related to the everyday life-world, and megalithic stone building) – large stones were used wherever possible. In his summary of the evidence, Masters says that it 'seems reasonable … to think of two broad traditions – that of the NM barrows of northern Europe and that of the chambered tombs of western Europe'.[12] The former developed as long barrows in England, the latter spread up the west of Britain, Ireland and Scotland.

The significance of death to Neolithic societies is vividly illustrated in Orkney by the prevalence of burial tombs in the archaeological record. In *The Chambered Cairns of Orkney*, Davidson and Henshall list 81 cairns known to have existed, although there were certainly more (**40**). It seems highly probable that every settlement had its burial cairn.[13] Drawing upon anthropological research, Shanks and Tilley have explained why this is likely to be the case. Neolithic mortuary practice fundamentally served to assert the community over the individual, and reinforced the solidarity of the social group.[14] The idea of the individual so familiar to us was hardly known amongst primitive peoples who, anthropologists remind us, saw the unpredictability of death as a threat to the social order. Hence, as in the other changes of an individual's state – birth, puberty, marriage – so death has to have its rite of passage. Bloch and Parry explain that this is 'to dramatise the victory of order over biology' such that 'death can be represented as part of a cyclical order'. They point to a surprising link between fertility symbols and funeral rites noted from anthropology. This they consider to be explicable by the irreversibility of time made manifest in death. Hence funerary rituals often 'commence from the fact of a changed state and develop an analogy with the idea of birth; rebirth; merging time's line, its irreversibility and its discontinuity, with time's cycle'.[15] Ritual is action orchestrated into a symbolic pattern. Often such ritualised action finds

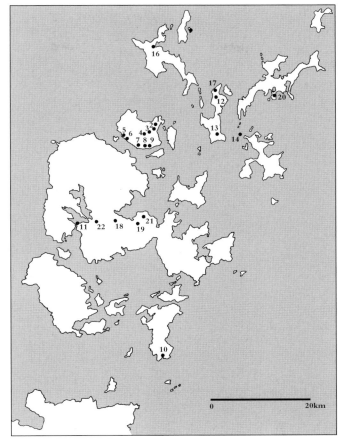

40 *Map of Orkney showing the location of chambered cairns to be discussed in this chapter. 1 Bigland Round; 2 Bigland Long; 3 Knowe of Craie; 4 Kierfea Hill; 5 Midhowe; 6 Knowe of Ramsay; 7 Knowe of Yarso; 8 Blackhammer; 9 Taversoe Tuick; 10 Isbister; 11 Unstan; 12 Braeside; 13 Eday Church; 14 Holm of Huip; 15 Holm of Papa Westray South; 16 Pierowall; 17 Vinquoy Hill; 18 Cuween; 19 Wideford; 20 Quoyness; 21 Quanterness; 22 Maes Howe*

an echo in the symbolic form of an artefact or construction, as we noted in the Dogon basket and house, for example. An examination of the location, setting, orientation, form and material of the cairns shows the archaeological record to be consistent with anthropological descriptions. The building itself can become the frozen witness, as it were, of the ritual event that called it into being. Holding on to this intersection of ideas, it is proposed here to review a selection of the cairns to see what light they might shed on the significance of death in Neolithic Orkney and to enquire what the building of these cairns meant to these communities negotiating the passage or transactions between life and death.

Stone and bone

I returned to Orkney the following Easter to begin my serious study of Neolithic remains. I knew now that there were two distinct kinds of passage grave on

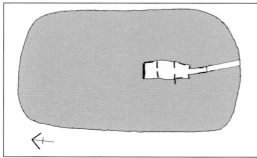

41 *View of Braeside chambered cairn looking along the line of its entrance passage*

42 *Plan of Braeside.* Redrawn after Davidson & Henshall

Orkney and that all those I had previously seen were of the Maes Howe type. My first Orkney-Cromarty type I encountered on Eday when I walked from the magnificent standing Setter Stone to the cairn on Vinquoy Hill. The exposed remains of Braeside, its chamber divided by two pairs of slabs, declared it to be a tripartite version, generally held to be the earliest of this type.

Returning later that day, my route passed Braeside again. Approaching from the rear of the chamber I was astonished to see that the entrance passage aligned with the Setter Stone (**41** & **43**). Archaeologists do not mention this. I re-examined the cairn and noticed that the passage was skewed at an angle of about 10° from the chamber axis, so it must have been deliberately aligned on the standing stone (**42**). This dramatic discovery, and its curious omission from Davidson and Henshall's comprehensive survey (the passage is drawn skewed but is not remarked on in the text), confirmed my opinion that defining evidence too narrowly would inevitably overlook an important aspect of a cairns' significance. For it was an objective fact, if not a material one, that the entry passage to the chamber had been built to give a line of sight to the standing stone. But what could be the significance of this, why would a tomb

43 *The Setter Stone on Eday*

have its entrance aligned on a standing stone, and what might be significant about relating bone and stone in this way?

Although acknowledging that we will never know exactly why Neolithic builders arranged materials as they did, it seemed inescapable that this alignment formed a significant part of their intentions. Here, the impossibility of understanding the significance of burial cairns without attempting to bridge the gap between material evidence and possible intentions was starkly shown. At the same time the links between these two structures open up a way to investigate the world of meaning. Examining the nature of this relationship from the point of view of the savage mind or mythical thinking might disclose something of the chambered cairns' meaning to their Neolithic builders. In the light of what we know about the symbolism of death, meanings might be extracted from the arrangement, the form and material of the burial structure itself.

Operating within our scientific world view makes it difficult for us to envisage that physical and physiological life can be considered sacred. Ceremonies and sacraments are ways by which primitive man communicated with a force that stood for life itself. This force might be made manifest in phenomena such as thunder or the moon, and a dead man's bones may contain his spirit or ghost.[16] A sacred force may reside not only in the substance but also in the form.[17] As in the last chapter we found that the intertwining of these two categories yielded insights into the Neolithic dwelling, so an examination of them here might shed new light on death, burial and the chambered cairns.

Amongst earlier peoples the sacred could manifest itself in many ways, not only in phenomena but also in ordinary objects such as stones, trees, or birds. The stone, tree or bird is venerated not for itself, however, but because it reveals something which is no longer simply stone, for example, but the sacred. In revealing the sacred, the stone, paradoxically 'becomes something else, yet it continues to remain itself'.[18] Eliade proposed the term hierophany to designate the manifestation of the sacred, defining hierophany as 'that something sacred shows itself to us'. For the primitive, continues Eliade, 'sacred is equivalent to a power, and, in the last analysis, to reality'.[19] In the case of stone it signifies some force greater than man. Erupting from the earth, as did all vegetable life so significant for these first farmers, boulders and rocks would strike men's minds by their solidity and steadfastness. Stone endured whilst everything else was subject to decay. Stone partook of the eternity that the mysterious driving force of organic nature only revealed in its endless cycles.

There are Greek myths explaining the origin of mankind that suggest how the savage mind might see the relationship between bone and stone. Although Greek mythology was collected at a much later period than we are concerned with, it does include a genealogy of the gods that gives a significant place to a beneficent Mother Goddess, Gaia, a vestige of more ancient myths considered to emanate from the first farming societies. Because of the extensive literature on Greek myth, it is possible to see how the familiar stories evolved from much earlier rituals. One myth places the origin of mankind after a great flood (a mythical theme from the East and one, of course, incorporated in the Bible) brought down by Zeus to exterminate an earlier race of bronze.[20] Deukalion was advised to make a wooden box, store in it all necessaries and then climb into it himself. This he did, and so was saved from this flood along with his wife Pyrrha, daughter of Epimetheus and Pandora. On disembarking, Deukalion made a sacrifice to Zeus and in return he was granted a wish. He wished for people, so Zeus instructed him to throw stones over his shoulder – those cast by Deukalion became men, those by Pyrrha became women. A variant of this Greek myth contains a stronger resonance of an archaic source and one more suggestive of what form such myths might have taken at the far corners of the farming world. In this account Deukalion and Pyrrha received instructions from an oracle to throw behind them the bones of their 'great mother'. Cast in the typical oracular form of riddle they might have taken this to be Pandora, but they cast bones of the Great Mother Gaia, i.e. stones, and from them sprang humans. In this way they were descendants of the Earth herself.

This originating myth is preserved in ancient Greek, because the word *laoi* means 'people' and the word for 'stone' is *laas* or *laos*.[21] Although one might see in this no more than a pun, Cassirer's work shows that in fact both myth and language originated in a common source, the pre-reflective, pre-categorising layers of the mind. This will be further discussed in the final chapter. Seen from this perspective, the myth outlined above and the etymological similarity between stone and people might be explained by a combination of mankind's anxiety about his own fate. As the remorseless passage of time submitted his body to decay, he perhaps saw in his own bones some essential, indestructible core that resisted the former as it partook of the latter in its striking resemblance to stone. In this way stone and bone might be homologised.

The first person created by these stones thrown onto the earth was Protogeneia. This name, Kerenyi informs us, 'means exactly the same as Protogonos "the first to be born", which is also a surname both of the goddess Earth herself and of a more famous ravished daughter, Persephone.'[22] The story of Persephone is perhaps the best known example of the Greek myths where natural phenomena are personified. Persephone's abduction by Hades and her subsequent release upon condition that she returned to spend one third of each year in the underworld is a story that explains the fundamental mystery of farming, new life from seed buried in the earth. That Persephone, standing for the seed that brought forth new life, could be given this connection to the birth of mankind from stone or bone in the mythical mind, is very suggestive and perhaps epitomises a root belief of the builders of chambered cairns such as Braeside. Like stone, the bones contained the essence of an indestructible force that poured through life. Burying bones in the earth was perhaps to seek some metaphoric relationship with the planting of seeds. In its maturity and death, the seed containing the essence of its own renewal served as the inspiration for the hope of life's rebirth in some other form. In this we see myth confirming Bloch's anthropology.

Another aspect of the myth of Persephone offers more direct insight into the relationship between stone and bone and opens up a possible interpretation of the alignment between Braeside and the Setter Stone. When he realised that Demeter had made the world barren in her anger at the abduction of Persephone by his brother Hades, Zeus sent Hermes into the underworld to retrieve her. It is in the derivation of Hermes' own name that we can see a connection between what has been said about stone and bone and his role in negotiating the passage between this world and the underworld. Pausanias wrote that; 'If one goes far back in time one sees the Greeks paying honour not to statues but to unwrought stones (*argoi lithoi*)'.[23] Eliade takes this up and explains how in pre-Homeric Greece stones had been set beside roads to protect the way. These were called *hermai*, which much later became the familiar stone column surmounted by a head found in Renaissance gardens (**44**). So from out of a theophany of stone specifically related to guarding paths came Hermes the messenger of the gods, who could pass from this world to the next and was the conveyor of messages between worlds. Hermes sometimes has the epithet Psychopompos, 'god of ghosts and the underworld' and is often portrayed standing beside a grave with his snake-staff, a symbol of reincarnation.[24]

All this seems suggestive of how the minds of the first Orkney builders might have been operating as they built cairns with a stone-lined passage to an artificially constructed otherworld encased in stone. It might also explain the alignment of the passage at Braeside with the Setter Stone. Perhaps the standing stone symbolised something like a prototypical Hermes figure, assisting in the

44 *Hermes as a standing stone depicted on a Greek vase.* Redrawn after Harrison

rite of passage. The vast stone stood like some eternally vigilant being never succumbing to repose neither in sleep nor death. Both of these suggestions can be shown to have a possible connection with shamanism, the practice of which allowed the shaman to move between worlds. Eliade argues that vestiges of shamanistic activity 'remain among all the European peoples'. Its persistence and spread across Europe and Asia resulted from a 'systematic reorganisation of magico-religious life' that was 'basically accomplished at a period when the proto-Indo-Europeans had not yet separated'.[25]

Traces of shamanism can be found in ancient Greece. The 'few figures of Greek legend who can be compared to shamanism are related to Apollo', says Eliade. These legendary figures are said to have come 'from the north, from the land of the Hyperboreans'.[26] He considers this significant, for it is in the vast steppes and forests of Northern Europe and Asia that shamanism persisted. In the developed mythology, Hermes was described as having been born in a cave and the cave is connected to the symbolism of the descent to Hades. His mother's name Maia is variously construed as 'good old woman', 'midwife' and the goddess of night, all attributes that can be shown to have links with shamanism. All these suggest possible meanings that might resonate through the nexus of bone, stone, cave, cairn and otherworld.

The possibility of whether there might be any relationship between shamanistic-like activity and Orkney cairns will be discussed when we examine the buried remains. But before we leave Braeside and the Setter Stone there is one other myth that hints at a meaning latent in the material and the relationship between the cairn and standing stone – the biblical story of Jacob's ladder. Eliade demonstrates that the symbolism of Jacob's ladder has close parallels with the cosmic tree, often symbolised by a notched birch tree up which the Siberian shaman climbs in rituals, evoking his journey into the heavens.[27] The stone laid down as a pillow, upon which he slept and dreamt of angels ascending and descending, Jacob set up as a pillar at Bethel, the house of God, when he awoke. In this way the stone pillar symbolises an *axis mundi* by which this world becomes connected to the heavens. The Setter Stone may have been imbued with similar ideas, for the *axis mundi* can link this world with an underworld as well as a celestial world. Jacob's ladder obviously refers to a belief system that acknowledges a god on high, but the act of setting up the pillar itself may symbolise a shift from more archaic beliefs encountered in the Old Testament. A principal difference for these pre-Christian pioneer farming peoples was that the sacred would have manifested itself as a chthonic force rather than emanating from on high. Like Hermes descending to Hades, the line from the Setter Stone to Braeside probably refers to an idea of an underworld.

A complementary interpretation of the burial cairn might be that the stones serve to constrain the dead rather than facilitate their passage from one world to another. If the bones contained the spirit of the dead – that force which might live on – and if stone embodied something of nature's eternal force, then perhaps any malevolence from the dead could be held in check by the benevolent potentiality of stone. Tribes in central India pile up stones over or near a grave to:

> fasten down the dead man's soul; ... the funeral megalith [sic] protected the living against possible harmful action by the dead; for death as a state of indetermination made possible certain influences both good and bad. 'Imprisoned' in a stone the soul would be forced to act only beneficently.[28]

Perhaps the curiously anthropomorphic form of the Setter Stone, its gigantic size, its location and the fact that its broad face is directed towards Braeside, played some similar defensive or supportive role. Perhaps it helped to face down the potentially malevolent spirits of the dead or gave interlocutors enormous support when entering the passage to this otherworld in which were housed the bones of the dead.

Tomb and house

Before any more questions of interpretation are asked we should describe the cairns in some detail. Bigland Round makes a good starting point as, along with the Knowe of Craie, Bigland Long, Kierfea Hill and Faraclett Head East and West, it constitutes a group of very similar, early passage graves in Orkney, all sited within a mile or two of Rinyo on Rousay (**45** & **46**). These are very similar to many found in Caithness.

Pottery finds at Bigland Round and the Knowe of Craie have been interpreted as being 'early in the Orcadian pottery sequence', and this group of cairns are established on typological grounds as some of the earliest in Orkney.[29] With the exception of Bigland Long, all these cairns are of the Orkney-Cromarty type having a tripartite chamber like Braeside but within a circular cairn. Bigland Round is the best preserved of this group. In looking first at Bigland Round we can also broach the relationship between burial cairn and settlement for there is a distinct relationship between its siting and that of Rinyo.

The cairn is roughly circular, approximately 12m in diameter. Its coursed exterior containing wall now stands only 0.3m high but originally rose to a height of 2.5 to 3m and was probably capped by a shallow dome of stones. About 1m within, an inner wall contains the chamber, 4.8m long and 2.1m wide. Pairs of standing stones divide it into three compartments, the walls curved or bowed between. A large stone terminates the back chamber. The innermost stones are the tallest, surviving to a height of 1.2m, and evidence from elsewhere suggests that the chamber may have originally been 2m high. The orthostats would have looked not unlike the stalls of a byre.

Low stones in the back chamber probably supported shelves. We know from Taversoe Tuick that such shelves were present and from Midhowe (amongst others) that bodies – skeletons or bones – might be laid on them. This arrangement, of course, is precisely that seen at the earliest houses at Knap of Howar, the back section of the house organised with shelves and 'bins' into a storage space. The plan form of these early chambered cairns is clearly developed in response to that of the house at Knap of Howar, with its distinctive configuration divided into three compartments by standing stone slabs.

45 *Bigland Round viewed from behind the closing stone and looking across the chamber and entrance to the farmland below. Rinyo is in the corner of the field above the left-hand stone*

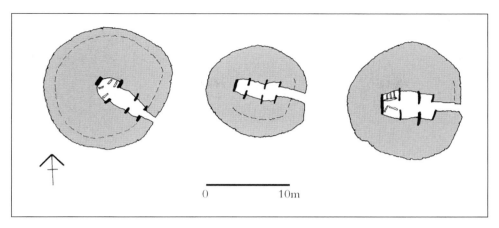

46 *Plans of (from left) Bigland Round, Kierfea Hill and Knowe of Craie.* Redrawn after Davidson & Henshall

These would appear to be houses for the dead. The deceased were in some cases laid out on the shelves that occupy the position of storage or sleep in the house. Possibly the symbolism inherent in both these positions was called into play, death seen as a kind of waiting before rebirth or as a mode of existence different from life, one more akin to sleep – the Greeks held that Thanatos (death) and Morpheus (sleep) were brothers. Such a relationship between the physical form of the house and a place for the dead constructed here as a visual, formal, or spatial metaphor has also been detected in the language of primitive peoples. Bloch and Parry describe a people – the Tikopia – whose social organisation is focused on the *pa*, a word which the authors say can be translated as 'house', 'lineage' and 'tomb'.[30] This will be examined in more detail when discussing remains found in the chambered cairns.

When discussing the possible transformation of basket to boat to dwelling in the last chapter, it was suggested that the significance of storage would have been immense to these first farmers, perhaps associated with the mystery of seeds bringing forth new life from within the earth. We noted in the course of describing the processes of adaptation and transformation peculiar to the savage mind how vestigial marks of basket-weaving were incorporated into the decoration of the first pottery. It is interesting to note, therefore, in this context where the interior space of the burial chamber has a metaphoric relationship with the house, that the external appearance of the cairn would have been rather like an upturned pot, remarkably similar in profile and proportion to Unstan ware but also not unlike early pottery found at Kierfea Hill (**47**). Apparently 'Unstan-ware vessels were often found in an inverted position within tombs'.[31]

In some later stalled cairns a herringbone pattern of stone appears immediately above the foundation courses, which makes a pattern very similar to the

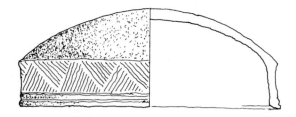

47 *Upside-down Unstan ware pot and decoration compared with herring-bone stonework at Blackhammer*

decoration of a pot rim. This will be discussed in due course. With their distinct wall the cairns would have struck the eye as more structural than the earth-mound they appear today. There may, however, have been some intended analogy with outcrops of stone, which are seen by many primitive peoples as sacred apparitions having their source in the soil. Stone's association with eternity might have been harnessed to harbour that human essence which persisted in the bone. In this context it is worth remarking upon the circular form of these early cairns. The circle is the obvious formal manifestation of the idea of a cycle, as well as the form of the sun and moon, those visible orches-trators of nature's eternal cycle into which, says Eliade, all rituals aim to weave human activity. This will be expanded upon in the next chapter.

Although at this early stage of the cairn's development the entrance passage is quite short, it nevertheless marks a distinct threshold; 'strait is the gate', as the Christian saying goes, between this world and the hereafter. The idea of two distinct domains, an inner space contained and circumscribed, is strongly suggested not only by the narrow, low passage, the restricted opening to the chamber and the entry portal, but also by the double wall. The wall to the inner space shapes the form of the house, a house for the dead; the outer defines the cairn as upturned pot, an enclosed form set apart from the everyday life-world. It is worth noting that where the cavity wall of the houses at Skara Brae and Knap of Howar was packed with midden to bring the stone to life, here in contrast, it was filled with stone. This was perhaps, as Eliade's sources suggested, to constrain the otherwise unpredictable movement of spirits asso-ciated with the dead.

The passage at Bigland Round was blocked by a large stone, its outer face flush with the cairn's perimeter wall. Whether this formed only part of a final sealing of the tomb or whether blocking stones were opened from time to time in the course of ritual activity is not certain, although the weight of evidence suggests there was a final closing. For the moment, however, it looks as if the burial cairns were less tomb than some kind of house for the dead, containing, controlling or storing the particular form of spirit energy or force associated with the bones.

Stone cairn and settlement

Rousay has been the site of some of the most illuminating work on the role of chambered cairns. Because of the remarkable survival of so many, the distribution and siting of cairns has encouraged theories to be advanced about the role of cairns for Neolithic communities. Renfrew initiated this line of research, which has proved fruitful on this classically shaped island with its tall, hump-backed centre and its farm land spread along the low-lying shore. By drawing a bisecting line between two cairns and then drawing one perpendicular to it, Renfrew constructed notional territories (**48**). Each of these hypothetical territories have the resources needed for pioneer settlements; the shore giving access to the sea, arable land, and moorland for grazing sheep etc. From this analysis Renfrew proposed that the cairns should be considered as territorial markers establishing a community's claim to a particular area of land, providing evidence to support Scarre's hypothesis mentioned earlier.

Two widespread characteristics concerning the siting of Orkney cairns that have been noted are that they were built both to be seen from and to overlook a particular area.[32] Davidson and Henshall point out that several cairns could have been sited more conspicuously, but proximity to potential sites of occupation seems to have been another important factor. We can see both these relationships at work particularly clearly in the relationship between Bigland Round and Rinyo (**49**). The Neolithic village of Rinyo lies half-buried in the hillside, against a cliff face that marks the present day boundary between the arable land at Bigland farm and the moorland above. From here the cairn of Bigland Round is clearly visible against the sky on the hillside to the west.

Moreover the cairn's entrance passage looks out over the farmed land which had been first worked by the ancestors interred there. In this way some kind of reciprocal relationship seems suggested between ancestors and descendants, an aspect that will be taken up later. For the time being, however, we can say that the people whose home was the village at Rinyo would be constantly reassured of their claim to this land by the stone cairn of Bigland Round containing their ancestors' bones – their ancestors who had settled, worked and claimed this patch of land. On the other side of the valley perhaps another group had settled, or perhaps one original family group had expanded and split into two, and this second group established its legitimate claim by building the cairn of Bigland Long.

Renfrew's hypothesis is particularly convincing when viewing the well-preserved chambered cairns along the southern side of Rousay. The topography of this side of the island clearly reveals its structure as distinct terraces made from the erosion of horizontal sandstone beds. Most of the cairns are sited conspicuously on a ledge above the arable land. The group of cairns from Midhowe to Taversoe Tuick forms a well-mapped part of tourist Orkney, and the visitor is inevitably struck by the visibility of the cairns. The Knowe of Yarso,

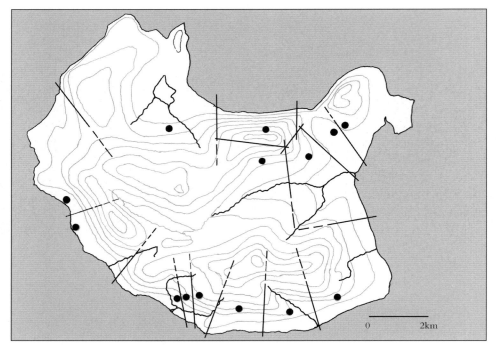

48 *Map of Rousay indicating hypothetical Neolithic territories.* Redrawn after Renfrew

Blackhammer and Taversoe Tuick each suddenly appear as pronounced silhouettes as one approaches from what would have been a neighbouring territory (**51 & colour plates 18 & 19**). Seen in this way, Renfrew's hypothesis seems to work, for not only do the cairns stake a claim for a particular group of settlers, but they serve as a distinct sign of this claim to neighbouring groups. This hypothesis, drawn from anthropological studies, has been summarised by Fraser who said that such a monument would 'give them a sense of belonging to their own special place, and would also have been a signal to be transmitted to outsiders, informing them they did not share in that sense of belonging'.[33]

Looking at this group one by one we can also see the development of the stalled cairn from the earliest tripartite. The Knowe of Yarso occupies the most dramatic site of this group: silhouetted against the sky on the edge of a terrace some 100m above sea level and with terrace after terrace stepping down to the shore (**50 & colour plate 20**). The terrace upon which it sits is much wider than those lower down, so when seen from the arable land directly below, the flank of the hill above it disappears from view leaving the cairn silhouetted against the sky. The terrace seems to have been carefully chosen because there is no comparable flat platform below and the hill above rises steeply to its summit. This reinforces the impression that the cairns were not merely mausoleums, nor were they simply territorial markers, but also sites for ritual. Half a mile to the east, Blackhammer stands on a less pronounced terrace but

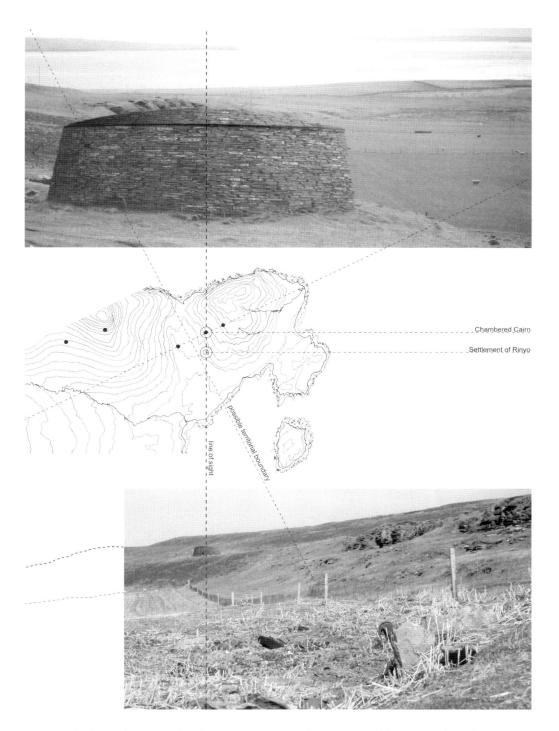

49 *Bigland Round as territorial marker. Top, reconstruction of cairn as it would have appeared according to Davidson and Henshall's description; centre, map showing relationship between Bigland Round and Rinyo; bottom, reconstructed cairn seen on the hillside from Rinyo.* Montage made by Harry Paticas

Chambered Cairn

Settlement of Rinyo

possible territorial boundary

line of sight

is equally visible as one approaches from adjacent land. Further east lies Taversoe Tuick sitting on top of a knoll that caps land rising from the seashore before it falls away to a wooded valley beyond which stands moorland. This knoll also marks a point where the coast and contour line swing sharply northwards; consequently the cairn makes a vivid impression up against the sky when seen from adjoining territory on either side. Seen from a distance in this way, Taversoe Tuick would have looked not unlike those early tripartite cairns such as Bigland Round, although slightly smaller in diameter (**52**). It is, however, a variant of the Orkney-Cromarty known as the Bookan type, with very small central chambers and side chambers constructed of upright slabs (**53, 54 & 55**). Yet the extraordinary point about Taversoe Tuick is that it is a two-storey cairn, one chamber constructed immediately above the other. The lower chamber is entirely subterranean, its masonry walls a lining to the living rock behind and the floor itself is the bedrock.

The Knowe of Yarso illustrates well how the tripartite became the stalled chambered cairn. Pairs of standing stones divide the 7.1m-long chamber into four compartments (**56**). A low kerb differentiates the end chamber from the others and a projecting perimeter ledge suggests a slab was supported here. In effect this is a tripartite chamber where the innermost compartment has been marked off as an elaborate storage area. The remains of at least 29 human skeletons were found during the excavation, most located in the inner chamber where skulls had been arranged along the side walls. It may have been the need or desire to house an increasing number of dead that prompted the development of the stalled cairn.

50 *The Knowe of Yarso as territorial marker. The island of Gairsay is beyond*

51 *Blackhammer as territorial marker*

52 *View of Taversoe Tuick chambered cairn showing entrance to the lower chamber*

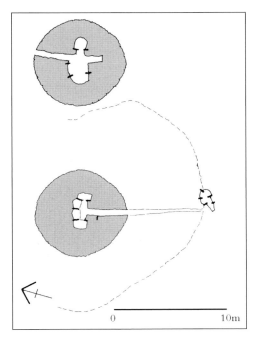

0   10m

53 *Plans of Taversoe Tuick.* Redrawn after Davidson & Henshall

54 *The lower chamber of Taversoe Tuick. A Bookan-type chambered cairn, and one of the smallest, it is unusual in having two central chambers, one above the other*

55 *Entrance passage to lower chamber of Taversoe Tuick*

Although the chamber has been greatly disturbed, Blackhammer illustrates the next step in the evolution of the stalled cairn, for the 13m-long chamber is divided into seven bays by six pairs of slabs. The lengthening of the chamber caused a change in the form of the cairns from circular to rectangular. The Knowe of Yarso is about 15m by 8m externally with slightly rounded corners. Above a projecting foundation course, the stone face is laid to a sloping course rather than horizontal. Whether this type of walling continued to the full height of the cairn is not known as only 1m survives. Blackhammer is similar to the Knowe of Yarso but longer, 24m by 10m. Along both its long sides the stones were laid herringbone pattern. This pattern-making in the stone wall is seen more clearly at Midhowe (**57**). The base courses of the outer face are laid obliquely. Above a string course set back about 120cm, the facing stones are set obliquely in the opposite direction, which gives a distinctive herringbone pattern. It seems as if once the circular, pot-like form of the cairn was abandoned, the decorative patterns associated with its rim became incorporated into the cairn. The savage mind's insistence on transferring resemblances from things known to things new — from woven basket to clay pot, from pot to cairn — seems to be at work here once more. The symbolism of containment, preservation and transformation that adhered first to the basket and then to the pot possibly continued to be necessary for the meaning of the cairn as it departed from its original form. In this we perhaps see an analogous procedure to that seen at the Knap of Howar houses. In the case of the cairn, as the form changed almost beyond recognition from its circular point of departure, a representation of its material origins seemed to become necessary.

West of the Knowe of Yarso are two long cairns, the Knowe of Ramsay and the Knowe of Rowiegar. Both survive as nothing more than long grassy mounds with a few stumps of uprights protruding from the earth. Both are approximately 27m long, the Knowe of Ramsay with fourteen compartments and the Knowe of Rowiegar probably with twelve. Two aspects of the Knowe

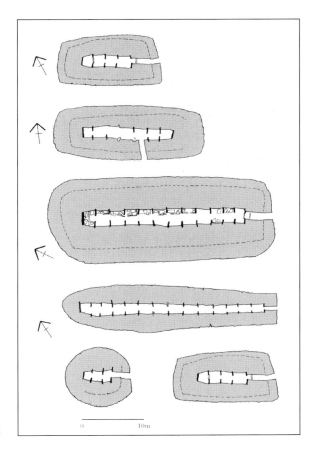

56 *Plans of stalled chambered cairns. From the top: the Knowe of Yarso; Blackhammer; Midhowe; the Knowe of Ramsay. Bottom left is Kierfea Hill, a tripartite cairn for comparison, and bottom right, the Knowe of Yarso.* Redrawn after Davidson & Henshall

0   10m

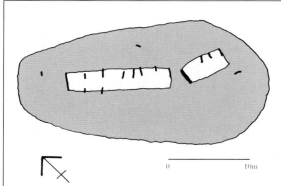

57 *Detail of herringbone stonework at Midhowe*

58 *Plan of Bigland Long.* Redrawn after Davidson & Henshall

of Ramsay are worth mentioning. Firstly, vertical joints in the external walls at about the position of the fourth pair of orthostats suggest that this may have been a cairn with the same number of compartments as the Knowe of Yarso, which was subsequently extended. (Interestingly the narrowest chamber is at the east end and has the same dimension, 1.2m, as the narrowest at Blackhammer, also at the east end. This is also the same width as the entrance chamber at Bigland Round.) Secondly, at the inner end, the last three chambers taken together have the same roughly convex plan shape as Bigland Round, to which they correspond in length. One would like to imagine that either of these suggestions could be true as this might produce evidence of the long stalled cairn's development. Yet is it possible for both to be true? Of course, just as it is possible that neither supposition may be correct so it is possible that both might be true. In Bigland Long, for example, we see two sets of chambers almost end to end, one divided into six compartments, the other a tripartite cairn, but their non-alignment preventing the possibility of them being joined as two might have been here (**58**).

Unlike these two very long stalled cairns, Midhowe has both an inner and outer wall, as did the earliest cairns such as Bigland Round. The effect of this outer wall is to make Midhowe a more squat rectangle 32.5m long by 13m wide. The interior of Midhowe creates the strongest impression of all the Orkney-Cromarty passage graves, partly because of its size but also because it is so well preserved that a direct grasp of its enclosure can be obtained (**colour plate 21**). Unlike the others where the visitor is always looking down upon the remains, here the interior masonry survives in places to 2.5m high, probably nearly its original height. Also the stones dividing the chamber into twelve compartments rise as high as 2.1m and 2.3m, the serried ranks of great stones standing on either side of the chamber's axis presenting an awesome sight.

Along one side of the chamber seven compartments had low shelves or benches on which were found the remains of at least 25 human skeletons. Most were lying on the benches, some more or less complete skeletons in the crouched position but others incomplete with the bones in a heap. The four compartments nearest the entrance have no benches and no human bones were found, whereas the end chamber had an elaborate system of shelves and kerbs. We can see in this very rare instance of complete skeletons found in Orkney cairns a possible explanation for the emergence of the stalled cairn. But it seems that there was no consistent pattern to burial; some communities may not have buried all bodies while others probably did, and some may not have buried the complete body at all. This will be discussed further, but for the moment let us note that it was perhaps the custom of burying their dead complete and crouched on a bench in the same position as the bed in their houses that caused these people on the south of Rousay to develop the stalled cairn from the first tripartite.

Midhowe and the Knowe of Rowiegar both sit close to the shore. Perhaps because the land near the shore slopes more gently and the hill inland rises more steeply and is without terraces, the communities felt that greater visibility might be obtained for the cairns if they were built down by the sea. The shore and the flanks of Ward Hill and Swarta Fiold turn north here consequently making any cairn located on the interior of these territories virtually invisible to its eastern neighbours.

In this analysis of a cairn's siting, we tend to break apart into separate categories something that must have been a larger, more complex unity to the savage mind, which sees everything in terms of a cosmos, a complex mental picture of the interrelation between all things. This form of understanding almost presupposes a multi-faceted aspect to things. As Eliade says: 'The same symbol may indicate or evoke a whole series of realities, which only profane experience would see as separate and autonomous'.[34] While the cairns may have been territorial markers, they may also symbolise a people's ideas about death; the eternal nature of stone and bone, stone as a bursting forth of the earth's latent power, and the cairns' pot shape or decorative pattern as evoking ideas of containment, protection and transformation. Both of these locations, against the sea or against the sky, might also have had symbolic significance. Water, continues Eliade 'precedes all forms and upholds all creation'. In nearly all cosmogonies, water is associated with potentiality, creation emerges from water. Consequently it is most obviously associated with new life, but in addition 'water symbolised the primal substance from which forms come and to which they will return'. All that which acquires form 'falls under the laws of time and life' and succumbs to change and decay and 'would cease to be itself altogether were it not regenerated' periodically.[35] Rituals for the primitive were aimed at emulating plant life which regenerates itself out of its own death. We can see from this widened context, from this idea of an interconnected cosmos, how the symbolism of water could overlap with and expand the associations between bone and stone made in the hope of connecting human life with nature's eternal life-force.

There may have been some such overlap in the primitive mind when they located their cairns to define their territory. A similar yet opposite set of possibilities also existed in the more general case when they sited them against the sky, where the idea of transcendence most obviously exists and was perhaps first noted in the transformation of matter into smoke through fire. This last notion is more problematic for what was clearly a fundamentally chthonic culture — although water is often present on the hill tops in Orkney where the low, rain-filled clouds come to rest. This will be returned to in the next chapter's discussion of stone circles. For the moment let us leave the exterior of the cairns with a sense of the potential interplay of material form and siting in calling forth the significant layers of meaning their presence suggests.

Chambered cairn as ritual site

There is some evidence from both within and outside the chambered cairns to suggest that they were not only territorial markers, nor simply tombs, but also sites of ritual activity. Two of the earliest type, Bigland Round and Knowe of Craie, had fires by the entrance — this practice might have been common but excavations have tended not to be as thorough or as fortunate as these.[36] Fragments of burnt bone, flint chips and pottery shards were found. Adjacent to the mouth of the long passage to the lower chamber of Taversoe Tuick is a curious miniature tripartite chamber only 1.6m long by 1.1m wide. Its role remains enigmatic but it is very suggestive that chambered cairns were more than mausoleums. Only a few remains were found in the two earlier cairns, but from Taversoe Tuick and others a clearer picture emerges. A crouched skeleton and fragments of bones were found on the shelf of one of the compartments in addition to one almost complete bowl, shards from as many as twenty others, scrapers, knives, an arrowhead, beads, and a polished mace-head.

This list of remains in itself does not establish that the cairns saw ritual activity, for these things could have been interred with the dead and the chamber sealed as an ossuary. However at Isbister on Mainland Orkney, aspects of the finds suggest that these might have been sites of recurring activity. Hedges' account of this chambered cairn was used earlier to portray a Skara Brae-type community. Its extensive remains will be used here to explore what purpose the cairns might have served in addition to housing the dead and acting as territorial markers. As well as the more everyday objects described above, a smooth-polished jet ring and a highly polished jet button which was drilled on one side to receive a fine thread, were found amoung the remains. Axes of haematite and of a fine grain greenish-brown rock were also found along with a mace head of speckled black rock (59). Twenty-one limpet shells found together with their apices removed suggest that they formed a necklace. Shells, as we have seen, were particularly symbolic and have been used by many peoples as amulets. Various other beads, bones, pins and pieces of flint were found, some of which were scorched. From this the obvious inference drawn was that some individuals were buried with favoured or prestigious belongings. Or, alternatively, that symbolically significant objects were placed in the cairn.

By far the most common material remains found at Isbister, however, were broken pottery shards. Hundreds of pieces weighing a total of 28.5kg from at least 46 different vessels were recovered. Half of the pots were Unstan ware (60). Two interesting facts emerged from the analysis of these remains; firstly, shards had apparently been burnt; and secondly, the pots had been broken after burning. We are familiar with the widespread idea that existence continues in some different form after death, so it comes as no surprise to find utensils and personal ornaments alongside the buried dead from primitive societies. Yet why would the pots be deliberately broken? Eliade sheds some light on this. He says that there are peoples of North Asia, who:

> conceive the otherworld as an inverted image of this world. Everything takes place as it does here, but in reverse. When it is day on earth, it is night in the beyond (this is why festivals of the dead are held after sunset; that is when they wake and begin their day); the summer of the living corresponds to winter in the land of the dead; a scarcity of game or fish on earth means that it is plentiful in the otherworld; and so forth. [...] And everything that is inverted on earth is in its normal position among the dead; this is why objects offered on the grave for the use of the dead are turned upside down, unless, that is, they are broken, for what is broken here ... is whole in the otherworld and vice versa.[37]

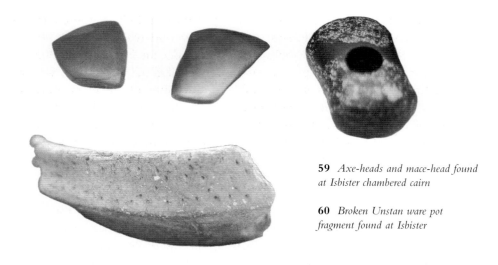

59 *Axe-heads and mace-head found at Isbister chambered cairn*

60 *Broken Unstan ware pot fragment found at Isbister*

Pursuing this kind of 'logic' a little further, we might surmise that burning the fragments represents a symbolic remaking of the pot for its new, otherworld usage. This incidentally gives some indication of how the inverted pot form might be symbolically appropriate for a container of the dead. The recently discovered Seahenge on the Norfolk coast exposed the remains of a timber circle with an upside-down tree at the centre, its roots sticking into the air. This curious apparition is perhaps also explained by Eliade's remarks.

Either way, it is clear from the large quantity of pots that the dead required nourishment. In fact, a large number of bones from domesticated animals were also found, the analysis of which showed them to have been butchered and deposited in the chamber with flesh on them. More than one thousand animal bone fragments were found at Isbister, analysis of which shows there to have been a distinct preference 'for joints of mutton or goat, particularly those of the legs, despite the fact that the majority of the carcasses available were of beef'.[38] A large number of fish bones were also recovered. It is quite likely that other more perishable food was deposited in the cairn for a number of seeds were recovered, predominantly barley.

All this tends to confirm that the dead were accompanied in some way to the otherworld with food and possessions. However, this still does not establish whether offerings were deposited at the time of burial or at periodic times thereafter – whether given once only to sustain the deceased on their journey or proffered repeatedly to persuade the dead to remain in their own domain. One clue that this practice might suggest a regular and repeated ritual rather than being connected to the haphazard occasion of death comes from folklore.

One of the best documented absorptions of pagan myths by Christianity was that of All Hallows Eve, which was followed by All Saints' Day. During the reign of Pope Boniface IV in the seventh century, the Pantheon (which housed images of the Roman gods and goddesses) became converted to a Christian church dedicated to all the saints.[39] In 'the old Celtic calendar the last night of October was old year's night' and the pagan new year is recalled in Hallowe'en, with all its superstitious practices of warding off an amorphous group of creatures of darkness, devils, hob-goblins, warlocks and witches. Following the malice and mayhem of Hallowe'en came All Saints' Day when the great legion of saints were invoked to re-establish order in the name of the Church. The next day was set aside for remembering more ordinary people, All Souls' Day. Customs associated with All Souls Day involved offering food to the dead, perhaps an echo of much earlier pagan customs. For example, there was the custom of 'soul cakes', where poor people would go from house to house begging for a bun, which seems to be a survival of an older custom where the poor asked for food to make a feast for the dead.[40] On the night of the feast doors would be left open so that the spirits might partake once more of earthly fare. Also lighted candles would be put in windows so that lost souls could take comfort.

All New Year festivals are fundamentally the renewal of time. Time for the primitive is corrosive, wearing away the human being, society and the cosmos, and has to be renewed by rituals that signify the birth of a new year.[41] These rituals usually begin by a descent into chaos, social confusion, orgies and extinguishing fires, and into this primordial confusion can enter the souls of the dead. All human life is hemmed in by time, but as the clock strikes twelve on New Year's Eve – a common motif in fairy tales – there is a small gap between years, a gap in time, and through this gap the spirits of darkness might pour. Folk tales and customs such as these are the habitual practices of earlier, more focused myths and rituals.

The connection between fear of the dead and food offerings is given additional significance by the evidence that most of the animal bones at Isbister were young, cattle less than 18 months old, and sheep or goats in their first year.[42] Archaeologists were able to establish that these joints were placed in the chamber immediately after butchering because there were no signs of gnawing by scavengers. Perhaps there was a seasonal killing of young animals when the pasture stopped growing as later took place at the Celtic festival of Samain. Perhaps these first Orkney farmers, predominantly pastoralists like the Celts, divided their year in a similar manner, marked by rituals associated with death that inaugurated the beginning of a time of darkness and apprehension. This darkest part of the Celtic year ended in February and was commemorated at Imbolc with offerings of food, a custom that may have shared a root belief with much older customs.

We may get no closer to understanding prehistoric rituals than by seeing what vestige of earlier customs survived amongst Celtic and Norse peoples. In her book *The Lost Beliefs of Northern Europe*, Hilda Ellis Davidson painstakingly assembles what these might have been from the fragments of evidence contained in historical accounts from the period and from the archaeological record. A number of parallels suggest how folk customs such as those just described could have derived from early Norse ritual, and how these in turn allude to yet more ancient practices and beliefs. For example, the beginning of winter and New Year was celebrated in Scandinavia (also at the end of October) with a feast known as the Winter Nights. This feast was, Davidson says, 'a dangerous time, when there was communication with the dead as well as the gods, and meetings with supernatural beings might take place'. This was the most important feast during the Viking Age 'when men sacrificed for plenty'. The essential element of this seasonal ritual was the feast itself, a communal meal shared with the gods. In the great hall of the chieftain the drinking horn would be passed among the assembly. Davidson describes a saga which tells us that first a toast was drunk to 'Odin for power and victory, second to Njord and Freyr for peace and good seasons, and finally to the memory of dead ancestors'.[43] Bearing in mind both the tendency of male heroes to supplant goddesses in the development of mythology and how later religions absorb earlier beliefs, we perhaps glimpse behind these legends a more ancient beginning-of-winter ritual in which a communal meal was shared with the gods or goddesses and the ancestors. This 'otherworld feast' formed part of the symbolic means of communicating between two worlds. In another of Davidson's examples a 'dead king is described as entering the hall of Odin after his last battle, to join the heroes feasting with the god'. She describes the motif of the dead hero being welcomed by a woman holding a drinking horn, 'a familiar symbol in the pre-Christian Viking Age' and one which she interprets as symbolic of offering sustenance to the dead or spirits after their difficult journey. Some visual evidence from carved memorial stones includes 'what appears to be a stylised hall which bears some resemblance to a burial mound'.[44]

When the human bones from Isbister came to be analysed they were found to be bleached and weathered, in contrast to the animal bones. The archaeologists saw this as clear evidence that 'the bodies of the dead had been excarnated – de-fleshed – outside the tomb' before the remains were deposited.[45] Analysis of remains elsewhere suggest this was not an uncommon practice throughout Neolithic Britain, allowing the temporal body to be obliterated or in some way left behind in the world so that only the bone containing the human essence would be conveyed to the otherworld.

Hedges considers that the bodies were not simply left on the ground because there are no carnivores' teeth marks on the bones. He suggests that the bodies might have been placed on a scaffold to de-flesh, perhaps the scaffold set up on the cliff-edge natural platform before the cairn. He cites parallels for this kind of custom amongst North American tribes such as the Dakota and the Choctaw.[46] We will consider this again in looking at the Stones of Stenness where there is some evidence for such a structure. Hedges explains the possible meaning of this practice by referring to the Tibetans, the Zoroastrians of Persia and the Parsees of India, who shared a belief that this reunited the body with the air, allowing it to take its place among the other elements of water, earth and fire. This might be a particular and developed mythology which shares a common Indo-European root; the fleshly body remaining in this world before the bones were finally put to rest. Renfrew's excavation at Quanterness indicated that bones in the chamber were not all in the same condition. Combining this anthropological comparison with Renfrew's report led Hedges to the view that the bodies might have been left to decay, not for any specific duration, but rather until the customary time or times when the cairn was opened. This suggests that the cairns were not simply thought of as ossuaries but as centres of rituals. Like most rituals, perhaps these focused on a particular time of the year; one individual's life's ending being woven into all of life's eternal cycle. Such a pattern of activity would be consistent with death being 'represented as part of a cyclic order', a key component of Bloch and Parry's analysis of primitive funerary rites.

It is worth remarking upon Ibister's location in relation to a cairns' potential as site of ritual. From the land it would have served, Isbister is seen silhouetted against the sky, for the ground rises gently up to it before plunging away to steep cliffs on the seaward side. Both the plan form of the cairn and its siting are very suggestive of a ritual setting, for the oval-shaped cairn had horn work of stone that encloses what might be construed as a roughly paved, natural stone-platform sloping away to the cliff edge. It is a very spectacular site. The craggy sandstone cliffs step steeply down to the sea with the north coast of Caithness seen across Pentland Firth, and it is hard to resist imagining some spectacle involving the community and the dead taking place on what is in effect a natural amphitheatre facing the sea (**61**).

Ancestors

Hedges' interpretation of the disposition of human bones at Isbister is that several stages were involved in the mortuary practice. In one or two places bones from the same individual were found together such that they corresponded to a complete body, which suggested to him that they were interred and remembered as a particular individual (complete skeletons had been buried at Midhowe and Taversoe Tuick). However, most of the bones at Isbister had been sorted into distinct piles where skulls and other post-cranial bones were collected together. He infers from this that they had ceased to be known as individuals but that their bones had become absorbed into some more general concept of the ancestors. Bloch and Parry remind us why primitive peoples do this. 'Having as far as possible erased individuality they reassert continuity by equating death with birth into the depersonalised collectivity of the ancestors, which is the continuing source of fertility of the living'.[47] In one particular case

61 *Isbister chambered cairn on the cliff edge of South Ronaldsay*

'...the tomb and the reunited dead within it represent the undivided and enduring descent group and as a result [are] the source of blessings and fertility of the future'.[48] At death the body reverts to a natural condition. It thus becomes necessary to transform the natural skeleton which remains after the biological process of decay into a cultural product. This is achieved, explain Shanks and Tilley, by 'the selection and arrangement of body parts ... the arrangements of skulls and long bones and variations in the occurrence of ribs, vertebrae, and hand and foot bones'.[49] In the long barrows of southern England they found clear evidence for this in the way that skulls and other bones are disarticulated and piled together in a basic body-like symmetry reconstituting a singular collective rather than an aggregate of individuals. A similar arrangement occurs at Isbister.

There is some evidence from elsewhere in Orkney that this sorting and moving of bones might also have embraced removal of some bones for ritual purposes. This is implicit in the relationship of stone and bone, for often, as Eliade says, 'the "soul" is presumed to reside in the bones and hence the resurrection of the individual from its bones can be expected'. Eliade here refers to both human and animal bones, going on to say that often 'the mythical animal ancestor is conceived as the inexhaustible matrix of the life of the species, and this matrix is found in these animals bones'. He describes several instances where animals have been resurrected from their bones, including the legend of Thor who used his hammer to bring goats back to life and the Biblical vision of Ezekiel where the word of God restored flesh and sinew to 'ye dry bones'.[50] The crucial point seems to be that 'the inexhaustible matrix of life' continued to reside in the bones, and that returning them to the earth would restore the life force allowing ancestors to continue playing a role in weaving together the complex web of a people's culture and cosmos. Eliade describes a shaman's costume that had, '…at least partially, the appearance of a skeleton'.

Eliade explains that amongst the Teleut and other Central and North Asian peoples 'the recently dead are feared, [whereas] the long dead are revered and are expected to act as protectors'. No dead person at first 'accepts his new mode of being', which helps explain rituals associated with transporting the soul to the otherworld and precautions taken to keep them there. But eventually as the deceased becomes absorbed into the spirit world of the ancestors, the dead become revered. They 'are invited to funerary banquets, [and] in time they come to be regarded as tutelary spirits of the ancestors'.[51] Davidson noticed something similar in Icelandic Sagas where, on the one hand the dead are portrayed 'as hostile to the living, grudging them life and desirous to deprive them of it'. On the other hand 'there is some indication that the dead might be regarded as guardian spirits, helping and supporting the living'.[52]

In one of Davidson's examples assistance was invoked from three sources. A very similar trio is called upon by one of the Asian people Eliade describes above. These are respectively Odin or fire, Mother Earth or good seasons, and thirdly, from both regions, the ancestors. Thus we can see that across long periods of time and widespread areas of northern Europe, practices associated with the dead were not merely to guide the deceased's spirit to the underworld, nor were rituals simply acts of remembrance, but rather the spirits of the ancestors were evoked for help.

In Norse mythology, dominated as it was by warrior gods, the main goddess Freyja seems to contain some trace of these ideas. She is described as 'Lady' (to the 'Lord' Freyr, her brother or husband). She '…was regarded as a giving goddess', continues Davidson, 'bringing bounty to the fields, animals and mankind'. She was also 'queen of the underworld, at home in the land of the dead'. In this capacity she took her lover, who was of royal lineage 'down into the underworld … so that he may learn his ancestry'. In this much later mythology we see many strands – mother goddess, ancestor worship, shamanism (Freyja had a '"feather-form", which enabled her to fly as a bird') – mixed together. This may simply represent confusion as a male hierarchy supplanted older, matriarchal lore. Or it may reflect the complexity of an earlier world view, a tapestry woven into a richly overlapping pattern from which single threads are not easily disentangled. In one of the Sagas, Freyr is represented as a divine king, 'continuing to bless his people from his mound'; that is, after he is dead and has become an ancestor.[53] Perhaps in this historically known Viking mythology we get a glimpse of what the symbolism of the ancestors meant in much earlier prehistory, in a similar manner to the way we know Christian symbolism absorbed and transmuted in Mithraic belief. It seems quite likely that Neolithic human remains were used in some ritualistic way to sustain the living human community. Like any tear in the social fabric, that of a death had to be repaired.

Shamanism

Perhaps the most intriguing find in the Isbister chambered cairn was the bones and talons of the white-tailed sea eagle (**62**). Of all the bird bones found, 97 per cent were of carrion-eating species and of these 90 per cent were of the white-tailed sea eagle. Isbister is known colloquially as the Tomb of the Eagles. Hedges estimates that as many as 20 of these magnificent birds might have been interred, which have a wingspan of 1.8m and can live for more than 40 years. Two interconnected lines of thought are prompted by this discovery. Firstly, it might well be that these carrion-eating birds were used to de-flesh the body, as in the case of the Tibetan and Iranian custom of exposing corpses to vultures. The 'Iranians put the bones in the 'astodan', the 'place of bones', where they await resurrection. We may consider this a survival from pastoral spirituality'.[54] This last point is particularly interesting in the context of Eliade's view that shamanistic activity emanated from belief systems held before the proto-Indo-Europeans had separated. Amongst the images made by some of the very first settled farmers at Çatal Hüyük in Anatolia were wall-paintings of vultures attacking a headless body. Other wall-paintings from the same settlement show a man holding two heads and what appears to be a mortuary structure. From these the excavator James Mellaart concluded that excarnation involving vultures probably took place before the bones were buried.[55]

In one of these wall-paintings Mellaart noticed that some of the vultures were drawn with human legs and feet. From this he deduced that there may have been a priesthood associated with rites of death and burial who dressed to look like vultures. Other paintings show figures wearing leopard-skin skirts and headgear dancing to a figure with a drum. Perhaps there were 'mythical animal ancestors' in whose bones the inexhaustible matrix of life resided. All this is very suggestive of shamanistic activity as described by Eliade and perhaps suggested by the sea eagles at Isbister. Of course Çatal Hüyük is very distant from the Tomb of the Eagles, both in time and space. But the fact that similar symbolic motifs can occur around 6000 BC in southern Turkey, in nineteenth-century Tibet, and even in twentieth-century Siberia (from where Eliade draws most of his anthropological evidence), suggests that setting the sea eagle remains in the context of shamanism is not unreasonable. Moreover, there is evidence for shamanistic activity much closer to Orkney. This returns us to Renfrew's hypothesis concerning the Celtic language that the oldest layer of Celtic mythology perhaps offers a glimpse into the deeper, prehistoric past.

Roman accounts of the Celts include descriptions of druids that place them unmistakably in the realm of shamanism. Pliny tells the story of a druid

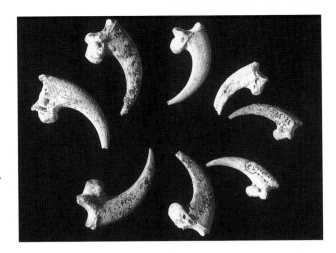

62 *Sea eagle talons, some of many found in the chamber at Isbister, which is colloquially known as the Tomb of the Eagles.* Copyright Charles Tait

climbing a sacred oak on the sixth day of the moon, cutting some mistletoe and then sacrificing two white bulls.[56] Druids claimed to understand the secrets of the gods. Caesar wrote that druids believed the souls of the dead passed from one body to another.[57] He may have thought this to be a doctrine not unlike the Pythagorean transmigration of souls, although his is probably a Romanisation of the strange 'shape-shifting' character of Celtic myth. Many Celtic stories tell of a malevolent flock of birds that emerge from the other-world at Samain, the Celtic New Year. One speaks of three ravens that come from the sea to a sídh each Samain to 'carry off three boys from the fairy mound'.[58] Another recounts how the hero Cú Chulainn destroyed an entire flock and bathed his hands in raven's blood. This contact with otherworld creatures imbued the hero with some of its prophetic and supernatural powers. Finally there are telling descriptions of the druids' appearance that support the link between what was found at Isbister 3,000 years before Roman historical accounts of the Celts and what anthropologists tell us of Siberian shaman 3,000 years later. 'The chief Druid of the King of Ireland is described as wearing a bull's hide and a white speckled bird's head-dress with fluttering wings, a typical shamanistic appearance'.[59]

In her study of the historical evidence for the Celts and the character of their culture, Ross says that druids 'do not seem to have differed so very basically from the Shamans of the Finno-Uqui peoples'.[60] With this in mind, let us return to Eliade to see how his anthropologically based study of shamanism might help understand the burial practices at the Tomb of the Eagles and other Orkney cairns.

Whether or not there were shamans who took on the appearance of the white-tailed sea eagle to perform rituals at Isbister we will never know. But the bones and talons in the chamber themselves suggest that some such belief system was held in common with the later peoples mentioned above, for a crucial role of the shaman was guiding the soul of the dead to the other-world. Furthermore, nearly all shaman have helping spirits in the form of animals or birds. All over the world, writes Eliade, 'learning the language of animals, especially birds, is equivalent to knowing the secrets of nature and hence to be able to prophecy'.[61] Hence the shaman might employ his helping creature in the rituals he performs or, more often, transform himself into it by imitating its cries, its movements, and donning a costume made from the animal's skin or feathers.

Eliade describes myths from several Siberian tribes where the gods decided to give mankind a shaman to combat evil, disease and death, and they sent an eagle to fulfil this role. He interprets this in relation to the fact that these people had sky gods and that the eagle, with its ability to fly immensely high, was an obvious symbol for how this world and the heavens might be connected. Perhaps the white-tailed sea eagle was ascribed a totemic role at Isbister because of similar attributes, its immensely high flight being complemented by its ability to plunge into the sea. Birds that can dive into the sea feature in many creation myths, bringing up the first particle of earth from the primordial ocean. Such a myth was common among peoples of northern Europe and Asia.[62] Combining in this way the two elements that represent respectively transcendence over matter – sky, and the pre-formal before matter – water, the huge white-tailed sea eagle would have been both an awesome spectacle and a powerful symbol. In several Celtic myths supernatural beings take on the form of an eagle for part of their existence. The Irish Fintan, for example, whose name is derived 'from earlier Vindo-Senos, "The white Ancient"'.[63]

Eliade describes scenes of shamanistic activity that fit well with what we have learnt from the archaeological remains. In one particular example he describes a Siberian tribe that has two funerary ceremonies, the second and 'great ceremony celebrated some time after the former and at the end of which the soul is conducted to the underworld'.[64] Anthropological studies suggest that this double event is quite common amongst primitive peoples. It is deemed necessary because, as we have seen, the deceased is not only a biological individual but also an integral part of a society threatened with disintegration by the death. The first part of the mortuary ritual thus deals with matters concerning the possible pollution caused by an individual's death, symbolised and experienced by the decay of the body, whereas the second part entails the recreation of permanent order using the bones that remain.

In Eliade's example the shaman captures the dead person's soul in a 'fanya' – a sort of cushion – and takes it to a banquet which may last for several days and at which all the extended family would be present. (In prehistoric Orkney, as in other cultures, we might presume the bones played a similar role). Eventually, at sunset, preparations for departure are made. 'The shaman sings, dances, and daubs his face with soot', (in another of Eliade's examples his chant invokes fire, Mother Earth and the ancestors) He invokes his guiding spirits (including, in this case, a long-necked bird), and climbs a notched tree (which represents the World Tree, an *axis mundi*) from where he sees into the other-world, and finally he sets off on a sledge with the 'fanya' containing the dead person's soul and 'a basket of food'. When he arrives in the underworld, the shaman searches for the close relatives of the deceased to entrust his spirit to them. The shaman then hastens home and gives an 'account of all he has seen in the land of the dead'.[65]

Eliade writes elsewhere that death is not seen as extinction but as a change in the mode of existence. The earth is imagined as 'living' because it is fertile, so the dead are returned to the earth 'to be regenerated and to absorb the forces needed to start a new existence'.[66] This is why the part of human existence that embraces the spirit has to be transported to its proper realm. But as we have seen, the principal concern is not for the deceased individual but what this loss might mean for the social group. Thus the shaman's task was not only to see the deceased's spirit safely home but also to ensure that the reciprocal relationships that existed between the spirit world and this world continued to function properly. In Greek myth we hear of the dead going 'to join the throng of vague 'ancestors' who year by year…send or rather bring back as flowers and fruit the buried seed'.[67]

The symbolism of the journey in this particular example is fundamentally celestial but in discussing a very similar account (which was observed and reported by an anthropologist in the 1920s), Eliade makes the point that the 'Tungus of Manchuria still remember a "time long ago" when shamans "shamanised towards the earth"'.[68] This is not the place to introduce Eliade's discussion of this shift to a celestial symbolism from an earlier chthonic equivalent, but simply to take note of the strikingly similar elements and structure described in this ritual to the archaeological remains found at Isbister and elsewhere in Orkney. The possibility of such a shift in belief system we will consider in relation to the stone circles.

Setting aside all scholarly caution for a moment let us put together the structure of the events just described by Eliade with the material remains of Isbister. The cairn stood on the highest ground of the tribe's land, an outcrop of stone breaking through the green. Man-made, it drew up the strength of the rock that forms the foundation of the earth and supports all that lives upon it. Silhouetted against the sky, it alluded to all that was transcendent. Containing the bones of the ancestors, it spoke more directly of this people's right to belong here. Its stone spoke of eternity, its form perhaps a reminder of the pots that stored the grain from one year to the next and helped transform raw nature into food. The inverted, pot-like form connected it to the laws of the otherworld. The cairn was not merely a symbolic monument however, but the focal point of the religious life of the community. In this, perhaps it was not so different from the parish church that orchestrated the religious beliefs of later farming people of Britain for more than a thousand years. For as long as 800 years the Isbister community came to the stone platform between the cairn and the cliffs to participate in rituals in much the same way that later peasant farmers came to Christmas, Easter and Harvest Festival services in the church. Instead of one God, the Son of God, the Mother of Jesus and Heaven on high, the Neolithic community perhaps called for help from a strange multiplicity of spirits that were somehow linked to the earth. Instead of calling to 'Our Father who art in Heaven' they might have summoned their fore-fathers whose spirits continued to exist in the bones that resided in the underworld, the passage to which was symbolised by the chambered cairns.

Among the ceremonies that wove their lives into the endless cycle of nature's fertile rhythms would have been rituals whereby the spirits of deceased individuals were transported to the underworld. Perhaps the body had been laid out for the sea eagle to peck the bones clean. (Incidentally, the etymology of Valkyrie, the name of the beings in Norse mythology who chose those who were to die in battle and helped transport heroes to the otherworld, is a compound of two words – *valr* meaning carrion and *kyrya*, to choose.)[69] At the appointed time the bones in which the spirit of the deceased resided would be taken into the burial cairn, through the 'strait gate', the narrow passage that connected this world to the underworld. Although the passages have varying alignments that may have particular astronomical and symbolic significance as we will see, the majority, including the Tomb of the Eagles, entail transporting the bones in a generally westerly direction, the direction of sunset. This is the way taken by shamans in most of Eliade's descriptions of the journey to the otherworld, and to which direction initiates are often turned to intone 'a hymn to the Spirit of Darkness'.[70]

Altered cairns

The entrance passage at Isbister arrives at the side of the main chamber as at Blackhammer. Isbister is a hybrid cairn incorporating a stalled chamber with Maes-Howe-type side cells. Unstan is another hybrid very similar to the Tomb of the Eagles. Both Unstan and Isbister have five stalled compartments with those at either end marked off by a distinct kerb-stone. Isbister has three side chambers and Unstan has one. That at Unstan is unique amongst side chambers in being terminated by an upright stone slab, a feature characteristic of stalled cairns. Earlier activity was found beneath Isbister itself and later additions had been made to it as also at Unstan. So it is evident that these cairns were subject to change and modifications. Both Isbister and Unstan have their chambers encased within a roughly circular cairn, although both are stretched along the perimeter to become oval, Isbister particularly so.

A careful investigation of the geometry of these two hybrid chambered cairns suggests that both may have been originally tripartite stalled cairns that were subsequently modified with some of the orthostats remaining in their original position. Taking Isbister first, if we inscribe the geometry found from the circumference at the cairn's southern end and project it to a complete circle, we would describe a cairn of almost exactly the same size as Bigland Round (**63**). Presuming the southern back stone to be the original closing stone we derive a tripartite chamber divided by orthostats occupying the position of the next two pairs. Assuming a passage directly on axis with the chamber, we would describe a plan where the passage would be almost exactly the same length as that at Knowe of Craie within a cairn of approximately the same diameter.

Unstan is much less of an oval-shaped cairn but nevertheless, it too is longer along the chamber axis. In Davidson and Henshall's plan and section three distinct walls are shown encircling the cairn. Between the outer and middle wall are shown two strips of wall foundation that project outwards like the horns seen at other cairns, for example Eday Manse or Fara. This foundation stops abruptly at the outer edge of the middle of the three walls which suggests that the whole outer section of cairn was a later addition. This middle wall has a more pronounced lengthening of its radius along the central axis than the perimeter wall. If, for argument's sake, we assume that this was the original line of the cairn's exterior − most have a distinct inner and outer wall − and if we describe a circle using the radius of the shorter side sections, then once again we have a cairn of almost exactly the same size as those at Knowe of Craie and Bigland Round (**64 & 65**). If the four pairs of orthostats that define the central chambers of Unstan occupy the positions of those in an earlier tripartite, this earlier Unstan would correspond very closely to that earliest group of tripartite cairns found at Rousay, Kierfea Hill, Knowe of Craie and Faraclett Head West.[71]

What is being suggested here then, in the broader context of an exploration of possible meanings developed through particular relationships, is that Unstan may have originally been a tripartite cairn, one of the first type to be used when Orkney became occupied from Neolithic Caithness. It is not difficult to imagine Unstan marking the site of an early occupied territory in Orkney, for it sits on the edge of a tidal inlet from Scapa Flow, the first protected water encountered

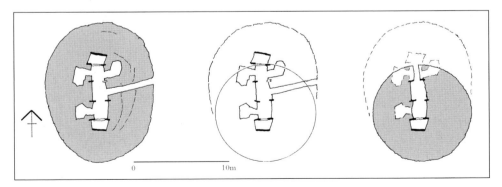

63 *Plan of Isbister. From left to right: the hybrid chamber as excavated; the chord of the southern perimeter inscribed as a complete circle; conjectured as an early tripartite cairn*

64 Left: *Interior of Unstan chambered cairn. The entrance passage is on the left and aligns with the Watch Stone.* Copyright Charles Tait

65 Below: *Plan of Unstan. From left to right: the hybrid chamber as excavated; the chord of the southern middle wall inscribed as a complete circle; conjectured as an early tripartite cairn*

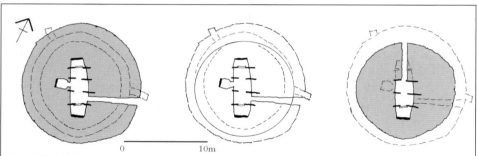

on the journey from Scotland. Furthermore its dramatic location on a low spur jutting into Loch Stenness suggests that, if cairns were territorial markers, it staked a claim for those who fished the loch and farmed the shore.

It is perhaps worth noting in relation to this argument that Unstan gave its name to a distinctive form of pottery found widespread only in Orkney, 'the north mainland and Hebrides'. A large number of these shallow, round-bottomed bowls (whose inverted form resembled the earliest cairns) were found here and this type of bowl has been associated with the early settlement of Knap of Howar. Grooved Ware, in contrast, we saw at the later settlements of Skara Brae, Rinyo, the Links of Noltland and Barnhouse. Fragments of small Unstan ware bowls have been found only at the older Orkney-Cromarty type of cairn, whereas only two Maes Howe-type cairns have produced pottery and both of these finds were of Grooved Ware. This led Davidson and Henshall to interpret Unstan ware as being 'early in the Orcadian pottery sequence'.[72] The pottery evidence suggests, therefore, that Unstan was an early cairn, but other evidence associates it with the later Neolithic.

There are only three known stalled-chambered cairns in Orkney where the entry passage rather curiously arrives at the side of the rectangular chamber. No obvious explanation exists for Blackhammer and Isbister, but at Unstan the reason is strikingly clear and introduces us to the significance of lines or alignments. Leaving the chamber, one sees straight ahead the Watchstone upon which the passage is aligned (**66 & 67**). In itself this might be seen as having no more, nor less, significance than the relationship between bone and stone which was discussed in relation to Braeside. Yet this line, when projected, passes through the centre of House 2 at the Barnhouse settlement – that larger, more significant house whose construction links it with Maes Howe. If this was the house of the chief, chieftains, or elders then this alignment may have been to help legitimise the power of these leaders. Locating it on a line that connects the Watch Stone (which embodies its associations of everlasting force) with the burial chamber at Unstan (where perhaps the ancestral bones of this particular tribe, or even the actual first settlers were interred), might give authority over the people who lived in close proximity to the Stones of Stenness.

In his short interpretative essay entitled 'Doorways into Another World', Colin Richards has argued that the 'architecture' of the stalled cairns with their parallel pairs of orthostats presents an image 'of a series of doorways'. This idea implies a line of possible movement formally organised in a not dissimilar way to the axis at Skara Brae. At Skara Brae the axis seemed to symbolise man's understanding of himself as a being oriented towards things together with his understanding of the force that produced all living things transformed through fire, which occupied the centre of his cultural production. Richards describes the arrangement of stalled cairns as 'the passage from the outside world to the sacred place of communication with the gods and ancestors'.[73] In the line from Unstan to Barnhouse we see, perhaps for the first time in Western Europe, all that is implied in the power of the organising line, or axis, being used to establish the authority of particular individuals residing in a significant dwelling. Although latent in Hodder's idea of the line from *domus* to *agrios*, the suggestion of control here seems to make for a distinctly new use of the axis.

To develop the hypothesis, at some point the cairn may have been altered, its passage relocated such that it aligned with the new dominant house at Barnhouse. Whatever power resided in the ancestors housed at Unstan could then be drawn upon to legitimise a new settlement whose leaders claimed extended authority. At the same time the cairn's form and plan configuration may have been changed. If Unstan did commemorate the original settlers, then perhaps metamorphosing a tripartite cairn into a stalled one with a hint of the Maes Howe-type (as we will see) played a part in symbolising this new

66 *The Watch Stone with the Stones of Stenness in the background*

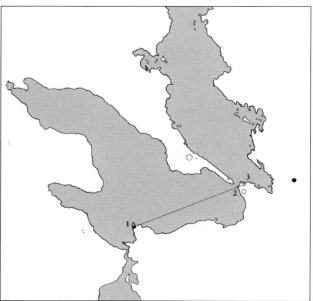

67 *Map indicating the alignment between 1 Unstan, 2 the Watch Stone and 3 Barnhouse 2*

authority over all the groups that occupied Orkney. All Maes Howe-type chambered cairns have their passage entering from the side of a long chamber, except for Maes Howe itself.

However complicated Unstan may appear in the context of Orkney chambered cairns and however speculative or wide of the mark the foregoing may seem to be, we are nevertheless left with two inescapable facts. Firstly, that the principal house in the settlement at Barnhouse is linked to Maes Howe through it's plan and masonry construction, and secondly that it is also linked by an alignment with the Unstan chambered cairn, where artefacts associated with the earliest form of settlement in Orkney were interred. This introduces us to the broader question of orientation in chambered cairns.

Orientation

There are four possible considerations in relation to orientation: 1) celestial or astronomical; 2) to natural features in the landscape: 3) to other cairns; and 4) to other man–made features such as the Setter Stone or the Watch Stone to which Braeside and Unstan were orientated respectively. Davidson and Henshall refer to Fraser's plotting of twenty-nine passage graves of which twenty-two face the quadrant between east and south. They explain away most of the exceptions that face the west half of the compass by exigencies of site (steep, west-facing hillsides for example) or construction (two storey chambers). The one exception that is clearly and deliberately orientated towards the west is Maes Howe, which raises questions concerning patterns of social change and systems of belief that will be discussed at the end of this chapter. Davidson and Henshall consider that entrance passage orientation 'probably had an astronom-ical basis', but the range of aspects indicate that 'an exact alignment for a specific event was not important'.[74] They follow Fraser in acknowledging that the midwinter solstice would probably have been of particular importance to these first farmers and note that a significant majority of passages cluster around the 140° azimuth, which is the bearing of midwinter sunrise in Orkney. It seems prudent to follow their lead in the matter of orientation, eschewing the complex precision demanded by archaeo-astronomy in favour of a calendrical focus. However, it should be acknowledged that to the savage mind a calendar was not purely or even primarily a practical matter but was inextricably bound up with notions of the sacred. Criticising the astronomical precision of such as Thom and Ruggles, Scarre says that 'the fundamental question at issue is one of prehistoric belief system'.[75] The nature of Neolithic belief systems will be considered in the next chapter. Because the savage mind tends to concretise time – light and dark, phases of the moon, seasons of the year, sowing, harvesting, breeding and birth of animals – it comes to acquire almost 'a material form in the minds of [these] peoples'.[76]

The cosmos of a primitive implies a complex interweaving of many possible phenomena, and given that these were pioneering peoples who might carry with them only a rudimentary mythology, such variation of cairn orientation seems understandable. Differing orientations might imply a connected group of associations, for primitive peoples' belief systems tend to be less systematic than more recent religions and were contingent upon a wide set of factors. In the Celtic world, for example, we know that there were at least four hundred different Celtic gods, for this number are recorded on Romano-Celtic inscriptions. That over 300 of these occur only once is taken to indicate that Celtic gods were disparate and strongly localised.[77] The fact that Neolithic cairns were constantly evolving makes this variety of orientations less perplexing. Perhaps only in much later Neolithic cultures could the intermeshing of ritual and astronomical events produce such a remarkably similar set of recumbent stone circles as those found in Aberdeenshire, a seemingly singular 'cause and effect' scenario that chimes more readily with our own cultural and religious predilections. Bearing this in mind it is proposed here only to consider a handful of passage graves whose orientation allows us to explore through Celtic myth what possible meanings they might have embodied. These have been chosen not only because my own fieldwork has taken me repeatedly to visit them, but also because they are cairns we have already discussed, thus allowing us to see a possible added complexity which sits happily with the notion of a cosmos.

The whole group of earliest cairns on Rousay – the Knowe of Craie, Bigland Round, Bigland Long (the tripartite within the cairn), Kierfea Hill, Faraclett Head East and Faraclett Head West – have their entrance passage orientated towards the rising sun in that period between midwinter and the spring equinox. This part of the year is associated with returning spring and new growth and is marked in the Celtic calendar as the festival of Imbolc or Oimelg. Burl has drawn upon a comparison with the Celtic year, its festivals and rituals, to help explain the possible meaning of stone circles. Acknowledging the danger of comparing customs of the Celtic world with those of people more than a thousand years earlier, he proceeds nevertheless to argue that it helps to repopulate ritual sites 'with people rather than with metempiric abstractions, and it reminds the modern reader of the interplay in early religion of the animal and supernatural world'.[78] Burl made this point in relation to Cornish stone circles which he noted were orientated to sunset at the Celtic festival of Samain. He thinks that this could be linked to 'the Celtic bisection of the year into two halves at the beginning of May and the beginning of November and dates from the time when the Celts were only a pastoral people'.[79] As the old year came to an end, animals would have been brought into winter quarters and many slaughtered to eke out the winter feed. In May they would be released again into the fields. In ancient Greece the year was divided into the 'fruitful' and the 'fruitless'.

Following Burl's lead we find a number of suggestions from the Christianised Celtic world that elucidate why this group of cairns might have been so orientated. Imbolc, on 1 February, for example 'celebrated the coming into milk of ewes and the return of light'. This festival was associated with Brigid who presided over a fire cult. Brigid was a significant figure of worship in the Celtic world, a fact we can deduce from the status of St Brigid in early Christian Ireland. Many of the legends accruing to the saint have their source unmistakably in Irish pagan myths. In his *Lives of the Saints*, Butler writes that 'Brigid's name is fancifully etymologised as *breosaiget*, i.e. fiery arrow'.[80] Butler is, of course, inclined to play down Celtic legends and establish Brigid as a historical person who became a Christian saint but, fanciful or not, the etymology is very suggestive of the rising sun sending a shaft of light into the passage-grave. It is worth recalling here that the 'sidh mounds where the otherworld people in Ireland lived after the coming of the Gaels were originally burial mounds'.[81] Celtic mythology consistently links Brigid with both power and fiery light. Brigantia, meaning 'high one' or 'Queen', gave her name to the British tribe Brigantes. That Brigantia gave her name to this pastoral tribe is a typical instance of Celtic people tracing 'their tribal descent back to a divine ancestor', a concept that has interesting similarities to the significance ancestors seem to have had for these first Orkney farmers and tomb-builders.[82] Christian legends that accrued to St. Brigid refer again and again to fire. St Brocan in the seventh century wrote: 'Brigit, excellent woman, a flame, golden, delightful. May she, the sun-dazzling, splendid guide us to the Eternal Kingdom.'[83]

This is an example of how a not-unsympathetic church in Ireland could transform pagan attributes into suitable metaphors for the Christian message. Also it explicitly links the sun with a rite of passage to a place of the dead. Another of the miracles attributed to St Brigid is that she restored a blind woman's sight as she watched with her the beauty of dawn. The setting for this tale is markedly pagan and in 'Old Irish *suil* means (both) "eye" and "sun"'.[84] In this we can also detect a characteristic of more recent religions where the spiritual world becomes abstracted and distant compared with the all-pervasive, animistic spirit world of primitive peoples.

In Christian art St Brigid is usually shown with a flame above her head, assimilated with Christian halos, and often with a cow near her, for she is held to be protectress of those engaged in dairy work. The cow comes with specific Celtic connotations. Christian history itself states that St Brigid was born in a druid's house at Tocharmaine, Ireland, in AD 453.[85] She was reputedly reared on the milk of a red-eared cow; the red cow is a common otherworld beast in Irish vernacular literature.

The specific attributes that Brigid brought from a much deeper past resonate through the Christian festival of Candlemas, celebrated on 2 February. Coming the day after Imbolc, this repeats the pattern of All Saints' Day following Hallowe'en. At Candlemas 'the Church blesses all the lights to be used in ceremonies throughout the year'. During the Mass the congregation receive the blest candles before the altar, the symbolism of which has been described as: 'the sun which first shone in the cave has given forth an ocean of stars.'[86] The deepest meaning of this symbolism and ritual is that of incarnation, that is the spirit becoming clothed with flesh. We are so familiar with this idea in the story of Christ's coming among us that we easily overlook its similarity with the widespread custom of Greek gods taking the form of mortals and animals. Such threads taken further back into the darkness of prehistory perhaps offer a faint glimpse of what these first cairn builders were seeking.

Arranging the passage to let in the rising sun at this time of year associated with the arrival of new animal and vegetable life constructed a correlation with the life in seeds concealed within the dark earth. Perhaps allowing the sun's fire into the cairn would re-ignite whatever spirit form the dead ancestors were believed to have taken from the bone remains.

Following Burl's lead we have found a number of suggestions from Celtic myth and legend as to why this group of cairns in the neighbourhood of Rinyo might have been orientated to this arc of the compass. We saw linked together fire, flame, sun-dazzling and the linking of the eye with the rising of the sun. Taken together with Brigid's concern for 'flocks and stock' this suggests why some cairns were orientated to sunrise at the time of 'the coming into milk of ewes'. From our Christianised perspective this suggests the idea of the spirit that lives on after death. Yet this carries with it a burden of individual person- ality which, as we have seen, is not significant to the savage mind. It is more likely that, just as the ewes' milk is one expression of that force of nature by which existence is carried on, so the light of spring symbolised life's renewal. Sunrise entering the passage grave may have been aimed at rekindling the spirit of the ancestors of the particular tribe or social group. Their bones had been returned to the earth, through which poured some vital life-giving force that began to reveal itself at Imbolc in the pushing up of new growth after a season of seeming death upon the land.

On first visiting Wideford Hill, I described noticing that the entrance passage looked across to the cairn on Cuween Hill. Two others seem to have their passage aligned on another cairn. The lower passage to Taversoe Tuick is aligned with Gairsay, a classically shaped island on the top of which appears to sit a burial cairn. Eday Church is a tripartite chambered cairn where the axis of the chamber points to the cairn known as the Holm of Huip, which caps the highest point of the tiny uninhabited island of that name. The meaning of this is far from clear; perhaps there was quite simply an attempt to suggest a community of the dead. In Norse sagas sometimes 'we find the pleasant idea of friends buried in neighbouring mounds conversing with one another'.[87] Or perhaps the people who gathered around Taversoe Tuick or Eday Church had come from Gairsay or the Holm of Huip respectively and the alignment was an attempt to strengthen their claim on the land. Linking their buried dead with the ancestors left behind but from whom they were descended extended, as it were, the ancestral line. In returning to Wideford Hill and Cuween Hill facing each other we find ourselves back on Mainland and in the presence of the Maes Howe type of cairn. A pattern of development can be detected in the Maes Howe type that helps clarify the meaning of Maes Howe itself. Maes Howe is the culmination of this phase of chambered cairn building and an elaborate special case which will complete our investigation into orientation, as it has a relationship with distinctive landscape features. In a different way to Unstan and Barnhouse, it also has a relationship with a man-made feature.

The Maes Howe-type of cairn

There are only ten Maes Howe-type chambered cairns certainly known in Orkney. This compares with more than fifty of the Orkney-Cromarty type. Five of the ten, including Maes Howe itself, occupy a stretch of land running across the centre of mainland from the south side of Loch Stenness to the east of Kirkwall Bay. The others are scattered across the northern isles; the extraordinarily long Holm of Papa Westray South, Mount Maesry and Quoyness on Sanday, Vinquoy Hill on Eday and Onziebist on Egilsay. Quoyness will be discussed in the context of the cairns as ritual sites and, along with Quanterness, will be analysed in relation to the development of Maes Howe itself. Wideford Hill and Cuween Hill provide a good starting point for a general description of the Maes Howe-type.

Both these cairns sit high up on steeply sloping hillsides into which they are set. Both are roughly circular, Wideford approximately 14m in diameter, Cuween around 16.8m. Wideford Hill was constructed with three distinct walls encircling the chamber that have been left exposed since excavation giving the false impression of a distinct façade with stepped revetments. Cuween Hill has been left as a grass covered mound. Wideford Hill and Quoyness have both been reconstructed with their concentric walls stepping up to an exposed central drum, but Davidson and Henshall are of the opinion that these cairns, much like the Orkney-Cromarty cairns, were 'faced by well-built vertical walls standing to a height a little less than the chamber they covered, the top of the cairn being gently domed and finished by a carefully laid capping'.[88]

Both Cuween Hill and Wideford Hill have a low, narrow entrance passage that emerges at the corner of a central rectangular chamber, approximately 3.5m by 1.8m off which are distinct and smaller side chambers, Cuween has four, Wideford has five. The main chamber is constructed of stone slabs that corbel steadily inwards reaching a height of approximately 2.3m and capped with large horizontal slabs. The much smaller side cells are accessed through low narrow openings and are constructed in the same way as the central chamber. Both these cairns were excavated haphazardly in the nineteenth century, both were already exposed, and the remains found have been subsequently lost, although the skulls of twenty-four dogs were found in the lowest stratum on the floor of the main chamber at Cuween Hill. The basic plan form of these cairns has been compared with the houses at Skara Brae, which have similar small cells off the central living space. The plan of these passage graves is much less regular than the houses, even more so at Vinquoy Hill (**colour plate 22**). This may simply be because the red sandstone on Eday is not so easily worked as that on Mainland Orkney. What we will see, however, is an increasing use of formal geometry as the Maes Howe-type of passage grave develops.

This increased formality, which reaches its conclusion at Maes Howe, reinforces the view that a hierarchical society emerged like that seen associated with Barnhouse. With the earlier Maes Howe-type such as Wideford, Cuween, Quoyness or Vinquoy Hill, there is no clearly ordered relationship between entrance passage, central chamber and side chambers, but at Maes Howe there is (**68**). Unlike the Orkney-Cromarty cairns where similarities persist, each of the Maes Howe-type differ one from another, suggestive in itself of changing belief systems. Vinquoy has a polyogonal chamber with four side chambers; Wideford and Cuween have rectangular chambers but the former has three and the latter four side chambers. Quoyness and Quanterness are quite similar in that both have six side chambers. Yet five at Quoyness have their entry in typical Maes Howe type fashion at the very edge of the chamber, whereas at Quanterness all six arrive at the centre of the side chambers, which are also distinctly rectangular.

Quoyness illustrates the beginning of this process. With its reconstructed stepped external appearance, it is one of the most striking of Orkney cairns (**70**). It stands up against the sky on the low promontory of Elsness when approaching along the shore of Sanday, or is silhouetted against the sea when seen from its hinterland as, like Midhowe, it is located on a slight rise close to the shore. The presence of loose stones and rocks on the surface of the ground becomes pronounced as one approaches the cairn. Sanday is a low, sprawling island with no major rocky outcrop, such that one wonders whether the cairn was sited here because of this greater presence of stone. Perhaps here with the rocky shore stepping away in great horizontal slabs to the sea, something of the eternal force that stone represented seemed to erupt from the earth, making this place propitious for a burial cairn.

Quoyness is surrounded by a roughly circular, low platform of stones, which might be interpreted as a consolidation of this idea, but which also conveys a suggestion of ritual activity associated with the cairn. The stone structure – fundamentally a symbolic form and an enclosure – is extended to define an external space materially related to the symbolism of the cairn on which rituals might take place. The presence of this stone platform complicates any attempt to imagine the original appearance of Quoyness, for it is described as sloping up to the outer casing such that only a low stone wall would be seen, capped by a rough stone dome. This description is drawn from Renfrew's conjecture of the original appearance of Quanterness, similar in size and ground plan to Quoyness, but is contested by Davidson and Henshall. They argue that the rounded profile of Quanterness is caused by falling building material and that it would have been surrounded by a vertical wall 4.4m high. Quoyness they believe to have been 4m high.[89]

One consequence of the sloping stone platform at Quoyness is that a distinct descent is made into the entry passage. At the point where the level floor of the passage meets the outer casing wall, there are curious recesses of different heights and shape that suggest they were contrived to enable a corpse or skeleton to be manoeuvred down from the stone platform and into the

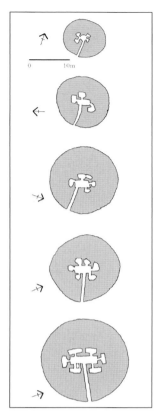

68 Above left: *Plans of Maes Howe-type chambered cairns. From the top, Vinquoy Hill, Wideford, Cuween Hill, Quoyness, Quanterness. Note the increasing size in the development of this type and the increasing formality. In Quanterness the side cell entrances are symmetrical and opposite one another.* Redrawn after Davidson & Henshall

69 Above right: *Interior view of Quoyness. Water-worn stones are a feature of the 4m-tall central chamber, perhaps because the cairn stands by the shore of Sanday*

passage. This gives the most distinct sense of descending to an underworld, penetrating through a contrived crust of rock into the bowels of the earth.

The exterior of Quoyness is matched by its interior, an impressive 4m by 1.8m and 4m-high central chamber built of mainly water worn stones, corbelling inwards as they rise (**69**). Only a few material remains were found; small pottery shards, two curiously shaped stone implements, a bone pin, stone discs and knives, a small quantity of animal bones, and various bones from ten or twelve humans. From these human remains we have only our second set of radiocarbon dates for the chambered cairns so far discussed, which show Quoyness to have been in use around 2900 BC.

The interior of Quanterness is a more formalised version of the Quoyness plan. Quanterness is, after Maes Howe itself, the largest of the Maes Howe-type. The entrance passage arrives almost exactly at the centre of the 7m-long rectan-

70 *Quoyness as rebuilt after excavation. The original profile of the cairn and the height of the surrounding stone platform are not certainly known*

gular main chamber, entrances to the two end chambers are located centrally on the end walls, and the four side chambers have their entrances directly facing each other. We saw a corresponding arrangement, although with open side chambers, in the principal House 2 at Barnhouse. This formality is brought to conclusion at Maes Howe, where the entrance passage arrives at the centre of one wall and openings to the three side chambers occupy the centre of the remaining walls.

Unlike any of these Maes Howe-type of cairns is the extraordinary long Holm of Papa Westray South, its main chamber 20m long with twelve entrances to side chambers irregularly arranged along its sides. Where Vinquoy seems to have initiated a process in which the passage grave plan resembles the house, by the time we arrive at the Holm of Papa Westray South the plan seems to have become a metaphor for a village-like settlement. The long, central chamber with cells either side presents a more geometrical version of the arrangement at Skara Brae with its winding passage and house-cells off to either side (**71**). Grooved Ware, which we discussed in relation to the emergence of village and hierarchical settlement, was also found at Quanterness.

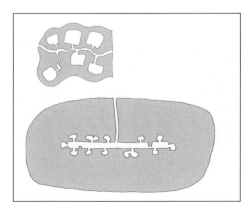

71 *Simplified plan of Skara Brae compared with the Holm of Papa Westray South chambered cairn. The plans are not to the same scale but suggest that the development of the Maes Howe-type of passage grave might reflect the emergence of village-type settlements having a cluster of houses*

Maes Howe

Although Maes Howe clearly evolves from the Maes Howe-type of passage graves such as Quoyness and Quanterness, its differences are very significant. Some commentators exclude it from a strict typology of Maes Howe-type passage graves, but Richards concludes that these differences are precisely what makes Maes Howe such a significant culmination of a process of development and change.[90] It is much larger and is built of much bigger stones, some of the slabs are estimated to weigh over three tons. Its actual appearance is also very different; the typical stone-wall, upside-down pot form being here replaced by a great mound, between 32m and 38m in diameter made from a tough mixture of stone and clay (**72**). It has been given a rounded domical form but was first reported as having a conical mound – although its top had been opened up by Viking grave-robbers. Uniquely among Orkney cairns it is surrounded by a ditch and a henge, roughly circular, measuring between 94m and 103m in diameter. This defines the area related to the cairn, covered with clay as was the area between the feast house and the surrounding wall at Barnhouse. Richards interprets this as making a place for public access to ritual as activity related to burial chambers came under greater control, an inference he makes from the longer passage at Maes Howe and its closing stone.

Renfrew has made an interesting study of the labour required to build Maes Howe from where the idea of a hierarchical society emerged. A retired country builder drew up estimates for quarrying, transporting and building a cubic yard of sandstone. From this, Renfrew first calculated that Quanterness would have taken approximately 6,500 man hours to construct, a figure he rounded up to 10,000 to take account of the absence of metal tools and wheeled transport. This represents about 250 working days for a group of around twenty having

72 *Maes Howe. The surrounding henge is clearly visible. The Stones of Stenness and the Watch Stone can be seen on the left silhouetted against Loch Stenness. Barnhouse is hidden behind Maes Howe on the shore of Loch Harray*

five able-bodied males. He concluded that a cairn the size of Quanterness could have been built by the members of the community it served in a single season, if given a little help by neighbours, or by the group unaided over a slightly longer period. Renfrew proposes a 10,000 man-hour class of cairn, to which all Orkney cairns would roughly conform except for Maes Howe, which he estimated would take 100,000 man hours to build. Adding to this an estimated 80,000 man hours to build the Ring of Brodgar and perhaps half that for the Stones of Stenness, he draws the obvious inference from the order of magnitude implied in the construction of this complex that it could not have been the work of a single settlement group and must have involved labour from many communities. This seemed to him to fit a pattern detected in southern Britain. Whereas the smaller Orkney 'chambered cairns were constructed by small-scale, autonomous, segmentary societies', the Maes Howe complex suggested to Renfrew, 'the emergence of [a] chiefdom society ... in the later Neolithic of Orkney [and] that we see the emergence of a larger social formation to which the population of the whole mainland may have owed allegiance'.

> The social organisation represented by those major works appears to lay more emphasis on group identity than on the personal eminence of the leader, and for that reason these may be regarded as 'group oriented' rather than 'individualising' chiefdoms. [91]

Hedges comes to fundamentally the same conclusion, although, drawing upon anthropological studies, he is more inclined to allow the possibility of a distinctly hierarchical society focused on the individual figure of the chief. He describes:

> a conical clan system [where] the chiefs of existing local lineages are seen as the product of a largely mythical ancestry that ultimately links them to a common founder but that gives them an order or precedence according to a rule of primogeniture. Hence, the eldest son of the eldest son of the eldest son of the ultimate ancestor will be chief of the whole area.[92]

A related possibility is found in the cultures that Eliade describes where the shaman increasingly came to be a particularly significant figure. One tribe traced their origin to a shaman and kept the skulls of dead shamans. These were venerated and used for divination; '..nothing was undertaken without recourse to divination by these skulls'.[93] Another tribe believed that 'in olden times' the shaman received 'the shamanic divine right' directly from the celestial spirits but that now they received 'it merely from their ancestors'.[94] In this we can see how possession of these powers could lead to the shaman coming to occupy a privileged position in the community. This might explain why in many Orkney cairns the remains of only a few individuals were found

as well as explicating the emergence of what appears to have been a hierarchical society that built this complex of monuments. Following Renfrew and
Hedges' stress upon the long line of ancestors provides a useful interpretative
framework to understanding the line of development leading to Maes Howe.

The plan of Maes Howe completes the formalising development of the
Maes Howe-type just traced but the arrangement becomes increasingly
geometrical. This formal development of the chamber plan may also be
connected with the principle of primogeniture described by Hedges. Double
the floor area of Quanterness, a bi-axial symmetry is introduced to the square
plan of the central chamber at Maes Howe, which is 4.7m across (**73** & **colour
plate 24**). The floors of the side cells are raised approximately 0.8m above the
central chamber floor and the openings to them are perfectly square, reinforcing the sense of formality.

In the line of development leading to Maes Howe, we saw that the
chambered cairn of Quanterness reflected the six bays in the dominant house
at the Barnhouse settlement. Some reciprocal relationship between house and
passage grave seemed to exist, similar to the relationship between the Knap of
Howar house type and the earliest tripartite chambered cairns. This transmutation takes a step further in the design of Maes Howe itself. For although it
incorporates the more precise geometrical qualities embodied in the dominant
house at Barnhouse, its plan form is square and has only three recesses.

The notion that the labour involved in building Maes Howe echoed a
change in the social structure of Neolithic Orkney finds support in the possibility that the plan can be read as a metaphor of primogeniture. Perhaps its
compression from the elongated rectangular chambers at Quanterness and
Quoyness to the square chambers here was not only for formal reasons but also
to embody the plan arrangement of the earliest houses seen at Skara Brae and
Rinyo. The early houses had two distinct bed recesses, one on either side, and
a more shallow recess opposite the entrance for the dresser (or altar). The plan
at Maes Howe returns to the original three bays, making more formal the
resemblance to the configuration of those early houses (**74**). This might have
been made as a metaphor for the spatial form of the first house. At Maes Howe,
inset into the innermost walls in the same place and perhaps symbolising sleep,
is the entrance to the repository of the bones for those contained there in the
eternal sleep of death. The side chambers, although rectangular, revert to the
form of the early cairn with the entrance-reveal running on directly as one side
wall. Perhaps, as Hedges says, being 'the eldest son of the eldest son of the
eldest son of the ultimate ancestor' was a necessary condition to become 'chief
of the whole area'. Embodying a reference to the first house of the first
farming settlers lends an appropriate form to this ultimate house of the dead.
In this way whatever significance the role of the ancestors had was brought into
the symbolic structure of Maes Howe through its plan form or spatial arrangement. Any dealings that were made with them through the matrix that resided

in their bones were enacted in a setting resonant with the first house. Just as perhaps one individual amongst many had become transmuted into an all-powerful ancestor, so the one small house that existed back in the beginning had metamorphosed into this singular, significant, temple-like tomb.

Certainly the organisation of Maes Howe, the small side chambers in relation to the large central chamber, and the unique blocking stones to each side chamber suggest that this was not an ossuary for all the bones of this particular community. Rather, the side chambers raised above the floor and sealed suggest that the bones of a few significant ancestors were kept here in casket-like conditions, perhaps those extending the lineage of the emerging chief or chiefs of the hierarchical social order.

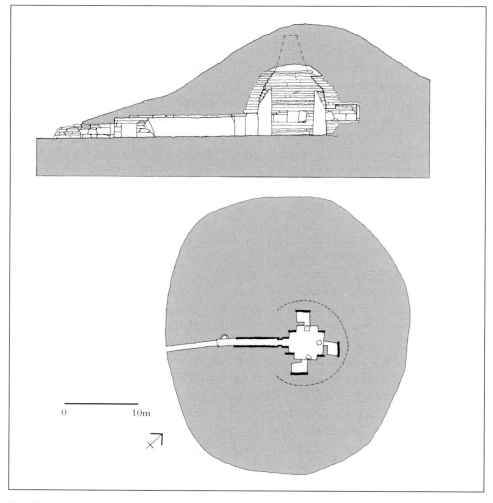

0   10m

73 *Plan and section of Maes Howe. Based on the construction of Quoyness, the broken line on the section indicates the possible original profile of the chamber now capped with a concrete roof. The scale refers to the plan only.* Plan redrawn after Davidson & Henshall, section after Gibb (1861)

The stone slabs used for the wall construction are vast, most courses being a single stone running from corner to corner. The stone courses begin to corbel inwards from above the side-chamber lintels at around 1.4m high, slightly at first but becoming more pronounced at around 2.7m high. When excavated in 1861 the chamber stood 4m tall but its top had been destroyed by Viking tomb-breakers. If it had the same profile as Quanterness or Quoyness its original height might have been as much as 6m. As the vault is a square corbelled one, it is perhaps more likely to have continued the stepped profile that survives, which would have made it about 4.5m to 5m high.

A particularly intriguing innovation at Maes Howe is the introduction of megaliths. In each corner rises a gigantic standing stone the tallest of which is 2.9m high. Often described as buttresses, they probably contribute nothing to the structural stability of the construction. However, they strikingly affect the appearance and also, subtly but significantly, the plan, so that it is more likely they played a symbolic role. Standing there in each corner they mark out the space in a way that seems analogous with the standing Stones of Stenness, and perhaps translate the symbolism enacted there to the burial chamber – possibly very early evidence of the complementary symbolism of square and circle. If there was a four-post structure in the Skara Brae-type houses, perhaps the standing stones in the corner of Maes Howe alluded to them. Their position in the plan also gives a faint, but discernible suggestion of side bays to the chamber, a feature associated with the significant House 2 at the Barnhouse settlement. Richards observed that it incorporated sophisticated masonry techniques using vertical stones in the same way as those at Maes Howe.

Of course large standing stones had formed an integral feature of the tripartite and stalled cairn – reaching truly megalithic size at Midhowe – but are not present in any other Maes Howe-type passage grave. A work of art can resonate with several meanings, and with the idea of a cosmos allowing us to see interconnected aspects of meaning in different kinds of resemblances, perhaps the standing stones in Maes Howe refer not only to the orthostats in the stalled cairn but also to the standing pillars at the corners of the beds in the later Skara Brae houses.

Enormous slabs contribute not only to the monumental effect of the chamber but also to the impression made by the entrance passage. Very long single slabs are used for the floor, ceiling and the walls. These were laid on edge rather than flat and coursed as in the chamber, which enhances the sense of vast size. The enormous length (12m) of the passage, its narrowness (0.7m) and low height (0.7m, but reconstructed to 1.15m) prompted Richards to interpret the entrance as denying access to but a few. At the entrance there are recesses to accommodate a blocking stone. This stone, 0.47m lower than the height of the passage, would leave a gap above similar to that at Newgrange in Ireland. An early drawing made by Gibb in 1861, however, shows the passage roof dropping down to the same height as the recess. This feature suggests that allowing access

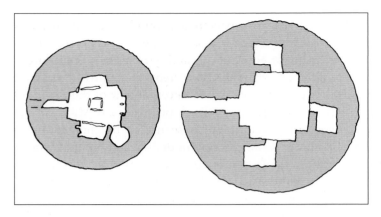

74 *Plans comparing the chamber of Maes Howe with the early House 9 at Skara Brae. See also the model of the reconstruction of Skara Brae in illustration* **30**

to the sun at a particular moment was more important that allowing access to members of the tribe. Before we discuss its particular orientation this might be the most appropriate place to review the possible influence from Ireland.

Orkney and Ireland

Pitchstone from Arran found at Barnhouse provides evidence for links between Orkney and the Western Isles, and carved decoration on a lintel at Pierowall on Westray shows a distinct resemblance to many such decorated stones from the Boyne valley passage graves, indicating a connection to Ireland. The nature of such an exchange in the later Neolithic remains problematic. Yet Renfrew, developing the concept of 'peer–polity interaction' advanced by Bradley and Chapman, has suggested that early local variations evolving as communities spread out might have had their counterparts later in exchange, promoting coincidences of 'beliefs and norms of behaviour':

> On this view it would be perfectly possible for the Orkney passage graves to have begun their development locally, from a starting point in the simpler Orkney-Cromarty cairns, and to have profited during their later development from contacts with the Western Isles and with Ireland.[95]

At the very simplest level, we can imagine that a society so obsessed with dead ancestors would have made an effort to retain contacts with living ancestral groups.

Henshall is more sceptical of this line of influence arguing that 'the building techniques are purely Orcadian' and that 'the design of the tombs have no more than a remote resemblance to Irish passage graves'.[96] This overstates the typological argument. Particularly in the case of such a non-transportable material artefact as a building, it is only to be expected that building techniques and traditions would evolve over time by craftsmen working with local material and that this would lead to a local character. But ideas and symbols transported from one culture can inform and affect adjustments or transformations in another. This seems a distinct possibility in the case of the development of the design of Maes Howe. We have seen how its plan form developed from the Maes Howe-type, whose origins remain unclear but which seems to be indigenous to Orkney, and that its precise masterly construction of dry-stone walling is wholly consistent with the development of local masonry traditions. Nevertheless, the orientation of the passage, its enormous length and the so-called 'letter box' feature at its entrance suggest the influence of ideas from Ireland. Moreover, Maes Howe also has a roughly cruciform chamber plan like Newgrange. This

75 Right: *Spiral decoration pecked into stones at Pierowall (above), and Eday Manse (below), chambered cairns on Orkney*

76 Below: *Spiral decoration found on a kerbstone at Knowth (left), and macehead (right), also from Knowth in Ireland.* Redrawn after Eogan

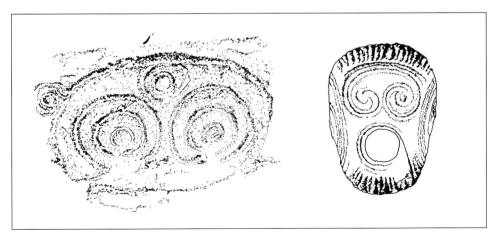

plan form is also found in the two other great mounds that dominate this 'cemetery', Dowth and Knowth, although all three Boyne Valley examples lack the precise geometry of Maes Howe nor are they as finely constructed. A much smaller example of cruciform plan is to be found at Fourknocks, Co. Meath.

Another feature Maes Howe shares with its Irish counterparts is the use of megaliths. All three of the enormous Boyne cairns have large slabs of stone lying on edge to form the lining to their passages, a culmination of a development from earlier Irish passage graves. The stones at Maes Howe are much larger, but this may be simply because larger stones were available in Orkney. Clearly the desire for megaliths was present in both cultures. The Irish graves also incorporate standing stones to define the perimeter of the central chamber, using these almost exclusively in the case of Newgrange, Dowth and Knowth. At Fourknocks they appear in conjunction with dry-stone walling, where the three small side chambers present a square face to the central chamber and are raised above its floor like those at Maes Howe. In his review of *Scottish and Irish Passage Tombs*, Eogan notes that 'the closest and most obvious links are between the major monuments of the Boyne valley and Henshall's Maes Howe group'.[97]

Many stones at Newgrange are decorated with motifs also found at Pierowall and Eday Manse in the Northern Isles, reinforcing the Ireland-Orkney connection. The motifs are spirals and circles of concentric lines pecked into the stone (**75** & **76**). The meeting pair of symmetrical spirals is a motif found repeatedly in much later Celtic art, i.e., on the bronze Battersea shield found in the Thames and another shield from the River Witham in Lincolnshire. Bradley uses the appearance of the decorations at the Boyne valley tombs as the principal support for what he calls a 'circular archetype' in prehistory. Not only are the enormous Irish passage graves contained within a circular mound, but also a ring of smaller circular passage graves cluster around Knowth, and a timber circle has been found adjacent to Newgrange. In conjunction with the decorated stones, these lead Bradley to say; 'in fact the image of the circle is all-pervasive here'.

He continues, 'the gapped circle, with a radiating line leading to its centre, is one of the dominant images in Irish rock-art'.[98] He refers to recent studies that point out 'that the organisation of space in this design is exactly the same as we find in the passage grave'. That is, a line of space penetrates the otherwise bounded perimeter of a number of concentric circles and leads towards the centre (**77**). It is interesting that this motif is found on the outside of Newgrange where, as at Maes Howe, there was a blocking stone to deny access to the interior. Perhaps this was a representation of its interior, just as the spiral (also found in the Orkney decorated stones) in the classical tradition symbolises the mystery of inner life. The symbolism of spiral and labyrinth is too complex to broach here, but it should be noted that the spiral pattern has funerary associations through its manifest connection to shells which, as we

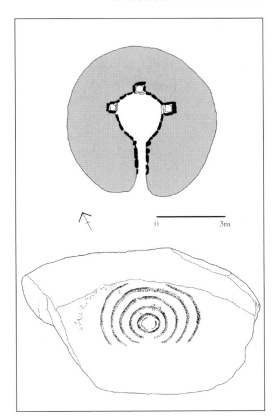

77 *Plan of Fourknocks, Co. Meath, passage grave (above) showing similarities with Maes Howe. Kerbstone from Knowth (below) illustrating Bradley's concept of a 'circular archetype'. Redrawn after Eogan*

have seen, 'puts the deceased into communication with the cosmic forces that rule fertility, birth and life'[99] (**78**). At the same moment as Maes Howe closes the interior of passage graves, there appears the new feature of a circular enclosure around the tomb; it seems as if, with the rituals of death emerging into the open, the circular archetype is used to contain it. Perhaps this also provided the impulse for the stone circle and for the circular wall around the nearby Barnhouse feast hall.

The sun at midwinter

The passage at Maes Howe is aligned such that the setting sun on midwinter's day sends a shaft of light into the chamber (**colour plates 23 & 25**). This is such a radical departure from the other Orkney cairns we have discussed that the symbolism suggested by it needs to be examined in relation to the undoubted significance of ancestors. Although Maes Howe shares with Newgrange the 'letter box' opening above a blocking stone, the drawing made by Gibb in 1861 shows a drop in the passage roof such that only if the stone was removed would a shaft of light pass down the passage at sunset on

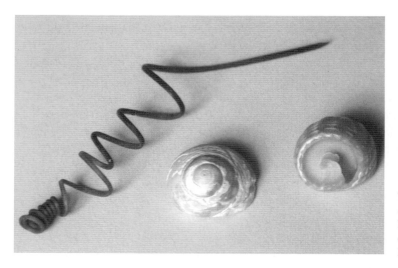

78 *Spiralling shells and tendril of plant.* Photograph courtesy of Harry Paticas

midwinter's day.[100] The particular meaning of Maes Howe's orientation to midwinter sunset might be broached by comparing it with the Christian symbolism embodied in the spatial arrangement of the church. In its classic formulation the church sets up a journey orientated towards the east which represents Christ the Light of the World, the rising of the light. The rebirth of day is thus symbolically re-enacted in relation to the sanctuary (with its east window) and the altar as symbol of the last supper (symbolically linked to feasts with the gods), so as to reinforce the idea that Christ's presence (and through him God) remains amongst us. In contrast Maes Howe connects itself to the setting sun which, as Eliade reminded us, carries with it strong associations of death as a kind of journey to the underworld where the spirits of the ancestors dwelt and which was their proper domain. Although other Orkney cairns were orientated to the general direction of sunrise at particular times of the year (connecting bones and sun, the social matrix with the cosmic life-force) perhaps Maes Howe was orientated to the setting sun because the significance of the ancestors themselves became elevated or the sun was linked with the idea of life's matrix in some new way. The idea of a sun king or ruler drawing his authority from a relationship with it, fusing the attributes of a solar god with his representative on earth, is so widespread and so well known as to need no further comment. One need not go so far as to suggest the existence of such a social structure in Orkney in noting the presence of such a symbolic structure. Perhaps the particular orientation symbolised the construction of Maes Howe as the ultimate place of the ancestors. It established a fundamental location and frame of reference for the enlarged community gathered around it, just as the sun, with its burgeoning warmth in spring, represents the ultimate source of life to farming peoples. Some such shift in belief system may be as plausible an explanation as the social/hierarchical one, a notion to be explored in the following chapter.

Marking midwinter has held significant sway over Western Europe since the beginning of historical time. That the celebration of Christ's birth was fixed in the fourth century AD to align with the Roman Feast of Sol Invictus and other pagan midwinter festivals is well known. The source of the sun's power as a symbol would seem to be connected with farming and farming peoples' heightened awareness of the fecundity of the earth. For if the sun's steady decline in the sky was not arrested and reversed then the slide into an ever colder and darker winter would continue. Midwinter festivals introduce a harbinger of new life at just that moment when the sun has reached its nadir before it begins its return to ascendancy. Without the sun's warmth the dark earth would not regain its fecund power. In this nexus of ideas between seed and soil, stone and bone, probably lies the root belief giving shape to all Orkney passage graves in some concept of regeneration. Perhaps by linking those ancestors given greater significance at Maes Howe with that pivotal moment in the year when the sun's apparent slide along the line of horizon was reversed and the cycle began again, would establish reciprocal relationships with this momentous event. This will be explored further in the next chapter on stone circles.

It is particularly interesting in this connection that the orientation of the passage at Maes Howe is not only to the setting sun at midwinter but also to a particular topographical feature. Skimming low over Ward Hill on Hoy the setting sun seems to descend into the Cuilags as if entering a gigantic burial mound itself. It might be worth remarking again on the new form of burial mound. All previous Orkney chambered cairns, whether the Orkney-Cromarty or the Maes Howe type, took the form of a distinct construction, defined by walls of stone. Dowth and Knowth are similar to Maes Howe, covered with a domical mound of earth, but both have a distinct kerb of large stones around the perimeter. So although this could suggest a cross fertilisation of ideas, perhaps it also reveals some development of built form in relation to a natural form. For the twin Hills of Hoy dominate the landscape of Mainland Orkney where Maes Howe is situated. It is impossible to ignore them and if one catches by chance — as I first did — the midwinter or near midwinter sun dropping into these hills it is profoundly affecting. It could easily be seen as a 'strange portent and prodigious token from heaven' given the savage mind's propensity to see things in relationships of resemblance and significance. It is easy to imagine the distinctive form of these hills as burial mounds. In Orkney there are no mountain ranges that might dissipate the impact of these hills with their distinct profiles upon the horizon. So perhaps the profile of Maes Howe was developed in response to that of the Cuilags to which it is given a formal correspondence through the alignment of its passage to the point where the sun sets, and a symbolic connection through its association with the midwinter sun. This could be construed as reinforcing the message of the significance of ancestors. It is a common myth that the sun daily enters the earth in the west to begin its night journey through the underworld. So perhaps here at midwinter (the final point in the year's descent into darkness) the sun – the primary 'cosmic ancestor' – seemed to be entering the otherworld to bring about the rebirth of the year. Such fixed points in the renewal of time were vital to the savage mind and perhaps here at Maes Howe the ancestors were put into some kind of symbiotic relation to this most significant point for the first farmers.

We will return to look at rituals in relation to the sun in the next chapter, but here let us conclude this consideration of formal and material influence from Ireland by examining what Celtic mythology might say about the relationship between sun and burial tombs. Before doing so we should recall that Eliade described shamans journeying to another realm that was imagined on high, but that they could also remember a time when they '"shamanised" towards the earth'. This folk memory suggests a shift of emphasis from the earth to the heavens, which is perhaps what we see emerging here in late Neolithic Orkney. We will come back to this when we consider the Stones of Stenness. Certainly such a focus had come into being by the time of the Celts. Surveying the type of art produced by the earliest phase of Celtic culture, Ann Ross writes that it 'seems reasonable to conclude that at this time there was a widespread European cult of a god associated with the sun'.[101] Miranda Green agrees, seeing the Celtic belief system emerging from 'some kind of pre-Celtic European cult-expression, quite widespread, and probably connected with fertility, power and the sun'.[102] In this milieu the Celtic goddess was 'more archaic than the gods, she remained tied to the land for which she was responsible and whose most striking natural features seemed to her worshippers to be manifestations of her power and her personality'.[103]

One reason why it seems reasonable to draw upon Celtic mythology to interpret Neolithic remains is that 'the Celts connected the burial mound with the entrance to the otherworld'.[104] A second reason is that many Celtic myths speak of goddesses who were overthrown by invading warriors, yet were accommodated such that their presence lingered on in particular topographic names. In association with these are stories of the underworld that intersect with the Celtic emphasis on sky and solar gods. From these earliest strata of Celtic myth, whose memory is preserved in the land, we find aspects that shed light on what meaning the cairns might have had, just as ideas adhering to Brigid carried us from the Christian history of saints back to Celtic or deeper pagan practice.

In *Lebor Gabála Érenn* ('The Book of the Taking of Ireland'), three women, Érin, Banba and Fótla request an invading warrior race, the 'Sons of Mil', to install Erin's name on the island. They accept her proposal acknowledging that this represents 'the established key to the island's sanctity'.[105] In one version of the myth, Érin forms an army to fight the invaders, an army composed of sods of peat and the mountains; i.e. these women are earth goddesses whose presence is embodied in the topography and material of the land. There are many Irish myths where mortal kings marry a territorial or topographical native goddess.[106] Male gods tend to be tribal heroes whereas the goddesses are often given local names, e.g. Boann, the River Boyne. Where gods or goddesses have consorts the male names often become Romanised, whereas the female retains a Celtic name. Again and again we find this pattern of a Celtic name and action laid over an older, always feminine, attribute that resides in the land itself.

The 'deities of Ireland were known as Tuatha Dé Danann, People of the Goddess Danu [herself] controlled by a great divine mother, nurturer of the gods and of the land with which, like all the Celtic goddesses, she was most particularly concerned'. Newgrange was alleged to be the house of the Danu (or Anu). Anu was also known as Aine; the Irish word aine contains the meaning 'brightness, glow, radiance, splendour, glory, brilliance', the goddess herself is always associated with the sun.[107] A burial mound in Co. Donegal, very similar in appearance to Newgrange, is called Grianan Ailigh or Ailech, grianan meaning 'sun house'.

One myth in particular suggests how the primitive mind understood the diurnal or annual movements of the sun in relation to topography and burial mounds. Etain (a goddess clearly connected to Aine, Anu) and her consort Midir ('whose name means Rays of Sun')[108] conclude their east-to-west journey across Ireland at a cave called Síd Sinche in Co. Roscommon. This cave faced the midsummer sunset. The couple had been accompanied on their journey by Etain's maid Crochen Croderg. She was enchanted by the cave: '"What fine house is this where we have halted?" she asks, "O Midir of the splendid feasts, is this thy spacious dwelling?"' Midir explained that his own home lay 'nearer to the sunrise' and he gave the maid this cave or sunset Síd. Crochen Croderg is 'the setting sun personified', her name derived from croch, 'saffron', and crod erg, 'blood red'. Thus her name embodies the visible transformation of the sun as it sinks to the horizon. Midir and Etain, meanwhile, hurried northwards anxious to start the next diurnal cycle.

The clearest suggestion of what underlies the orientation of Maes Howe to the midwinter setting sun is illustrated by our final example. There was an epic battle between Finn (or 'Fionn of bright aspect' – a solar demi-god from Leinster, i.e. the east, the rising light) and Goll, – a giant of the Fir Bolg, the mythical Men of the Bag. This giant has one eye in an earth bag because he was of the underworld (the Fir Bolg were from Connacht, i.e. the west). 'On the west bank of the Shannon, Goll fought a losing battle on the side of the dying day and sinking year.' But Finn did not kill Goll, rather the giant retreated, defending fiercely although he 'behaved as if he knew he must lose'. In the course of this battle Finn becomes trapped by three hags of winter – 'Carrog (meaning a small bag, which suggests that she was related to Goll), Cuilleann (Holly) and Iornach (spindle, or skein of yarn)'. Finn is ultimately rescued from what Dames, who relates this myth, calls 'this Trinity of Neolithic winter deities' by the intervention of his nemesis Goll.[109] In this story we see the bright light threatened by the forces of winter darkness. Yet it is ultimately rescued from the trapping web of perpetual winter by an archaic mythical being that is partly of the earth (the one eye in the bag, the setting sun, or sun sunk beneath the horizon).

One should stress, however, that the liveliness that permeates myths such as these or that of Brigid are largely a product of the later Christian traditions and the nature of folk tales. Nevertheless, Gimbutas, author of *Goddesses and Gods of Old Europe* said that the legends and rituals of Ireland 'preserved many elements which in other parts of Europe vanished long ago'. She went as far as to say that 'the ancient spirit of Ireland is closer to the Old European (fourth millennium BC)'.[110] Yet the traces of this preserved in Celtic myth tell a darkened and subdued story of earth goddesses clinging on to the land, responsible for its fertility but perhaps subject to assault from the deteriorating weather as well as warrior invaders. Nevertheless, the earth continued to provide, and it is perhaps in the simple cadences of folklore, legend and myth that we catch a faint echo of pioneer life 2,000 years before a distinctive Celtic culture.

4

LINES ON THE LANDSCAPE, CIRCLES FROM THE SKY

Stone circles remain mysterious and enigmatic. One thing is certain, however; they evolved in some way from causewayed enclosures and henges ultimately to replace, or exist alongside, burial mounds. Burl captures the fundamental character of this change in the principal monuments of the Neolithic; 'Open-air rings of the sky replaced tombs of darkness and earth'.[1] The origins of stone circles remain bedevilled by puzzles and problems, but Burl draws some overall conclusions from his lifetime's study. At several points his general interpretation coincides with particular evidence from the two Orkney stone circles. Reviewing the detailed archaeological investigations at the Stones of Stenness in conjunction with evidence from my own fieldwork allows us to enlarge upon Burl's overview. My fieldwork has necessarily been limited to observation, but this has the possible advantage of setting the stone circles in the context of the surrounding landscape.

The likely significance of landscape in the Neolithic has been recognised in a number of recent archaeological studies. Scarre gives an explanation for this; 'any attempt to understand a prehistoric monument which fails to consider the landscape setting is omitting one of the most salient characteristics'.[2] It is easy to get lost in the details of material culture and archaeological remains with the consequence that the overwhelming presence of the landscape fades into the background. Yet its sheer physicality as well as its appearance would have always been the highly visible context against which a Neolithic people's rituals and everyday actions found their meaning. This is particularly the case with stone circles as, in comparison with burial tombs, these are open structures that suggest relationships might have been made to the surroundings. In this chapter we will look up and around from the Stones of Stenness to see what relationships there might have been, and when we find them we will explore what they might signify (**colour plates 29** & **31**). The intrinsic symbolism of the form and material of circle and stone will also be considered. We are reminded of the enormous significance of the landscape for these people whenever we encounter one of their great ritual sites; Avebury, Stonehenge, Callanish, or the Maes Howe − Stenness − Brodgar complex. The immense labour invested in megalithic circles indicates the profound meaning located in these places by the communities who built them. Each of these places is unique but each seems to gather together the surrounding landscape in some intense and dramatic way.

Landscape has been defined as 'a tract of land with its distinguishing features and characteristics'.[3] This seems a sufficiently neutral or objective term. Yet the definition contains inherited shades of meaning that specifically refer to landscape as an object of gaze. It alludes to the distancing that we need to acknowledge and be alert to before we can begin to grasp what the landscape might have meant to much earlier people. Raymond William's discussion of the derivation and development of the word concludes that the very idea of landscape implies separation and observation. Landscape descriptions such as 'wooded', 'arable' and 'picturesque' are our way of looking at the earth's surface from an objective and passive rather than being lived-in.[4] This essentially modern perception applies equally to landscape painting and photography as well as to geography, indicating a pervasive sensibility. Tilley discusses this in the introduction to his book *A Phenomenology of Landscape*, where he puts forward the case for the importance of landscape to primitive peoples and for the landscape to be understood as specific, particular or concrete places rather than space. Rather than objects of observation or analysis, spaces are constructed from the 'day-to-day praxis or practical activity of individuals and groups in the world'.[5] This is similar to Bourdieu's notion of 'habitus', the routine, preoccupied practices through which people experience the world and which plays a large part in how they form their conception of the world. However, Tilley argues that it limits our understanding of the prehistoric past when we see adaptation as simply a practical matter of resources or overlook the consequence of rituals enacted in a particular place with which they may have been inextricably involved. He suggests instead that it is the symbolism of these aspects that is critical to an understanding of early human activity as it established patterns of land occupation. For farmers, unlike hunter-gatherers, the land was not simply a surface to be traversed, but, says Burl, it was the 'life blood'.[6] This earlier idea of a landscape is produced through action and recognition. As Tilley says:

> significant locations become crystallised out of the environment through the production and recognition of meanings in particular places and through events that have taken place.[7]

He refers to anthropological studies to show that the landscape is not 'natural' for primitive peoples but is 'totally socialised'; it has been created by the gods and/or ancestors with whom each culture develops particular relationships. The landscape thereby becomes a fundamental reference point for symbolism and mythological events with the consequence that topographical features such as ridges, stony patches, waterholes, creeks and so on are assigned meaning and significance in the Australian Aboriginal case he illustrates. He draws upon such anthropological evidence to explore Neolithic remains to see if their relationship to particular landscape features might elucidate their meaning.

Bradley has criticised Tilley's phenomenological method as being subjective. Phenomenology takes up Heidegger's neat inversion of the Cartesian subject-object duality by saying we are 'thrown' into the world and find ourselves 'beings-in-the-world'. We are involved in the world as we might be in love or in pain. Such formulations suggest a sensibility but hardly help find forms of analysis. Nevertheless, I propose to follow Tilley's lead and examine that group of Orkney remains that has a discernible relationship with one of the island's most distinctive topographical features. The basic principles of analysis used earlier in investigating the existential spatial structure of the house will help counter the charge of subjectivity. A distinct axis and directed line of sight, for example, provide clear evidence of a constructed relationship, as we saw at Braeside and Unstan. We will find a number of archaeological remains linked to topographical features through lines that emanate from the newly arrived form of construction, the stone circle.

Burl's considered view is that stone circles represent a change in Neolithic belief system. He thinks this may have been caused by a deterioration in the climate between 3200 and 2900 BC, for which there is pollen evidence. The old belief systems focusing on ancestors and tombs perhaps appeared to fail with the consequence that 'people turned to those powerful skies,' he says, and 'unroofed enclosures were constructed'.[8] The labour involved in erecting these enclosures, continues Burl, indicates a shift from a relatively 'self-sufficient existence' to larger 'cohesive societies,' a tendency we saw developing in Orkney at Barnhouse and Maes Howe.

The particular form of the stone circle itself may have emerged from the earlier causewayed enclosures of Britain that were in use from approximately 3800-3200 BC. These seem to have been places set apart for more general purposes of assembly. A more specific candidate Burl favours for the emergence of stone circles is the court cairn of Northern Ireland. Some of these cairns incorporate vertical stones interspersed with horizontal coursing not unlike Irish passage graves such as Fourknocks. The development of a roughly semi-circular forecourt defined a large space for gathering before the tomb and brought ritual activity into the open air – something similar perhaps to what we saw in the stone platform at Quoyness or the natural stone platform at Isbister. Reviewing the distribution of court cairns, Burl notes that the relatively small number with a completely circular court occurs in regions where there are no stone circles. He suggests that the semi-circular forecourt evolved and detached itself to become the stone circle in the other locations. The 'cemetery' at Carrowmore he sees as significant in the final phase of this process, demonstrating how burial within a circle of boulders may have led, step by step, to proper stone circles.[9]

The Boyne group of tombs he considers to be important in the dissemination of the idea of stone circles and perhaps in the origin of the form itself. The enormous cairns at Knowth, Dowth and Newgrange are much bigger than required to cover the chamber, so for a considerable time during construction it is likely that they would appear as a large ring of kerb stones. In support of the idea of a changing belief system, quantities of Grooved Ware were found associated with a circular wooden structure close to Knowth. The evidence of stratigraphy and ceramics, continues Burl, quoting from the excavation report, 'argue[s] for the emergence of a separate and culturally different phase of prehistory in the Boyne valley and by extension in Ireland'.[10] Burl extends this to those areas of Britain where Grooved Ware has been almost always found in the contexts of large henges or circles, including the Stones of Stenness. Richards has pointed out that for a considerable time during construction, the stalled Orkney cairns would have presented themselves as lines of standing stones.

A further potential connection between Ireland and Orkney emerges from Burl's consideration of the distribution of stone circles. The unusual cluster of stone circles on Machrie Moor on Arran he interprets as a place of seasonal exchange, the centre of extensive trading routes between Ireland and Scotland. He considers that a similar array of stone circles around Callanish on Lewis 'may have served a similar purpose for craft crossing the sea from eastern Ireland to the Orkneys'.[11] The inner sea route between the Hebrides and Scotland would have been avoided because of the whirlpools and fearful tides of the Minch. The circles on North Uist are much larger than those associated with Callanish, which Burl thinks may reflect settlement rather than passing trade. Each Uist circle is built near a Hebridean passage grave, which is similar to the Orkney-Cromarty type. The Hebridean passage grave evolved to replace the Clyde tombs, one of which is adjacent to the settlement of Eilean Domhnuil.[12]

The Maes Howe-Stenness-Brodgar complex is situated on low land beside lochs Harray and Stenness, encircled by rolling hills never very close but discernibly more distant to the west. Bradley noted this sense of surrounding landscape here in developing his hypothesis of a circular archetype. This shallow bowl seems to define the landscape and contain at its centre the new type of monumental structures, perhaps most dramatically seen from Staney Hill to the west of Loch Harray (**colour plate 1**). Coming over the brim the scene below is dominated by water as lochs Harray and Stenness merge, albeit now separated by a narrow bridge. On one side stand the Stones of Stenness and on the other the Ring of Brodgar. On a not untypical Orkney day with low, dark, broken cloud, the space of the world seems compressed and the veiled sun casts sparkling silver threads across the grey water. The promise in the sky is taken up in the landscape below. In this largely treeless landscape of islands the sky dominates perception now as it would have done then. Beyond and looming over it all, significant players in the scene because of their size and shape, are the two sugar loaf hills of Hoy: Ward Hill and the Cuilags. Scarre considers the interpretation of monuments most accessible where they can be seen to relate to landscape features.[13] The Stenness stone circle does, as we will see.

Not only is it an incredible spectacle but this view also evokes a strong sense of being a mythical landscape, for rarely is there such a suggestion of land emerging from the waters. This association is triggered by the two promontories on which the stone circles stand almost meeting like fingers, extremities from which the rest of the body of land extends. As well as land almost meeting, two waters do meet and mingle. It is interesting to note that Loch Stenness is saltwater and Loch Harray is freshwater. This unusual juxtaposition calls to mind the Babylonian creation myth which 'tells of a watery chaos, a primordial ocean, apsu and tiamat; the first personified the ocean of fresh water on which the earth was later to float, and tiamat was the salty and bitter sea'.[14] The Watch Stone stands beside the point where Stenness and Harray meet. Vicki Cummings has remarked how often 'Neolithic sites seem to have been located near to watercourses, particularly at points of transition'.[15]

The epicentre of this gathered landscape is the Stones of Stenness sitting just 50 yards from the Watch Stone and 200 yards from the Barnhouse settlement on the shore of Loch Harray. Standing in the stone circle one has a distinct sense of a divided, or contrasted landscape within the orbit of enclosing hills, particularly around the time of midwinter. To the south-east is a strong impression of a dark earthy landscape over which the sun barely creeps, whereas opposite it is light, full of sky reflected in the waters of the two lochs (**colour plates 28 & 30**). Celtic peoples who came to occupy so much of the Neolithic landscape divided their year into two, a light and a dark half, celebrated by the festivals of Beltane and Samain, as we have seen. Reviewing the claims for stone circles' relationship to the heavens, Burl rejects alignments to stars, but finds repeated evidence for some calendrical focus on the sun and the moon. 'It is clear that the turning points of the year, particularly the time of change from darkness and cold to light and warmth, were of very great importance to prehistoric people.'[16]

The circle is entered from the light, watery side, the same side where Barnhouse sits beside Loch Harray in the direction of the high dark moors. While this can be but conjecture supported only by the 'feel' of entering and walking towards the dark hills presided over by the sun, it is nevertheless a fact that the entrance is due north of the circle such that one enters on a line orientated towards the sun's point of maximum power. (A fundamental polarity in many creation myths contrasts the dark, fecund, harbouring earth with the warm, up-drawing sun.) We noted when looking at Maes Howe the alignment of the cairn's passage with midwinter sunset. So at Stenness and Maes Howe (clearly visible from it) we see the sun at both its strongest and weakest points marked by alignments. The contrast between these two aspects echoes Burl's comments about a shift to 'open-air rings' from 'darkness and earth'. We also noticed at Maes Howe a distinct and particular increase in the use of geometry, which found a response at Barnhouse. At both Maes Howe and Barnhouse Structure 8 there was an encircling bank or wall around the building itself, a feature that is also found at the Stones of Stenness. Each is different however; a stone wall surrounded Barnhouse Structure 8, a low earth mound Maes Howe, whereas both a bank and ditch surrounded the Stones of Stenness. Furthermore, a resemblance between the plan of Barnhouse Structure 8 and the Stones of Stenness has been noticed. Two particular aspects of this structure have been interpreted as linking it directly to the Stones of Stenness. Firstly (and more allusively), it has been observed that if 'the wall of the inner house within Structure 8 is removed and the circular wall expanded, then it mirrors the spatial organisation of the Stones of Stenness'.[17] Secondly, the entrance to the interior of the building 'was flanked on either side by two stone monoliths standing proud of the walls', a grouping of features that finds a close parallel within the Stenness circle.[18] This has led to the suggestion that, while the Barnhouse structure with its double walled enclosure might reflect increasing control over ritual in the later Neolithic, the Stones of Stenness might have been its counterpart, its perimeter ditch and circle of stones allowing more open access. Clearly these three monuments in such close proximity were related in some way. A detailed review of the Stones of Stenness will help clarify this, and out of the comparisons and structured relationships may come an enhanced understanding of the purpose of stone circles.

The use of lines or alignments hinted at in the entrance to the Stones of Stenness can be shown to organise relationships between several monuments in the vicinity of this extensive ritual site and with certain features of the landscape itself. Distinct alignments have been detected that encompass Unstan, Barnhouse, the circles of Stenness and Brodgar, the Watch Stone and other outlying standing stones, as well as the alignment of Maes Howe to midwinter sunset. There can be little doubt that this complex web of inter-related lines and monuments formed part of a pattern of meaning for the people who built them. By examining things in the light of lines established between monuments as well as what has been ascertained about particular material remains, we might come closer to grasping something of the late Neolithic cosmos and hence understand more about the meaning of the remains themselves.

The Stones of Stenness

The Stones of Stenness form the remains of a henge monument, a class of structure found throughout Britain. Often, as at Stenness, a circle of standing stones occupies the space within the perimeter ditch and bank. The earliest date for Stenness is just before 3000 BC. The ditch (from which material for radiocarbon dating was obtained) was originally 7m across and 2m deep, the lowest metre or so cut into the bedrock. This last point led the excavator, Graham Ritchie, to consider it likely that the idea of ditch-surrounded henges was imported to Orkney on the grounds that such a laborious undertaking probably originated in softer ground conditions elsewhere.[19] This kind of rationalist argument misses the obvious point that all the time and effort involved in constructing such monuments hardly represents a logical or practical use of labour. Nevertheless Burl's survey of henge monuments led him to agree that stone circles probably originated elsewhere. Just outside the ditch the excavation revealed the remains of a bank, much ploughed down. Two trenches cut through the bank disclosed a 6.5m spread of clay, probably taken from the upper levels of the ditch but now no more than 0.4m high. An obvious point made early in the antiquarian interest in megalithic remains is that henges did not originate for defence because the bank is outside of the ditch, reversing the necessary arrangement. Much more likely is that this enclosure marked off some kind of ritual space and controlled entry to it.

Although often associated with a stone circle, henges were frequently constructed simply as a causewayed enclosure. They present complex problems of interpretation which have been reviewed by Edmonds. He sheds little light, however, on the Stones of Stenness, as interpretations tend to focus on patterns of settlement or economic activity in relation to Neolithic life more generally. In the course of his review Edmonds summarises the typically tripartite structure of ritual; one of 'separation', 'liminality, which in turn is followed by one of reincorporation'.[20] He goes on to suggest that the physical form of causewayed enclosures lends them a distinct sense of being a ritual site. The evidence found from these sites often has associations with funerary practice, feasting, or exchange of prestige artefacts. For Bradley, henges concluded the Neolithic engagement with what he calls a 'circular archetype'.

In many causewayed enclosures the banks were made tall enough to preclude looking in, but the Stones of Stenness was always a visually open site. There are a number of features within the circle that offer a unique opportunity to interpret such a site, but nothing was found that allows us to understand why the ditch was dug (**79** & **80**). Given the above, one particular characteristic of this circle is that the ditch and causeway organises movement in a particular way and the line of entry sets up an axis upon which significant things are located. If this represents one form of control by directing movement in an otherwise visually open ritual structure, another might be that the ditch and causeway limit or direct the life-giving matrix that runs mysteriously through the earth. The ditch breaks its continuity and the causeway becomes a narrow conduit connecting it to the topsoil within the circle. Tilley refers to anthropologists who have pointed out that many Melanesian societies have two planes of existence; one is fixed, the land of the dead and ancestral forces, and

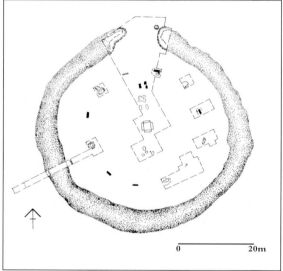

79 *View of the Stones of Stenness from the south-west*

80 *Plan of the Stones of Stenness showing the extent of excavations.* Redrawn after Ritchie and showing the extent of his excavations

the other is the fluid world of all life's forces. The former is perceivable, the latter invisible or underlying. The invisible place of existence can become 'visible' through the metamorphosis of animals and plants or mountains and rocks. This generalised notion of the underlying, invisible order of things made visible is most easily grasped by Greek myths, in particular that of Persephone and her abduction by Hades where personification explains natural forces such as the mystery of planting. Harrison describes this as 'the notion of a sort of continuum of mana, a world of unseen power lying behind the visible universe'.[21] Consequently, continues Tilley:

the land becomes ... replete with ancestral energies that require care and constant sustenance through ritual magic. Beneath the apparent surface of the landscape, but intimately bound up with it, there is a hidden topography best known to (and influenced by) ritual experts in these societies, but emotionally and cognitively pertinent to all.[22]

It is with such possibilities of control (or attempts to intercede) in mind that we might best approach the circle and the 'events' within.

Within the space marked off by the bank and ditch was a circle of twelve massively tall stones, the tallest of the four surviving measuring 5.7m. The stones are flat slabs approximately 30–40cm thick and more than 1m wide. One stone re-erected in 1907 was estimated to weigh between 9 and 10 tons. The circle has a diameter of approximately 30m. The very tall, flat, wide stones, their face running with the circumference of the circle, create an exceptionally strong sense of enclosure, or of being within a space set apart from the world. This is much more evident here than at any other stone circle, excepting perhaps Stonehenge and the smaller diameter Callanish. From within the circle, the three surviving stones that stand in close proximity to one another rise up above the horizon of the nearby Ward Hill, catching the sky between their pointed peaks. Perhaps because such gigantic slabs of easily split stone were more readily available in Orkney than elsewhere in Britain or Ireland, the impression gained here is that the early circle builders intended to make a ritual centre rather than an astronomical observatory, as has been suggested by Thom and others. Not that the arrangement of the circles was without its astronomical factors, as we shall see, but that these formed a part of the broader aims of such a ritual centre. In his consideration of stone circles as places of assembly, Burl attempts a rough calculation of how many people could gather there. He does this by proposing 1.8m² per person and assuming that half the circle would be reserved for officiants, although he acknowledges that there is no data for this. Yet it allows him to track the development of circles in relation to what appears to have been the consolidation of regions of especial power or significance. This calculation shows that 2,000 people could be accommodated within Stanton Drew, for example.[23] Using Burl's method suggests that approximately 200 people might gather in the Stones of Stenness.

Circle and earth

I would like to examine what possible meanings this ritual circle might have held by considering it from three perspectives: firstly, a further consideration of alignments set up or gathered by the circle and features within it; secondly, what might be inferred from the remains and their arrangement within the circle; and thirdly, to consider the symbolism of the circle. The first two of these are inextricably linked, as we shall see immediately.

As mentioned, the causeway makes entry to the circle from almost due north so that one walks towards the sun at its highest and most powerful. While this might be considered as purely conceptual, the physical act of approaching across the causeway is dominated by the more concrete 'facts' of landscape and constructions. Although only a matter of feeling, one has a strong sense of the standing stones coming to master the dark backdrop of Ward Hill the closer one approaches. Also, the Hoy Hills away to the right gradually appear to come into ever closer conjunction with the stones. More immediately and demonstrably, the line of approach is dominated by the close proximity of the so-called 'dolmen' that stands roughly on the centre of the line of approach across the causeway when projected towards the centre of the circle. This puzzling group of three stones was re-erected in 1907 in what is believed to have been their original positions. Ritchie did discover a series of other features that occupy the same line; an arrangement of post-holes, a stone-lined hearth at the centre of the circle and a series of stone-lined pits and buried pots beyond.

The arrangement of stones called a dolmen is more generally known as a cove. As at Stenness, they comprise a pair of stone slabs with a back stone so that they do indeed resemble an uncapped dolmen or portal tomb. Burl sees the presence of these as evidence for the view that stone circles came to take over the role of chambered cairns. Reviewing the dozen or so known throughout Britain, he concludes that they might be 'imitations of those disused cells'.[24] Generally the side slabs face one another but at Stenness they are adjacent. This arrangement, Burl continues, is 'identical to the projecting side slabs and back stone of the chambers in Unstan'. As we have seen, Unstan was modified to align its entrance with the Watch Stone and the line projected on to the principal house at Barnhouse, 200m from the Stones of Stenness. In the setting up of a cove that imitates the single side chamber at Unstan, we find more evidence of the interrelationship between this group of monuments and changing ritual activity. Even more intriguingly, the cove sets up a framed view and alignment that reinforces and extends this.

Stenness to Maes Howe

If the dolmen stones were reset in their original positions, as Ritchie considers likely from the evidence of earlier topographical drawings, then the narrow gap between the two standing side by side frames the mound of Maes Howe, estab-lishing an alignment to it (**81** & **82**). So once again we encounter a standing stone, or in this case a pair of stones making a portal, set up in a very specific manner to face a chambered cairn. Maes Howe we noted has its entrance passage aligned to the midwinter setting sun. Tilley concludes that a significant

81 *The 'dolmen' at the Stones of Stenness framing an alignment to Maes Howe*

82 *Map indicating alignment between 1 the Stones of Stenness; 2 Maes Howe; 3 the standing stone at Deepdale; 4 Unstan chambered cairn*

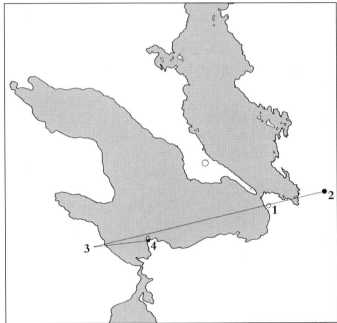

aim of Neolithic structures was to 'freeze perspective through the architectural lens of the monuments themselves'. His argument finds support here in this framed relationship between Stenness and Maes Howe. The focus Maes Howe gives to the sun setting into a particular feature of the landscape adds to the significance of this. 'Experience of the ancestral past now came into being within the specific setting of monuments and their relationship to the outside world'.[25] As we will see, the features unearthed within the stone circle and the lines associated with it further indicate that the Stones of Stenness could be seen in the way Tilley describes.

Early in the discussion of the chambered cairns we saw evidence of ritual activity – hearths and remains – associated with the cairn entrance. Although the ditch and platform surrounding Maes Howe have never been fully excavated, the architecture of the entrance suggests that it was considered more of a mausoleum than a place of regular rituals involving frequent access to the chamber.[26] Perhaps here the significant ancestors had their remains placed, reinvigorated by the midwinter sun, and whatever power or force they contained or commanded was transferred to the Stones of Stenness by the alignment set up by the two framing stones of the cove. Perhaps then, within the ring of stones, new rituals were enacted. The particular arrangement of the cove lends itself to such a reading for, as we have seen, they do repeat the essential elements of the tripartite or stalled cairns, a pair of portal stones and a back stone centred on the axis between. All this seems to provide firm evidence for Burl's view that ritual activity associated with burial cairns became transferred to stone circles. The main, inescapable fact of all megalithic monuments, as Thomas says, is that they dominate the landscape and hence impose themselves upon future generations.[27] The monumentalisation of ancestors at Maes Howe might in itself have accelerated changes in both social and belief systems.

Yet more intriguingly, if the line established from Maes Howe to the cove at the Stones of Stenness is projected, it aligns with the isolated standing stone at Deepdale that sits high above the western shore of Loch Stenness. This stone, tall and flat, is turned in such a way that its broad face is directed towards

83 *The standing stone at Deepdale turned to face Unstan chambered cairn*

84   The 'dolmen' at the Stones of Stenness framing a view of the standing stone at Deepdale

Unstan (**83** & **84**). The Setter Stone stands in the same relation to Braeside and we will see other standing stones set up to face another. 'Face', or 'to face', comes from the Latin *facies*, which means 'form' or 'shape', especially the front of the head. This yields 'façade' and 'fascia', both building terms bound up with facing. 'Facing up to' (a problem) and 'facing down' (an enemy) are habitual expressions of this that derive from the distinctive sense of human verticality and frontality. In this way we begin to see how a web of lines was laid down on the landscape binding together these significant ancestral remains with emerging forms of new and more elaborate ritual centres.

While it is incontrovertible that the dolmen face Maes Howe, close consideration of the stones' position, in relation to their own long axes or faces, raises another possibility which casts some doubt on – or supplements – this particular hypothesis of cove as a representation of burial chamber. Ritchie's excavation of the approach causeway led him to the view that the narrower section of the ditch on its western terminus was 'an afterthought, or later cutting'.[28] The causeway therefore had once been wider and subsequently narrowed. The most obvious explanation for this would be that those responsible wanted it aligned more closely to north, the final axis drawn through the centre of the causeway from the hearth being within 2° of true north. The two portal stones of the cove are located on this line. A similar line drawn from the hearth through the centre of the causeway before it was altered passes across the face of the third stone of the cove (**85**). Perhaps we see in this a repositioning of significant standing stones like that we know took place, for example, with the

153

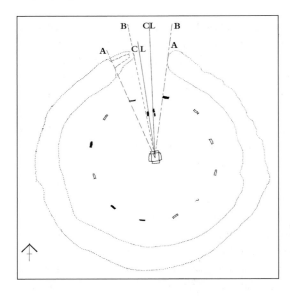

85 *Plan of the Stones of Stenness indicating the position of the 'dolmen' in relation to the first and second centre lines of the causeway entrance. The ditch was extended – see broken line on the left – narrowing the cause-way and bringing the axis of entry almost due north-south*

Heel Stone at Stonehenge. The conceptual significance of the line due south at Stenness could have been used to locate this feature. Standing immediately inside the entrance to the space marked off by the ditch, this stone feature draws to itself the forces associated with the ancestors, represented in its form and gathered by its alignment, as well as the sun at its strongest point.

Mortuary structures

The archaeological evidence suggests that there were two (or possibly three) features between the hearth and the causeway. In addition to the dolmen or cove there was a pair of standing stones possibly associated with a structure made up of four wooden posts. Because so few remains have been found in other circles, Ritchie reminds us that in no case 'can the central features of a henge monument be fully interpreted'. He discusses the evidence of the remains between dolmen and hearth as a single entity or possibly as some sort of 'ribbon development' as rituals expanded out from the central hearth. Ritchie considers there to be insufficient evidence to propose firmly that coves were symbolic representations of megalithic tomb entrances. Nevertheless he compares the central features found at Stenness with those at Balbirnie, Fife, which he discusses in relation to 'cult houses' or 'mortuary houses' found in Denmark. At this point he speculates that 'it seems possible that the central setting at Stenness may be the foundation of such an enclosure, designed to receive offerings, sacrifices or bones, and [that] the timber setting, with what must have been impressive stone portals, may also belong to a similar tradition'.[29]

Ritchie's inference that the pair of stones formed a portal to a timber mortuary structure approached from the close proximity of a hearth has compelling likeness to the entrance portal of the feast hall at Barnhouse. Discovered some 10 years later, this has formed the basis of later comparisons between the two plans. Beyond the portal stones the size of the Barnhouse building makes it almost certain that some kind of timber structural posts would have been visible within the space. This might have found an echo in the two stones and four posts arranged together in the Stenness circle.

This was before the publishing of *The Stonehenge People*, where Burl describes how a wooden mortuary building had existed on the site of Stonehenge around 3300 BC before the erection of the stone circle.[30] He describes how mortuary buildings in Neolithic Wessex had developed from quite small, possibly open enclosures, to huge long ones that finally became encased in long barrows. This formed the background to his view that rituals associated with burial became transferred to stone circles. The archaeologist largely responsible for discovering the remains at Stonehenge, William Hanley, also unearthed post-holes near the centre of Stonehenge which he tentatively suggested might have been 'a wooden passage grave'.[31] The proximity of the great trilithons prevented further excavation, but Burl compared the evidence from Stonehenge with that of a similar structure found at Saggart Hill near Dublin. 'Like that at Stonehenge, it was aligned north-south, 30ft long and 6ft 3in wide (9m by 1.9m) and it led towards a rectangular hearth in which the soil has been burned a deep red "by the kindling of many fires over a long period"'.[32]

If we take the structural features within Stenness as a single entity then we have almost exactly the same arrangement as Burl describes, in this case a structure measuring 7.5m long by around 2m wide and, as his other two examples, aligned north-south leading 'towards a rectangular hearth'. Attempting to conjecture the appearance and meaning of a structure from the few faint traces that remain in the ground is always problematic, so whether the structure at Stonehenge was a passage grave as Hanley speculated, or mortuary building as Burl leans towards, may prove impossible to say conclusively. It is even difficult to say whether they represent a single structure or a group of connected features (as seems quite likely from the evidence at Stenness). However, both suggestions link the presence of some kind of structure or structures within the circle with rituals for the dead. Burl finds confirmation of this in the fact that the mortuary building at Stonehenge 'faced towards the major rising of the full midwinter moon'.[33] The moon is almost universally associated with the dead, something that will be discussed shortly.

Another reading of the central features at Stenness tends to support this view. In his paper *Mortuary Structures and Megaliths*, J.G. Scott reviews the evidence for mortuary buildings – implying enclosures – often unearthed in long barrows. From this he proposes instead what he calls a three, four or six point mortuary

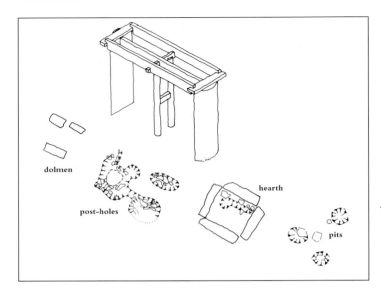

86 *Plan of remains found within the circle of the Stones of Stenness (below) and reconstruction of possible mortuary structure (above).* Redrawn after Scott

structure – a platform on which the dead were placed for excarnation.[34] This is the kind of structure Hedges proposed in relation to the buried remains at Isbister. While the evidence for any typical form for such a structure is at best slight, Scott nevertheless makes a reconstruction drawing of one – the four point – perhaps because it is most suggestive and there is more evidence supporting it (**86**). The crucial and most intriguing aspect of Scott's reconstruction is that both end supports for such a platform were found, from the evidence of post-holes, to 'be massive split tree trunks'.[35] These were clearly symbolic rather than utilitarian because the central pair of supports were comparatively slender poles, quite sufficient for the purpose of such a structure. Moreover, even substantial structures such as houses could be built from nothing larger than slender poles, as we saw earlier. What the symbolism might be is difficult to suggest with any conviction. Yet given that all Scott's examples are situated on densely forested mainland Britain, and given that we know tree worship or symbolism to have played a significant part in later cultures occupying such terrain, perhaps there was something significant in the dead being placed between the two halves of a split trunk. It may be that in this way the body was located within the force of life's matrix, symbolised by the tree's trunk, until the final internment. The tree, seeming to die each autumn only to be born again in spring, provided a symbolic link to what was sought on behalf of the dead. Excavations in the Etruscan region of Lazio have unearthed bodies buried between a split and slightly hollowed tree-trunk, an example of which can be seen at the Etruscan museum in Rome. Drawing upon ethnographic parallels from Madagascar where stone is used to represent ancestors and standing stones are known as *vatolahy* ('man stones'), Parker-Pearson and Ramilisonia contrasted wood circles and stone circles as places for the living and the dead respectively.[36]

I earlier discussed the symbolism of stone and, while the meanings associated with wood as a material are not so obviously relevant here at Stenness, it is worth a brief etymological digression to elaborate upon this, as it sheds further light on the way peoples once thought about their world. Our words matrix, material and matter all derive from the Latin word *materia*, which meant the hard part of the tree, timber or the stuff of which a thing is made. *Materia* is closely related to the Latin word *mater*, meaning mother. The trunk of the tree thus produces branches or offshoots as a mother produces offspring. So material, the basic stuff of cultural production, has its roots in reproduction – the mother as a perennially generative being just as Mother Nature was eternally regenerative. In these relationships of meaning we can perhaps detect something of a world view that had been held from a much earlier period and was captured when words first fixed ideas and things. Wood remains the material for coffins and stone for graves, so it seems more likely that distinctive ideas of regeneration and eternity were in play in mortuary structures than a simple polarity between the living and the dead.

If we consider the Stenness group of structural features as a single or connected entity then perhaps we see certain similarities with the mortuary platform proposed by Scott. Instead of the split trunks at either end we might have two sets of portals made of stone within the field of what might be a mortuary platform supported on four poles. Here in treeless Orkney, stone might have fulfilled a similar purpose to the split trunks, being ascribed with related properties of resisting time and decay as we have seen.

Hearth

At the centre of the Stones of Stenness the excavators discovered a hearth in which they found the burnt remains of bones, a few fragments of pottery and some organic material, including a quantity of what they term 'cramp' – burnt seaweed.[37] A not uncommon sight in present day Orkney are piles of 'tangles' – the thick stems of seaweed – drying on a wooden rack or stone wall beside the sea shore, as this can be used as fuel. Seaweed was also commonly used in the past by crofters as fertiliser, particularly in the 'lazy beds' of Harris and Lewis. So it is intriguing to consider its burning here as possible further evidence of rituals associated with the earth's fertility.

That the fundamental role of this hearth was a ritual one there can be little doubt, for its excavation revealed two curious facts. Firstly, that the earth at the centre of the hearth was natural till, the trenches for the kerb cut around it and the stones then set in place without disturbing it. This formed what Ritchie described as a 'natural hump' in the hearth. This might be taken simply as the desire to retain the original earth's surface within what seems to have been the marked off central hearth – although even this would not be without its significance. Yet between this hump and one of the kerbs was a looser fill in which traces of a post and slot could be made out. As the archaeologists stripped away the earth they found that this post and slot continued below the hearth.

What this seems to represent are the remains of an upright post with a supporting horizontal beam in the slot (presumably with a junction timber, rather in the manner of an inverted gibbet). The upright and its supporting beams were the reasons for the construction of the stone setting in the position in which it was, the existence of an upright timber provides the best interpretation for the way in which the central hump remained undug when the main slabs were set into position.[38]

Although Ritchie is reluctant to use the word, his detailed description leaves little doubt that this was a totem pole or something similar, one that clearly predated the building of the hearth and around which the Stones of Stenness were built. There is little firm evidence for totem poles among farming communities but Harrison discusses Pausanias' description of 'the festival of the Laurel-Bearing' in Ancient Greece, which opens; 'They wreathe a pole of olive wood with laurel and various flowers'.[39] Maypole ceremonies she considers to be a vestige of similar native rites. From anthropological parallels, she finds the belief in a 'group life' centred on a 'totem animal', which contains the tribe's matrix that never dies. When 'a man dies he goes back to his totem animal'.[40]

Richards has described this complex collection of stone monuments as 'creating the centre of the world in late Neolithic Orkney'.[41] Whenever Eliade deals with the creation of such places by primitive peoples he uses the term *axis mundi*, a term Richards utilises but does not fully explore. By *axis mundi*, Eliade means a place where the various levels of the cosmos are linked, normally requiring at least three levels; an underworld, this world and a world above. A totem pole is frequently found in association with this idea and the place in which it is found is always a sacred place marked off from the profane world, to use Eliade's helpful if not unproblematic polarity. Bradley discusses this concept in his *Archaeology of Natural Places*, where he considers the belief system of Lapland Saami. 'Communities in Arctic Europe', he says, 'made a vital distinction between this world, an underworld and the sky'. For the Saami these three spheres correspond to the air, land, and water or forest tundra for the underworld. (In symbolism the forest and water can both stand for the preformed or subconscious.) Each of these regions is occupied by particular creatures; birds in the sky or celestial realm, reindeer in this world, and fish in the underworld. 'Particular places were especially important in allowing communication between these different domains', continues Bradley, echoing a theme we touched upon when considering the possibility of shamanistic activity at passage graves. In Arctic Europe these three domains are often connected by a cosmic river or tree, a belief we saw extensively enacted across Siberian Europe. The *axis mundi* is sometimes found 'on the

Saami (shaman's) drum ... represented by a pillar or by a drawing of the sun'. The similarity between these practices or beliefs and what has been found at the Stones of Stenness becomes clear when we learn that Saami sacred sites are often associated with a mountain, lake, peninsular or island, and that they were sometimes 'ringed by a circle of antlers. In these cases the main focus was a cairn'.[42] I will return to this when discussing the symbolism of the circle, but let us first look at the other, more puzzling features found within the Stones of Stenness.

Sacrificial pits or *mundus*

On the line of entry projected beyond the hearth a group of small pits dug into the earth were found. This repeats the hearth-storage tank arrangement we noted when discussing the axis at Skara Brae. The largest pit measured 1.05m in diameter and 0.6m in depth. Two upright stone slabs were found, with two more lying among the filling suggesting that the pit was lined like those containers found at Skara Brae and Rinyo. In with the earth fill were found a number of organic remains. In a smaller pit immediately beside it carbonised cereal was discovered. A third pit contained several carbonised cereal caryopses. A fourth pit was a small hollow in which sat the base of a pottery vessel, the upper part of which had been destroyed by recent ploughing. Adjoining this was a shallow pit 0.9m by 0.85m containing reddish burnt material from which no organic remains were discovered. The essential aspects of this find – organic material and burnt earth in the pits with an adjacent hearth – are so strikingly similar to aspects of the Roman *mundus* that it is worth looking at the rituals and beliefs associated with it. For in the *mundus* we have historical accounts that can supplement archaeological and anthropological evidence.

Ovid gives a description of the making of the *mundus* that incorporates aspects of what was found at the centre of the Stones of Stenness:

> *A ditch was dug down to the firm clay*
> *Fruits were thrown to the bottom*
> *And earth from the neighbouring fields*
> *The ditch was filled again and an altar put on it*
> *And the new hearth*
> *Was decked with kindled fire.*[43]

Plutarch describes the founding of Rome as involving the digging of a circular trench called a *mundus*. Romulus sent for 'men of magical wisdom from Etruria to do this. Into the *mundus* were deposited specimen offerings of all things esteemed good by custom or necessary by nature, and a portion of earth brought from the country from which each man came'.[44]

Under the principal temple of the Roman colony of Cosa, archaeologists discovered a levelled site within which they found, on the axis itself, a natural crevasse around 2m–2.5m deep. In this way archaeology corroborated legend. The excavators reported that the crevasse was 'the receptacle of a mass of vegetable matter, which combined as it rotted. Given the religious context, it is to be presumed that this vegetable matter consisted of offerings deposited as part of a ritual act'.[46]

From his survey of Roman authors combined with archaeological evidence, Joseph Rykwert considers that the *mundus* went far back into the Etruscan period. The word probably had an Etruscan origin and its meaning was 'almost exactly corresponding to the Greek *kosmos*'. He demonstrates how important aspects of Roman city-planning and rituals were derived from the Etruscans (who in turn inherited them from 'a culture called Terramore early in the Bronze age, or even towards the end of the Neolithic period').[47] Like all western European cultures, the Etruscans, or their ancestors, must have been affected by the Neolithic revolution as the first farmers entered from the east. In view of this long thread and in conjunction with the universal spread of agriculture throughout Neolithic Europe, it is perhaps legitimate to see a common core of beliefs explaining curious events history records in such disparate places as the Roman *mundus* and found by archaeologists in the pits full of offerings at Stenness.

A large number of extraordinary deep shafts dug by the Celtic peoples attest to the antiquity and the widespread nature of these or related customs. Found as far apart as northern Britain and Bavaria in southern Germany, the pits often contained remains that have allowed archaeologists and historians to interpret the meaning they had for Celtic peoples. In the bottom of a 24ft-deep circular pit at Swanwick, Hampshire (*c.*1200–1000 BC) stood a central wooden post packed around with clay. A horizontal band of charcoal indicated that vegetable matter had been deposited in addition to clay loom-weights, fragments of a quern and traces of dried flesh or blood. Swanwick and its contents, including post, are strikingly similar to those found in the Iron Age religious earthwork at Holzhausen in Bavaria.[48]

Many of these shafts incorporate a well. Ross suggests that wells, springs and pits, many of which have been found to contain Celtic votive offerings, were regarded by Celtic peoples as 'entrances to the otherworld'.[49] Green describes a shaft at Deal in Kent in which was found a chalk figurine. Steps carved into the side suggest that access to the pit was intended, leading her to interpret the shaft as a shrine 'for communication with underworld powers who inhabited regions deep below the earth. Human beings and animals were sacrificed to these deities and they were propitiated also by offerings of food and other items'.[50] The enigmatic 'mystery of the twenty-nine steps' down into a subterranean chamber at the recently discovered Iron Age Mine Howe in Orkney may have involved similar associations with its Celtic counterparts.

1 *Orkney. View over Lochs Harray and Stenness to the Hills of Hoy in the distance. The Stones of Stenness stand on the isthmus separating the two lochs on the left and the Ring of Brodgar is on the far right*

2 *View from Rousay where the Atlantic meets Eynhallow Sound. Midhowe broch lies down by the shore and Costa Head, the northernmost point on Mainland Orkney, is visible in the background*

3 *The entrances to the two adjacent houses of the Knap of Howar*

4 *Detail of Knap of Howar House 2. Note the shelves or cupboards built into the walls of the inner compartment. The house is divided into distinct areas by very thin vertical slabs of stone. On the floor and to the right can be seen a quernstone*

5 *Basket-making; as the second set of willows are woven into the base, the starburst arrangement transforms into a distinct spiral*

6 *Basket-making; nearing completion of a shallow basket. The vertical staves are turned down and twisted together to make the rim*

7 *An Orkney basket made by William Watter of Melsetter House, Hoy. The position of the handle pulls the sides in giving a shape similar to House 1 at the Knap of Howar*

8 *Unstan ware from Isbister chambered cairn*

9 Above: *The early House 9 at Skara Brae*
10 Opposite above: *Hut 8 at Skara Brae is considered to have been a workshop*
11 Opposite below: *Exterior wall of Hut 8 with entrance to Skara Brae passage beyond*

12 *Photo-montage reconstruction of a Skara Brae house showing the conjectured roof structure. The reconstruction is based on the following: evidence of post-holes at Rinyo; post-hole positions in other Neolithic houses; the logic of vernacular timber-framed buildings; Hebridean Blackhouses. Hazel bark-lined drains at Rinyo suggest that the waterproof attribute of bark might have been deployed as roof tiles; if this was the case, there would have been a covering of turf as in Scandinavian vernacular houses. The roof plan below is from the model made to investigate the structure.*
Photo–montage made by Harry Paticas

13 *Detail of entrance to Skara Brae House 1. Note the jambs lined with thin vertical slabs to make a good fit for a door, perhaps a wood frame or woven and covered with skin*

14 *Looking down on Skara Brae House 7*

15 *Interior of traditional croft at Kirbister. The open fire with simian rope above for smoking fish is very suggestive of domestic life at Skara Brae. Built into the far wall to the left of the fireback is a bed not unlike the arrangement at Skara Brae House 9*

16 *Barnhouse. Looking across House 2 and Structure 8 to the Stones of Stenness*

17 *The principal house at the Barnhouse settlement. Reduced by ploughing to its foundations, the walls have been built up 3 or 4 courses since excavation. The Watch Stone is visible in the top right-hand corner*

18 *Taversoe Tuick, Rousay, as a territorial marker. Seen from neighbouring land to the east, its profile against the sky would have been a clear indicator of an ancestral claim to the land on which it sits*

19 *Knowe of Yarso from above. The hill drops away steeply immediately beyond the cairn to the farmland down by the shore. Beyond Eynhallow Sound lies Mainland Orkney*

20 *Knowe of Yarso as territorial marker*

21 *Midhowe stalled chambered cairn on Rousay is one of the largest of the Orkney cairns, 32.5m long with masonry surviving to a height of 2.5m*

22 *Interior of Vinquoy Hill. The thicker laminated sandstone of Eday may have contributed to the relative irregularity of this chamber*

23 *Maes Howe in snow. The all-enveloping gloom conveys something of the fear Neolithic farmers must have felt at the sun's decline in winter*

24 *The central chamber of Maes Howe.*
Copyright Charles Tait

25 *The midwinter setting sun casting its light down the passage of Maes Howe.* Copyright Charles Tait

26 *The Barnhouse Stone with Maes Howe in the background*

27 *A pair of standing stones on the Brodgar promontory. They align with the Barnhouse Stone, which is just visible silhouetted against the patch of light to the left of the stones in the foreground. The Stones of Stenness can be seen to the right of the telegraph pole*

28 *Midwinter sunrise over the Stones of Stenness, looking towards Ward Hill*

29 *The Stones of Stenness from the south-west*

30 *Midsummer sunset from the Stones of Stenness. Looking towards the Watch Stone and Loch Harray, centre right*

31 *The Stones of Stenness from the north-east looking towards Ward Hill and the Cuilags of Hoy. These two cairn-shaped Hills of Hoy are the only pronounced mountains in Orkney*

32 *Sunset at the Ring of Brodgar. Its relatively elevated position and distance from Ward Hill gives a better view of the moon setting into the Hills of Hoy than from the Stones of Stenness.* Copyright Charles Tait

33 *The Ring of Brodgar. The Stones of Stenness are just visible to the right of the right-hand stone of the circle*

We cannot be so specific in what we read from the archaeological evidence in Neolithic Orkney, of course. However, the pits found at Stenness would seem to suggest a connection to the basic belief system inferred from the Celtic shafts, that they represent an offering to supernatural forces that resided in the underworld. Green thinks it is reasonable to see the Celtic shafts performing a similar role to the *mundi* of the Graeco-Roman world, 'pits which linked the underworld to earth, ... used in acknowledgement of the dualistic chthonic and celestial powers'.[51] By the time of Celtic occupation of Britain there were well-established beliefs and practices focused on the sun. It might well be that such had become the emphasis on the celestial that it was more difficult to communicate with the chthonic, hence the extraordinary depth of so many of these shafts. The whole background to Neolithic Stenness, in contrast, is dominated by the chthonic, each settlement's passage grave offering 'doorways' into an associated underworld. In such a context the offering pits would perhaps not need to be very deep, whereas the stones have to rise to an enormous height as Neolithic peoples reach out perhaps for the first time to the celestial.

That the mythical accounts of the origin of Rome have Romulus digging a *mundus* is testimony to the antiquity of this theme. It formed an important and typical part of the myths that articulate the emergence of culture from nature – represented most strikingly, of course by Romulus and Remus being raised by a wolf, a myth of separation yet embracing reciprocal relations.[52] As Rykwert makes clear, the origins of town-founding rites have roots that go back deep into a more agrarian past. The essential rites in founding a Roman town remained the very 'savage' ritual sacrifice of a bird or animal, tearing its entrails out and reading auguries on the site. If auspicious, the place was then marked off by ploughing a furrow around its perimeter. Although sophisticated city dwellers, Romans needed to cosmogonise their world to make it habitable. Nor were such offerings only a part of a foundation ceremony. Rykwert goes on to describe another Roman account of 'a *mundus* devoted to Ceres, goddess of the crops, which had a special priesthood'.[53]

As has been suggested, there seems to be a fundamental idea that the earth, with its mysterious matrix of fertility, is sacred. Romulus carried the plough over the earth where the gates were to be (Latin *port*, meaning to lift, gives us our word portal) as he cut the ditch making out the boundary of the city because the Romans, as Plutarch says: 'considered all ploughed land sacred and inviolate'. The business of those who followed the plough 'was to see that whatever was thrown up should be turned inwards towards the city, and not to let any clod lie outside'.[54] The earth is the provider, the matrix from which all life stems. Lifting the plough over the entrances allowed the fertility of the earth to run into the town, which might have been the role of the causeway at Stenness. The sacred space of the Roman temple is etymologically derived from this. The Latin *templum* stems from the Greek word *temenos* or precinct, a place 'cut off from the common land and dedicated to a god'.[55]

We know that some North American hunter-gatherers would not plough or dig the earth because they saw it as cutting the skin or belly of their mother. Yet farmers had to cut the earth's surface by necessity, hence the huge significance placed on rites of propitiation or making offerings to the earth. To farmers the earth does not simply give but returns multiplied what has been placed into its care.

Rykwert also records why earth itself might be buried in pits. He quotes an interpretation of why the inhabitants of a new place threw clods of earth from their old town into the *mundus.*

> That is where their hearth had been; that is where their fathers lived and were buried. Now religion forbade the abandonment of a place where the hearth had been fixed and the deified ancestors rested. In order to be absolved from all impiety each of them had to make use of a fiction by taking with him, in the form of a clod of earth, the sacred ground in which his ancestors were buried, and to which their *manes* remained attached. No one could move without bringing his earth and ancestors with him.[56]

Much of what has been recounted here has to do with the foundation rites of much later towns, but it conveys something of the peculiar world view ancient people had. At so many points one can see correspondences with the kind of activity that the archaeological evidence suggests may have taken place at the Stones of Stenness. Rykwert even finds related meanings that carry an echo of what we have discussed in relation to the transference of ritual activity from cairns to circles;

> in some way *mundus* was a shrine of the *manes*, the propitiated souls of the dead. It was opened three times a year and the days on which it was opened were dangerous and all sorts of public business ... were forbidden. On those days the spirits of the dead came among the living.[57]

This curious conjunction of fertility (seeds and fruit), relocated homeland (clods of earth) and the otherworld (spirits of the dead) that gathered around the Roman *mundus*, reinforced by what we can glean from Celtic myth, strikes a chord with what we know to be perhaps the deepest meaning of the earth's association with death. To these first Neolithic settlers, existence could only continue if new bodies sprang into being as did corn from seed. Hence perhaps the widespread linking of the meaning of burial rites – placing the dead into the earth's care, hoping that ancestors might live on like seed – with those concerned with fertility and harvest. These conjectures upon what significance the activity that took place within the Stones of Stenness might have had for its builders can only remain as such, tantalising as they may appear. Yet in the alignment to Maes Howe and its links to Unstan we perhaps have specific pieces of evidence establishing that links to death and the ancestors were present at the Stones of Stenness.

Stenness, sun and sky

There is another significant alignment associated with the Stones of Stenness that weaves this web of connected ideas yet tighter and leads onto a consideration of the symbolism of the circle. The possibility has been mentioned that the north-south axis might have been to align entry with the sun at its maximum height and power – the Greeks sometimes described noon as 'Helios is King'.[58] Seen from within the circle of stones the midwinter sun sets into the Cuilags on Hoy at the same moment of the day and year when it illuminates the passage at Maes Howe (**87** & **88**). Silhouetted against the luminous evening sky in particular the Hills of Hoy appear to have the profile of a burial cairn. This linkage in a very brief space of time between the closed world of Maes Howe and the open structure of Stenness would seem to be very significant. At the same time as the bones or spirits of the ancestors were being illuminated by the sun in the depth of winter, the sun's own descent into the underworld was brought into a relationship with the Stones of Stenness through its location relative to the Hills of Hoy. Similar examples have been noticed elsewhere. In Ireland the sun sets into 'the sacred mountain of Carn Uineit' at Imbolc and Samain.[59] On the island of Islay the ring called Cultoon has its tallest stone in the direction of the mountain Slieve Snaght, into which the midwinter sun sets.[60] Interestingly the stones on either side of the line to this spectacle at Stenness have their tops sloping in opposite directions; the stone to the left has its slope the same way as the sinking sun, and the stone to the right slopes upwards as the rising sun will the next day. Because only three stones survive to their original full height this might be serendipitous. Nevertheless, it is suggestive of how the savage mind might develop relationships between the world they observed and the monumental things they made.

Although we saw relationships established between built structure and the sun in early cairns, it was much less decisive than here. In his *Patterns in Comparative Religion*, Eliade sums up the chapter headed 'The Sun and Sunworship' by stressing that 'it is worth underlining the close connection between solar theology and the elite – whether of kings, initiates, heroes or philosophers. Unlike other nature hierophanies, sun hierophanies tend to become the privilege of a closed circle, of a minority of the elect'.[61] While it is tempting to see Eliade's conclusion lending support to Renfrew's hypothesis of an emerging hierarchical society in Neolithic Orkney, we should take heed of his phrase 'solar theology', for it well describes the later and historically

87 *Midwinter sun setting into the Hills of Hoy*

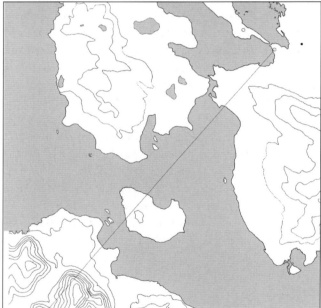

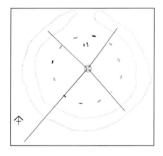

88 *Map indicating the relationship between the Stones of Stenness and the two distinctive Hills of Hoy, the Ward Hill and Cuilags*

accessible religions that form his source material. He warns his reader that, because the sun and solar symbolism have 'become one of the commonplaces of what is in a vague sense religious experience', consequently 'the sacred meaning expressed in the sun is not always clear to the modern Western mind'. Eliade's investigations enable us to see what the sun meant to earlier societies so very different from ourselves who have come to see 'only what remains after a long process of rationalisation has worn it away'.[62] Sticking close to the particular conjunction of lines and circles we find at Stenness, Maes Howe, and the dominant cairn-like feature of the landscape, provides us with a constraining framework by which to review some of his examples.

Eliade sets the scene for his discussion of the sun with a chapter on *The Sky and Sky Gods*. 'There is an almost universal belief in a celestial divine being who created the universe and guarantees the fecundity of the earth (by pouring rain down upon it)'. Often there is more than one divine being but always these emerge from the background of the sky as such, which has its own religious significance. 'The sky shows itself as it really is: infinite; transcendent'. 'Most High', 'power and changelessness' and 'infinite, immovable' are attributes found again and again applied to divine beings that are drawn from contemplation of the sky. 'The transcendence of God as directly revealed in the inaccessibility, infinity, eternity and creative power (rain) of the sky. The whole nature of the sky is an inexhaustible hierophany'.[63]

From out of this generalised observation of the heavens by early mankind, continues Eliade, 'the divinities of the sky showed themselves, or took the place of the holiness of the sky as such'.[64] His list is enormous: Anu, Shamash, Sin, Helios, Hekate, Zeus, Jupiter, Odin Thor, Woden, Donar and Taranis to name only those familiar from European mythology. These gods often personify natural forces associated with the sky such as thunder, lightning, dawn or storms. But 'in many cases the sun god replaced the sky god', concludes Eliade. 'The sun then became the giver of fecundity and protector of life.'[65]

The transcendence of the sky in many cases is expressed largely in terms of weather or natural phenomena, and its 'power' is often 'an unlimited reservoir of seeds', the meaning ascribed to rain as it fertilises the 'Great Goddess' or 'Great Mother'. A similar relationship exists in Greek mythology where 'the beginnings of things' are described in the form of Ouranos and Gaia, the earth goddess, from whose coupling descended the pantheon of gods. In many places in Ancient Greece, including 'the Acropolis of Athens…there was a Place of Coming…left open to the sky, … left in communion, as it were, with the source of their *mana*'.[66] The presence of a Father Sky and Mother Earth is extremely widespread. Here we will concentrate on the associations that the sun has with death, for this keeps us close to a connection known to exist at the Maes Howe-Stenness complex.

Strictly speaking, Eliade reminds us, the sun is not associated with death as such but rather its night journey is understood 'as a descent into the lower regions, into the kingdom of the dead'. In several Oceanic cultures, for example, the sun sets through the western 'gate of the sun' where it guides the souls of the dead. In this way the sun 'becomes the prototype of the 'dead man rising again every morning'.[67] It is interesting to find that in Greece 'the entry in Hades is frequently called "the gate of the sun"'. Through this gate went not only Hermes, the 'stony', shaman-like messenger of Zeus, and Orpheus (who also has distinctly shaman-like attributes), but also Helios, the Greek father sun-god. Earlier we saw the phrase 'Helios is King' sometimes used to describe noon; in fact Kerényi (from where the reference comes) adds 'only sometimes,' for 'the phrase is commonly used to describe the sunset'. Kerenyi explains that the setting sun was taken by the Greeks 'to mean simply that Helios had another dominion, either on the other side of the earth over the men [whether living or dead] who dwelt there; or in the depths of the sacred darkness of Night'. [68] Eliade takes the myth of Helios to illustrate that 'the sun, which, looked at superficially from the point of view of reason alone might be thought to be supremely an "intelligible" hierophany of the sky and of light, was being worshipped as a source of the "dark" energies'. He continues to say that this was not only 'with both the earth and the underworld' but also his 'organic connection with the plant world'.[69]

Something like this last point may have been crucial in the evolution of symbolic structures such as the Stones of Stenness for, as Eliade says, 'throughout the north the gradual shortening of the days as the winter solstice approaches inspires fear that the sun may die away completely'.[70] The first farmers would probably have had greater awareness than hunter-gatherers of the necessity of the sun's summer warmth (associated with its longer summer path across the sky) to generate vegetable life. Consequently their grasp of its annual cycle would have taken on greater significance. In this context it is easy to imagine how the reciprocity between cycle, circle and sun would have been noted. In reflecting upon these reciprocal relationships we can see how the generalised background of the sky could become the very specific stone circle. 'Awe of the heavens and gratitude that its cycles order and sustain life give the circle special symbolic status'.[71] As the most frequently perceived, as well as the most perfect, appearance of the circle in nature, it is not difficult to see why the sun would form the basis of such a place as Stenness.

If the sun had emerged from the passive background of the sky as a particularly active agent or god, then it was perhaps at sunset that it was most accessible, for the eye can look directly at it. Those gathered in the circle at Stenness might have taken special notice of the redness of the setting sun – which we saw embodied in Celtic myths and names such as Crochen Croderg – as a reminder of life blood even in the dead of winter. At this same moment the midwinter setting sun was sending a shaft of light into Maes Howe where the white bones of the ancestors lay. The symbolism of this had been utilised in Orkney long before the Maes Howe-Stenness complex had been built. Red ochre is often associated with Mesolithic burials and has been interpreted as representing life blood.[72] What is particularly noteworthy here is how the symbolism of the sun directed into passage graves, rekindling the spirit of the ancestors, becomes turned outwards. As the year itself dies, like a hall of mirrors the sun's rays are deflected from Maes Howe to the dolmen and from the fire at the Stones of Stenness back towards the sun again just at that moment when it descends into its own 'burial cairn'. Returned to the earth in death as were the ancestors, the sun too might be rejuvenated and continue to play its part in sustaining the cycle of life that springs, or is drawn forth, from the earth.

Eliade has described all primitive man's myth and ritual as efforts to wedge his own existence into nature's 'eternal return'. This would seem to be a particularly apt description of the building of the Stones of Stenness, the creation of a setting for just such a world view. Given the huge significance of the theme and the vast effort involved in the construction of the stone circle, it becomes clearer why it is possible to call this place an *axis mundi*. For seen from this particular place, the heavens do appear to be connected to the under-world through the long established form of the passage grave – a 'doorway' to another world. From within the form of the stone circle, time, which to the primitive mind appeared cyclical not linear and which could be worn out or run down, could be renewed each year. Many ancient cultures such as the Kogi have what they call a 'sun-turning' ceremony that helps the sun begin its ascent to summer when it has reached its midwinter nadir. Eliade describes the sun's daily death and resurrection as a prototype of the dead man's return to life. If we replace cause and effect with reciprocal relations, then perhaps we get a glimpse of what was here intended. Eliade adds that ancestor worship and sun worship 'which seem to spring from quite different lines of thought, are none the less closely linked in fact'.[73]

Circle symbolism

In her pioneering work on the persistence of archaic layers in Greek myths, Harrison describes numerous examples of ritual acts from European folklore. Many of these involved dancing. She explains that the Greek word for ritual, *dromenon*, meant 'the rite done', i.e., rituals began from enacting perceptions. Investigating how ritual transmutes to art and how *dromenon* (the thing done) becomes drama, she describes how first something has to be perceived, such as the significance of the returning sun, and then year by year it is recalled through ritual action until its personification 'is finally conceived'. This comes in a chapter of her book on *Ancient Art and Ritual* entitled 'Seasonal Rites' most of which, she says, are cast in the form of death and resurrection in relation to concerns about the food supply and its link to the seasons. 'The sun then had no ritual [until] it was seen that he led in the seasons; but long before that was known, it was seen that the seasons were annual, that they went round in a ring'.[74] From within the standpoint of savage thinking, the resonance between the circle and the cycle would make the stone circle an obvious form of monument to celebrate a belief system focused on the sun. Its form, like that of the moon, the raindrop on still water, and also the eye, is the perfect geometrical form, its perimeter making an unbroken circle as the seasons form an endlessly recurring cycle. If Harrison is right that conception succeeds perception and ritual action, then perhaps the circular form also echoes the most typical form of ritual action.

The significance of the circle can also be understood by contrasting it with the line. At Skara Brae I suggested that the axis focusing on the altar could be interpreted as recognition of human beings' fundamental orientation towards things. This device we saw extended with alignments at Barnhouse possibly utilised to demonstrate power over things and others such as was to become a stock in trade in the later history of architecture and landscape gardens. It has been said that; 'vision and locomotion apparently conspire to make linear movement more convenient for humans, and thus the intensity of feeling experienced in circular movement is heightened by its infrequency'.[75]

This special 'psychic experience' is linked with dancing in many cultures, and participation in a circular dance is associated with seasonal change the world over, maypole dancing in England being the most familiar to us. Most often such dances turn 'sunwise'. In other cultures, such as the Hindu, circling to the left is associated with death and ancestors. In our own, 'widdershins' has been considered unlucky, ill fated, or sinister.

Burl has drawn attention to a number of stone circles that have names associated with dancing; the Trippet Stones on Bodmin Moor, the Fiddlers associated with Stanton Drew, the outlying Pipers at the Hurlers stone circle, and the Haltadans, or 'limping dance', in Shetland.[76] Jacquetta Hawkes earlier observed how many stone circles are popularly known by a name that incorporates a woman and bond such as Long Meg and her Daughters, the Nine Maidens, etc. She suggests this is because everyone in the traditional culture from where these folk names emerged had a sense of the earth as a woman and that in many legends humans also turn into stone.[77]

Among the best known dances associated with such ritual activity by primitive people are those of the North American Indians. Perhaps the most vivid is that of a seasonal festival at the Powhatan village of Secota in North Carolina drawn by John White in the late sixteenth century (**89**). A group of men and women holding, or bedecked with, plants, each with a gourd on a stick looking rather like a castanet, are shown dancing in a circle around a ring of wooden posts. A contemporary description said 'they meet on a broad, open plain enclosed by tall posts carved into faces resembling those of veiled nuns'.[78]

The Sun Dance of the Sioux took place in a circular sacred lodge, at the centre of which was a 'cotton-wood tree symbolic of Wakan-Tanka, the Great Spirit, who is the centre of everything'. The dancers move 'first towards the west and back, next to the north and back, next to the east and finally to the south and back, thus beating a path in the shape of a cross'. They are, of course, also moving in a circular direction following the course of the sun. This was an annual dance 'held in June or July when the moon was full'. Black Elk, a tribal chief, noted that 'the growing and dying of the moon reminds us of our ignorance which comes and goes; but when the moon is full it is as if the eternal light of the Great Spirit were upon the whole world'.[79]

89 *American Indians dancing round a timber circle at the Powhatan village of Secota in North Carolina.* Drawn by John White *c.*1584. Copyright the New York Public Library

The conjunction of the full moon with the sun at its full summer power made this moment a particularly propitious one where the cyclical flux of life stood at its fullest ebb, the opposite of the midwinter solstice. It is perhaps not without significance that the dance moves to each cardinal point before ending at the south where the sun resides in its maximum power. The dance was to the accompaniment of drums. 'The drum,' said Black Elk, 'is especially sacred to us. Its round form represents the universe and its steady strong beat is the pulse, the heart, throbbing at the centre of the universe'.[80]

Perhaps the most poignant dance was the Ghost Dance of the Great Plains tribes introduced when the white colonists eliminated the buffalo herds upon which they depended practically and symbolically. Circling sunwise, they danced and chanted for 'an immediate regeneration of the earth, with the disappearance of the White Man, and the resurrection of both the buffalo and all the Indian dead'.[81] As their world collapsed, they turned to dance, the circle and following the sun's course as the basis of a ritual to recreate their world, to abolish historical time (which was represented by the 'progress' that was destroying them), and return to the original time and nature's eternal return. Drawing upon Bloch's anthropology, Whittle says that Neolithic monuments 'existed in and for a ritualised time'.[82]

A legend associated with dancing at the Stones of Stenness may be more pertinent to our line of investigation, but it reveals the tangled sources from which folklore arises. While it is extremely unlikely that folk tales preserve anything from prehistory, nevertheless it is worth following Burl and Hawkes a little further into this territory. As Hawkes suggests, traditional cultures that worked the land for millennia with very little change in their basic way of life held a world view that may have contained certain root similarities with that of much older farming people, a point also made earlier by Anna Ritchie. With these words of caution let us turn to an eighteenth-century account in the Revd George Low's *A Tour through the Islands of Orkney and Schetland* of a custom that took place in and around the Stones of Stenness. He describes how on '…the first day of every new year the common people, from all parts of the country, met at the Kirk of Stainhouse (Stennis), each person having provision for four or five days; they continued there for that time dancing and feasting in the kirk'.[83]

This gathering 'seldom failed in making four or five marriages every year' and the 'solemn engagements' were made by the couple in an elaborate ritual that utilised both the Stones of Stenness and the Ring of Brodgar. At Stenness, called according to Low 'The Temple of the Moon', the woman knelt and prayed to 'the god Wodden (Woden)' promising herself to the young man. The couple then went to the Ring of Brodgar, called 'The Temple of the Sun', where he reciprocated. The ceremony was completed by the couple clasping hands through the circular hole of the Odin Stone that formerly stood about 100m north of the Stones of Stenness (**90**).

The derivation of these customs from the period of the Norse occupation of Orkney is apparent from the name, Wodan. Moreover, it is relatively easy to see how the Vikings could associate this place of monumental circles adjacent a massive burial tomb with Wodan or Odin, for among his attributes was the ability to guide souls to the underworld. Also they swore oaths on rings 'reddened with the blood of sacrifice'.[84] The idea of a ring set in stone, a completely new phenomenon for the Vikings, would surely have suggested oaths and solemn contracts.

The other details of the folk tale, and the pattern of the whole, suggest the archetypal structure of myth. A striking feature of this custom is the time at which it takes place, the New Year. During the course of the three or four cold winter

90 *The Odin Stone that stood to the north-west of the Stones of Stenness.* Copyright Charles Tait

nights of this revelry, it is not difficult to imagine that sexual activity was common and that the solemn rites of betrothal sworn upon the Stones were partly the essential precautions taken after the event. A persistent feature of New Year celebrations is acts of dissolution – most strikingly to our mind, and not uncommon among primitive peoples, sexual orgies – followed by rituals that re-establish order. For the primitive, as mentioned earlier, there is a fear that time can be worn down, and rituals that celebrate New Year often symbolically enact the re-creation of time itself. Hence acts of dissolution that symbolise the primordial chaos are fundamental in such rituals, so that order can be re-established in the new year. Time begins again and everything is returned to how it was created at the beginning of time – a process not unlike that the Church adopted for All Saints' Day immediately following the pagan chaos of Hallowe'en.

Considered by some to be the first art, dance plays an important role in many such ceremonies as suggested above. 'To disclose the mysteries is as Lucian put it, "to dance out the mysteries"'.[85] It is interesting to consider a fundamental characteristic of folk dances such as Scottish dancing in this light. The band strikes up and complex patterns of movement in lines and circles are woven so that they seem to deny the original order, or any readily graspable order. A chaotic whirl of fleeting encounters ensues as partners are exchanged one after another, only for order to be re-established as the dance comes to a halt and the original couples are reunited. It would of course be unwise to infer from this any such activity in Neolithic Orkney. However, it is interesting to consider that the crofting community, with its traditional conception of time governed by seasons and cycles, came to see the Stones of Stenness as a significant part of their setting for New Year rituals. Not only this, but their celebrations included such timeless activities as dissolution of social conventions, feasting, dancing and solemn pledges made among the standing stones.

Ritchie discovered fragments of Grooved Ware in the ditch surrounding the Stones of Stenness. This type of pottery has been found at many of the larger henges throughout Britain, and its association with particular contexts rather than geographical locations has been taken as support for an emerging elite.[86] Evidence for their use as containers of alcoholic drink has been inferred from plant remains found in them. Formal drinking of alcohol has been common in Europe since antiquity. Alcohol may:

> have a ritual origin and significance. Such drinks as these are often felt to partake of divinity, and … enable those who imbibe to transcend the limits of their ordinary human condition … Such potent fluids are also regularly offered as sacrificial libations … [to] gods, demi-urges, spirits of the dead, or the natural order itself.[87]

Perhaps the pits at the centre of Stenness were not only for 'first fruits' but also for such libations.

Burl discusses the discovery of henbane – a hallucinogenic plant – in such a context and describes how two recent researchers applied a medieval witch's potion incorporating this, upon which they both fell into a long, troubled sleep where they experienced dreams of flying. In *The Birth of Tragedy*, Nietzsche writes of Dionysian mysteries known to have incorporated drinking, dancing and sexual revelry. 'In song and dance man expresses himself as a member of a higher community; he has forgotten how to walk and speak and is on the way to flying into the air, dancing. His very gestures express enchantment, he feels himself a god, he himself now walks about enchanted, in ecstasy, like the gods he saw walking in his dreams'.[88]

In the previous chapter we noted Celtic myths where the sun set, circular and blood-red, into a cairn-like mountain. Describing a Celtic cult of sun and sky veneration associated with fertility and death, Green advanced the hypothesis 'of a dualistic religion in which a celestial high god has power over, but is inextricably linked to, the earth and underworld'.[89] In the Romano-Celtic period a spoked wheel frequently represents the Celtic solar god. Our word Yule derives from the Germanic *jol*, which means 'turning wheel'. It has been remarked that 'the Germanic midwinter Yule feasts celebrated the reappearance of the sun and had a marked funereal character'.[90]

We discussed earlier Bradley's formulation of what he calls a 'circular archetype'. He suggests that this might have been a structuring concept not only throughout the Neolithic but also into the Bronze Age, where it could explain the emergence of circular houses and barrows. Perhaps this continued on to the Celtic period in the image of the wheel. A crucial point for Bradley is the first appearance of causewayed enclosures which, although at first associated with settlement, eventually moved to the margins. Here, he says, they 'symbolise the relationship between these places and the landscape that extended away on every side'.[91] Referring in particular to the Stones of Stenness, he says that the later stone circles 'epitomised a circular perception of space, ... but at the same time they may also be important symbols: representations of the landscape as a whole'.[92]

In this way stone circles brought to a conclusion the concept of a circular archetype in the Neolithic that Bradley saw particularly well-represented in decorated stones etched on the Boyne valley tombs and also occur in Orkney at Pierowall and Eday Manse. The motifs were concentric circles and spirals that form the image of a circle but were drawn from a line. Perhaps in this we see Hodder's idea of a line (between *domus* and *agrios*) developed into, or counter-pointed with, Bradley's suggestion of a 'circular archetype'. Archetype is a well-chosen word in this context, for Jung describes archetypes as emerging from the psyche as mysteriously as crystals from a liquid solution. Archetypes are innate, potential forms of the psyche, says Jung, 'universal images that have existed since the remotest of times'.[93] The archetype is not so much an external form as a propensity to arrange and order material in fundamental patterns. The most fundamental, according to Jung, is the 'mandala' which appears as a cross contained within a circle, curiously like the plan form of Maes Howe and also the pattern formed by the Sioux sun dance. Jung describes the mandala as a 'protective circle against chaotic states of mind'.[94] Given the importance of the habitual practice of weaving baskets and coiling pots, the tendency to produce circular forms must have seemed as natural as the cycle of the seasons. With this new focus on the sun, the circular archetype facilitated reciprocal relationships to be developed through the form of the stone circle, perhaps initiated by the almost universal custom of circular dance. It is interesting to note in this context that the spiral motifs in all Orkney examples are coupled together to form a connected pair of circles. Striking a chord with pairs of eyes and ears, the coupled circles perhaps refer to the pair of significant heavenly bodies, for the moon too is associated with the Stones of Stenness.

The moon

There is another enigmatic line on this landscape that weaves together the twin themes of circle and line. Just before and after its minor standstill it seems that the full moon sets into Ward Hill on Hoy, the other burial mound-like hill seen from the Stones of Stenness, after barely skimming the long slope of Mid Hill in the foreground. On the year of its minor standstill the full moon may not be visible from Stenness itself, although as it hangs in the sky beyond the nearest hills its glow would be noticeable. Throughout the 18.6-year cycle from its minor to major standstill the full moon in July never sets further north than the Cuilags, as seen from Stenness (**91**). This strange drama of the other significant celestial body acting out its curious movements over the Hills of Hoy must have added to the charisma of this place. Burl describes the complex movements of the moon well, and has interpreted a line of post-holes at Stonehenge as an attempt to record them. These may not have the precision of astronomy, he says, but are sufficient 'to show the pale moon rising over the frost'.[95] In their comparison between Madagascan custom and Stonehenge, Parker-Pearson and Ramilisonia report a saying that 'Dancing and singing should be conducted *fari-bolana* ('round like the moon')'.

Only in these northern latitudes (from 58° north) does 'the major moon between its rising and setting seem to skim the horizon', says Burl. The ancient Greek historian Diodorus Sicilus, on a journey around northern Britain, described a 'spherical temple' where 'the god (the moon) visited' every nineteen years. Investigating this, Burl considers that the 'temple' described must have been Callanish where the rising moon at its major stand-still does appear in close proximity to the circle, a phenomenon that Thom chanced upon when sailing into Loch Roag.[96] Something similar would have

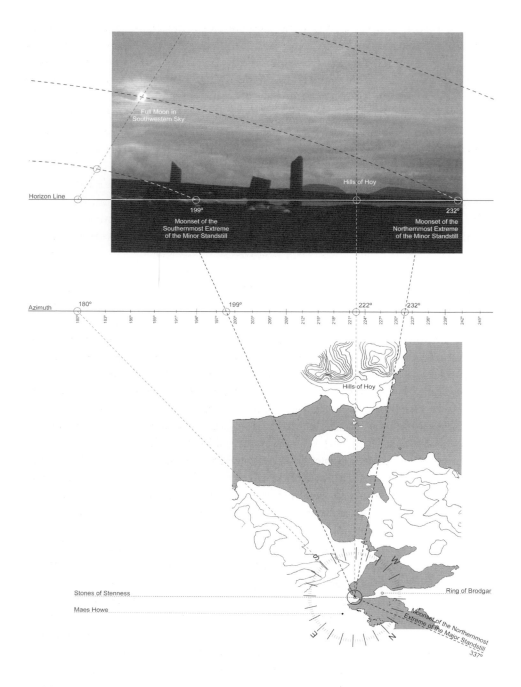

Full Moon in
Southwestern Sky

Hills of Hoy

Horizon Line

199°

232°

Moonset of the
Southernmost Extreme
of the Minor Standstill

Moonset of the
Northernmost Extreme
of the Minor Standstill

Azimuth

180°   199°   222°   232°

Hills of Hoy

Stones of Stenness

Ring of Brodgar

Maes Howe

Moonset of the Northernmost
Extreme of the Major Standstill
337°

91 *The full moon over the Stones of Stenness. The map indicates the range of the summer moonset along the horizon as seen from the Stones of Stenness. Using the Starry Night Backyard computer program, a typical cycle of the moon was plotted centred on the year 3000 BC and extended 20 years either side to cover its 18.6 year journey from major to minor standstill. The line at the bottom is azimuth 199° from the Stones of Stenness, the moon's minor standstill in 3019 BC.* Montage made by Harry Paticas been seen from Stenness. Diodorus' description reminds us that these circles were more temples and tributes than astronomical tools. Almost certainly it would have been known from other inhabitants at other vantage points on the islands that the moon at its minor standstill did in fact take to the sky. Perhaps this explains the location of the standing stone on Staney Hill, for from its higher position the profile of the Hills of Hoy can be clearly seen to the south (**92**). It is worth noting that the Barnhouse Stone standing before the entrance to Maes Howe has its broad face turned to this isolated standing stone visible on the hill above (**93** & **colour plate 26**).

If the sun had emerged as a particular sky god then it is likely that the moon would have also, and at about the same time. Eliade informs us that the 'oldest Indo–Aryan root connected with the heavenly bodies is the one that means "moon"'.[97] Later the Sumerians gave us the word 'planet' – which literally means 'wanderer' – for those stars noticed to be deviating from the regular procession of the night sky. So it seems quite reasonable to assume that the sun and the moon, being both the most obvious to the eye and clearly having some significance for life's rhythms on earth, would be the first to be marked out in some way. It does not really matter whether the moon was considered a mythical being, the dwelling place of a divinity or the resting place of the soul, for whatever form it took the moon itself seemed to share 'in ultimate reality'. The moon in many cultures is the measure of time; 'The moon is thus called "the measurer" in Greek (μῆν), the "radiant" in Latin (*luna, luc-na*)'.[98] In Ancient Greece there were three seasons analogous with the three phases of the moon: waxing, full and waning. Trobiand islanders had an elementary astronomical calendar based on the moon. The fact that its monthly cycle corresponded to the menstrual cycle of women (unique among the animal kingdom) and that it had a rhythmic relationship to the tides must have contributed to its power. This is particularly so in this landscape of water and burial cairn–like mountains that seemed to have some relationship to the moon at its lowest ebb.

The moon is known among many cultures as 'the first of the dead'. It is subject to the overwhelmingly apparent universal laws of becoming; it waxes, wanes and disappears. Agriculture emphasised the connection between the moon and the earth in the symbolism of the seed as a form of life that 'dies' for a period of time in order to be 'reborn'. The moon both 'lives' and yet is immortal; it 'dies', but only as a form of rest or regeneration. The moon's association with fertility rests upon this image of its endlessly recurring re-creation, the sense it gives 'of inexhaustible life'. So the moon must have had striking force for these first farmers surrounded by the presence of death. The moon dies but regenerates, says Eliade – something man tries to emulate: 'this is the destiny to which man is trying to conquer for himself in all rites, symbols and myths'.[99] Particular rituals focused on the moon serve the purpose of absorbing its powers and attributes into man's own life. There is no better way of

92 *The Staney Stone. From its elevated position overlooking the Stenness-Brodgar-Maes Howe complex a better view would be obtained of the moon setting into the Hills of Hoy. This might have been important at the time of its minor standstill when the full moon skimmed very low over the horizon*

93 *The Barnhouse Stone with its face tuned towards the Staney Stone just visible in the patch of light to the right of the telegraph pole in the centre middle distance*

concluding these observations on the moon than by quoting Eliade and spec-
ulating that some such belief provided the impetus for the construction of the
Stones of Stenness. 'Clearly, man's integration into the cosmos can only take
place if he can bring himself into harmony with the two astral rhythms,
'unifying' the sun and the moon in his living body'.[100] The question of why
the sun and the moon might have emerged as particularly significant will be
discussed shortly.

Lines on the landscape

In my fieldwork, I have detected several other lines on the landscape that
should be mentioned before offering an interpretation of the deeper meaning
of the line in this context. One line connects the Barnhouse Stone, which
stands before Maes Howe, with two standing stones on the bank of Loch
Harray across the causeway from the Watch Stone (**95** & **colour plate 27**). It
is not at all clear what role this line might have played, but it does point in the
general direction of the Ring of Brodgar at which the other two lines
converge. At the time of completing this study, a geophysical survey undertaken for the Orkney Archaeological Trust has indicated that there are
extensive settlement remains in the vicinity of this pair of stones. Another of
these lines, if projected from the Barnhouse Stone to the Watch Stone, passes
through the centre of the Ring of Brodgar. A third line runs from Maes Howe,
through the Comet Stone and on to the centre of the Ring of Brodgar (**94**).
These two lines combine as if to triangulate the Ring's position by reference
to the ancestors and whatever forces were thought to be embodied in the
standing stones. An early antiquarian account describes a broken standing stone
at Applehouse Farm. This standing stone was sited such as to make an
alignment with the Staney Stone and the Ring of Brodgar. In addition a line
running from the Stones of Stenness to the Staney Stone crosses the porch with
the hearth at the entrance to Barnhouse Structure 8. We will return to
consider further what meaning the line might embrace or from where its use
was derived, but first let us look briefly at the Ring of Brodgar, where several
of these lines converge.

Much less is known of the Ring of Brodgar than of the Stones of Stenness,
for modern investigation has been limited to an accurate survey by Thom and
three trenches cut through its encircling ditch by Renfrew. The Ring of
Brodgar is much larger than the Stones of Stenness at 103m across, with around
half of the original 60 standing stones in the circle remaining (**96**). It is
'surrounded by a deep rock-cut ditch, cut into tough, laminated bedrock'.[101]
When first dug, the ditch was probably 10m wide and 3.4m deep and may have
been the source of the standing stones. Renfrew points to the immense
quantity of material that would have been thrown up from the ditch and

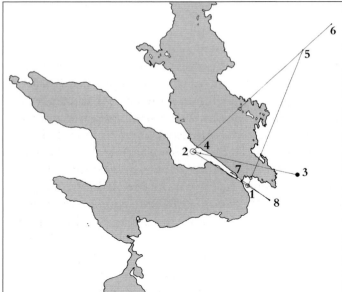

94 *The Comet Stone with the Ring of Brodgar on the crest of the hill beyond. A line from Maes Howe to the Comet Stone when projected passes through the centre of the stone circle*

95 *Map with lines linking isolated standing stones; 1 The Stones of Stenness; 2 the Ring of Brodgar; 3 The Comet Stone; 4 Staney Stone; 5 Applehouse Farm; 6 the pair of Standing Stones on the Brodgar peninsular; 8 the Barnhouse Stone*

suggests that we should imagine an encircling bank 'at least 3m high'. Although no vestige of a bank is visible today and the excavation revealed no more than a 40cm cover of topsoil in any one of the three trenches, Renfrew cites a nineteenth-century description that suggests recent farming had dispersed the material forming the bank. It proved impossible to find material to radiocarbon date the Ring of Brodgar, leaving Renfrew to postulate that it was probably built at approximately the same time as the Stones of Stenness.

96 *The Ring of Brodgar. The Stones of Stenness can be seen between the second and third stones from the left*

The alignment to Unstan, Maes Howe and other standing stones associated with it, suggests that the Stones of Stenness may have been erected first. Burl tends to this view, his own argument based partly on size and partly on the large number of adjacent circular cairns, which he presumes date from the Bronze Age. The evolution of stone circles seems to be associated with increasing densities of population, so Burl considers the Ring of Brodgar to have been built to hold the increased number of people associated with the labour required to build the monuments. He calculates that the Ring of Brodgar was 'capable of housing 1,600 people', approximately ten times more than the Stones of Stenness There are two causeways across the ditch that are not quite opposite one another and whose azimuths are 127° and 307°. These have no precise astronomical significance but the entrance facing south–east may, Burl says, 'have been directed towards the minor moon, ... the minor moonrise over Mid Hill three quarters of a mile away'.[102] Perhaps the moon demanded its own ceremonial site, or perhaps this site was chosen because its elevated position gives a better view of the sun and moon setting into the Hills of Hoy at the same time as offering a panorama over the Maes Howe Stenness complex (**colour plates 32 & 33**).

Thom has described the Ring of Brodgar as the best lunar observatory in Britain; it is extraordinary, he says, in presenting four lunar foresights.[103] The setting moon at its minor standstill, Thom calculates, would slip behind the cliffs of Helia on Hoy. Reviewing the evidence for this, Ruggles is dismissive of the sweeping nature of Thom's claim, for the three other foresights are insignificant, with two – at the Kame of Corrigall and Ravie Hill – almost impossible to see without a theodolite. Moreover, the phenomena Thom depicts at the Cliffs of Helia would have happened 'around 1700 BC, or possibly around 1500 BC' – dates much too late for setting out the Ring of Brodgar. From his precise surveys of a huge number of megalithic remains Thom found what he called a megalithic yard present in nearly all British stone circles. From this he inferred itinerant astronomer priests, a specialist ruling elite that is now considered to be more a reflection of Thom's commitment to mathematics and astronomy than a true feature of the Neolithic. From evidence of prehistoric measuring rods found in Danish Bronze Age tombs, Burl concludes that yardsticks were almost certainly used in the Neolithic and were probably calibrated with units based on the human body, not unlike those of more recent times, such as the foot. Even from within the field of archaeo-astronomy, Ruggles concedes that the notion of 'alignments', for example, 'may not be meaningful outside the western cultural context. A sacred mountain or astronomical event might have been conceived to be "in the same direction" as an architectural feature, and hence symbolically associated with it, even if in our view they are orientated many degrees apart'.[104]

We have discussed Hodder's development of the concept of *domus* in a polarity with *agrios*. The *domus*, he says, obtained 'its dramatic force from the exclusion, control and domination of the wild'.[105] The polarity *domus-agrios* found its most clear expression in the LBK long house, but was a more general concept symbolising cultural control over nature. Hodder argues that it could be extended to explain other aspects of the Neolithic as it unfolded:

> A linear ordering of space is created in which the movement along graded space to the heart of the *domus* defines society and its boundaries. The *domus* is that which has been controlled and dominated in the domestication process but which has also been brought in.[106]

Hodder goes on to say that, as social groups enlarged, the focus on the individual household frustrated its symbolic formation with the consequence that the *domus* concept became transferred to the tomb. Paradoxically, the increasing population forced people to settle in marginal land, hence the wild (the *agrios*), became more significant in the culturalisation process. As the *domus* concept became extended to incorporate ever more of the wild – upland resources, secondary animal products, wild animals and death – so the *agrios* became more central.[107] As these expanding communities dispersed, the long house disappeared. Yet by the time the first farmers had reached southern Britain, the *domus* concept had been transmuted into the long barrow, a long house for the dead. By a reciprocal relationship, dispersed settlements involved a more active utilisation of the *agrios*, and the consequent sublimation of the *domus* concept in the tomb allowed dispersed settlements to cohere as a single social body. Summing up, Hodder says that tombs 'provide the channel for transforming the *domus* into the *agrios*'. This process reflects the increasing importance of the *agrios*, whether as wild nature or death itself. He suggests that this concept and its evolution might explain the increasing monumentality and linear organisation of the landscape, as in long barrows where the ratio of tomb cover to tomb chamber increases enormously. He goes on to wonder whether the working out of *the domus-agrios* concept might explain the emergence of the cursus and other enigmatic lines of Neolithic Britain. 'Through time, therefore, the *domus* extended beyond the individual tombs to act as the focus for large tracts of landscape'.[108] Extending the line outwards led eventually to the *agrios* or wild being brought to the centre. Perhaps this explains what we see in late Neolithic Orkney. The wild, which can mean both untamed nature and the unrestrained, the wayward, the unpredictable, becomes controlled by a web of lines woven across the landscape. In this instance these lines have their source in lines to the sun and moon, the guarantors of nature's more predictable rhythms. Such a process, continues Hodder, could explain the emphasis on bounding space and controlling access to that space. Yet, as has been argued here, this was not the 'brutal' control over nature that Russell, for example, ascribes. It seems more likely that, if the *agrios* was being brought into the cultural realm in some new way, then the combination of gigantic standing stones, the circle, and the ditch cutting off the surrounding landscape from its potentially dangerous focal point, would make for an appropriate new form of monument. The line and the circle combining in a new, expansive form bring human life into some reciprocal relationship with what Eliade describes as 'the two astral rhythms'. As Bradley has said of later Scottish recumbent stone circles; 'the monuments connected the earth to the sky as they linked the living to the dead'.[109]

Objections have been raised against the far-reaching nature of Hodder's linear, *domus-agrios* concept. He argues, however, that the similarity between megalithic cultures along the Atlantic façade comes not simply from diffusion but 'from a common cultural background', i.e. one orchestrated by something like the *domus-agrios* concept. This chimes not only with Thomas' *Rethinking the Neolithic* but also with Renfrew's notion of the later 'cumulative Celticity'. Such an underlying principle or archetype might have been re-deployed by dispersed cultural groups in a range of ways as they encountered new conditions and circumstances and as the memory of the originating culture faded. Thomas remarks that the 'simultaneous emergence of "linear" monuments and an enhanced interest in celestial phenomena is worthy of note'.[110] Perhaps this concept became reactivated as dispersed settlement in Orkney reached the land's full capacity, coinciding with village-type settlements and the emergence of leadership able to mobilise sufficient labour to erect these monuments. Interestingly, the extensive use of the line as an organising principle at the Maes Howe-Stenness-Brodgar complex might relate to the expressive use of the axis focused on the dresser at Skara Brae, just as the cruciform plan form of Maes Howe seems to be a response to the earlier houses of that settlement.

Although we can never know the activity that took place in and around the stone circles it is nevertheless clear that, with their construction, we see not only a monumentalising of the sites of ritual but also an increased complexity to the ritual activity itself. The Stones of Stenness were linked to Maes Howe and to the setting sun at the turn of the year, the bones and spirits of the ancestors joined in some way to the eternal turning of the seasons. Within the ring of stone a number of seemingly significant activities were carried out. Beyond the circle were a number of enigmatic standing stones and beyond these were the Ring of Brodgar (linked possibly to the moon and certainly to Maes Howe) and Maes Howe itself, connected to the dominant house at Barnhouse by a similarity of plan and construction. Taken altogether, the social hierarchy detected at Barnhouse seems to have been projected onto the landscape. Furthermore, through the conjunction of built constructions and significant natural places the sacred realm became manifest in a series of circles and tombs, lines and links. Orme has said that 'as chiefs became more powerful and their position more hereditary, so their ritual role increased'.[111] Do we have any way of understanding this process? The pioneering American anthropologist Paul Radin made a distinction between magic and religion. In this we find a conceptual framework that has close parallels with the fundamental shift of ritual sites from many territorially-dispersed burial cairns to this pair of enigmatically placed stone circles.

From magic to religion

Radin defines magic as 'the coercion of an object so that it will comply with the wishes and desires of the performer'.[112] Among what he calls the 'simplest societies' magic is rooted in everyday life: it is all pervasive, folklorist in kind, its use is compulsive, and what he calls 'religious leadership' tends not to be found. Religion emerges from a number of possible causes – societies becoming more complex, trade leading to change, the desire to fix the dynamic flux of the world – and it is shaped by what Radin calls 'the religious formulator', which is his crucial notion. Radin says that despite there being no traces of religious leadership in the 'simplest societies' nevertheless 'the shamans or medicine men' will 'indulge in some type of speculation concerning those problems that loom so large in religion proper, and that some attempt will be made to co-ordinate and evaluate the multifarious and inchoate folklorist background'.[113] From this background, things of value to the people are shown to be in danger by the emerging religious formulator, whose task is to free magical activity from its former compulsive character. 'This task takes on two general forms' says Radin, 'its socialisation, and ... a transference of the coercive power from the subject to the object. In both cases there is a definite development away from extreme types of subjectivism to some form of objectivism'. The first indications of objective thinking are found in relation to disease and death, he continues, for these 'could not very well be attributed to any intrinsic desire of the ego for the self-infliction of pain or for self-destruction and had to be charged to some outside agency'.[114] He argues that it is the personality of the religious formulator – shaman, diviner, medicine man or priest – and 'his life, his symbolic death and rebirth and his hallucinatory experiences that form the concrete mould into which the supernatural has been thrown'.[115] Through reflection upon this process and its objectivisation or externalising, ghosts become transformed to spirits, and 'with the aid of certain social and economic forces, transform spirits into deities'.

Although this presentation of Radin's suggestion of religion succeeding magic has overtones of the now discredited evolutionist views of the first generation of 'armchair' anthropologists (particularly Tylor and Frazer), in fact his understanding is much more subtle. Written in 1937, *Primitive Religion* formed part of a wave of revision by anthropologists who based their writing on their own fieldwork. Such writers include Malinowski, Radcliffe-Brown and Evans-Pritchard, whose seminal work *Witchcraft, Oracles and Magic among the Azarde*, published the same year, is referred to by Radin.[116] Radin's own fieldwork was among the Winnebago Indians of North America. All of this group of writers continue to make a distinction between magic and religion although, unlike their predecessors, they do not see the latter as simply replacing the former, which then continues as something archaic and essentially 'dead'. In contrast they stress the interpenetration of these two modes of thought, the one being informed by the other while being subject to differing and particular forms of practice.

As all his generation, Radin was influenced by the sociological interpretations of ethnographic material put forward by writers such as Durkheim, Mauss, and Levy-Bruhl. From this perspective religion is seen as always embracing a collective practice, whereas magic is often performed simply by one individual for another. It is out of this framework that the idea of the 'sacred' as a separate realm emerges, for religion is seen as a ritual whose function is 'to fortify the faith of the group', an attribute lacking in magic.[117] Religion comes to refer to the fundamental issues of human existence and sets out a coherent view of this, whereas magic, while having its own 'system of thought', always turns around specific and concrete problems or desires. Religion comes to have 'a belief in spiritual Beings'.[118]

Radin argues that 'true deities or gods' can only emerge where economic development is such as to allow specialised reflection upon the spirit world. Such conditions of surplus labour are evident in the Maes Howe – Stenness – Brodgar complex as we have seen. Malinowski's view that 'magic is dominant when control of the environment is weak' might also support the contention of a shift to a 'higher' form of belief as manifest in this complex of monuments that demonstrate greater control over the environment. The vastly expanded effort in making the stone circles, the novel form of the monument and the evident complexity of ritual activity all combine to suggest an elevated significance of belief system akin to Radin's shift from magic to religion. Radin links a shift in spiritual practice to a change in economic and social conditions.

> True deities and gods do not develop where the totemic structure still functions significantly; ... they do not, in other words, develop where there is no social–economic basis for them.[119]

In this context it is interesting to remember how the position of a possible totem pole or maypole at the centre of the Stones of Stenness implied that certain features, such as the construction of a hearth, grew up around it. Perhaps the whole circle complex can be seen as the working out from totem pole to hearth to circular enclosure of a new form of ritual site to act as an appropriate setting for new religious practice.

What Radin calls 'true gods' occur 'only where supernatural spirits are fashioned into idols, are honed in special and sacred structures, and have true theogonic myths associated with them'.[120] While one of these three criteria is absent and another cannot be known, it is nevertheless reasonable to think of the great stone circles as 'special and sacred structures'. Radin provides anthropological evidence for rituals 'to attract the tribal deity to his temple and his prophet', which was the principal task of the religious formulator who was then in a position to communicate the needs of his people. Although Renfrew considers that a change in social structure can be inferred from the evidence of Maes Howe, Stenness and Brodgar, he remains sceptical of any distinctive form of primitive thinking, as mentioned in the introduction. Nevertheless, several of the factors he considers necessary to provide evidence for religion are present at the Stones of Stenness. For religion or religious activity to be detectable in prehistory, says Renfrew, 'a liminal zone' needs to be inferable, incorporating 'offerings of food or drink or goods', 'attention-focusing devices' such as altars or hearths, significant natural features such as mountain tops, a special building and 'repeated actions of a symbolic nature which are directed ... toward non-terrestrial and therefore transcendental forces'.[121]

Quite independently of Radin and coming from the very different discipline of philosophy, Cassirer also describes the shift from magic to religion. Cassirer's identification of a distinctive form of mythical thinking is discussed in the next chapter along with Renfrew's objections. In essence he postulates that behind any developed form of thought must lie an earlier form. As we will see, he sets out to describe what he calls mythical thought by back-tracking logically from more recent, rational forms of thought. Of particular interest in this context is his section headed the 'discovery and determination of the subjective in the mythical consciousness'. After citing evidence for the fact that primitive people do not have the sense of individuality that we moderns do, he goes on to say that, logically, the subjective cannot be discovered if 'the I and the soul were the beginning of all mythical thinking'.[122] There is no fixed 'I' nor objective reality; these are terms that have to be established. Cassirer goes on to say that the 'I' emerges not from meditation but from action. By this he means that mythical ideas adhere firstly to the efficacy of things, a view attested by the fact that the 'I' seeks to bend all things to its purpose by way of magic. He says this suggests that the 'I' has yet to be secured, because it is 'totally dominated, totally "possessed" by things'. At this early stage of primitive thinking there is no concept of the soul separate from the body in the individual; the soul is 'life itself, which is immanent in the body'. Thus any part of the body might be a vehicle for the life force that runs through the world of things and phenomena, which accords with the possibility that the bones of ancestors might have been used for magical/ritual purposes because the life force could reside in them. Similarly there is no hard and fast distinction between life and death; 'the deceased still "is"', says Cassirer, even if only seen as a shadow. Eventually people 'progress from the mythical to the ethical self' where ideas of judgement and guilt begin to weigh upon the individual soul. In this, Cassirer concludes, 'man rises from magic to religion, from the fear of demons to the worship of gods, and this apotheosis is not so much outward as inward'.[123]

The shift from magic to religion is a slow process and involves several aspects that Cassirer touches upon and to which we will return in the next chapter. One worth mentioning at this point in relation to the pits and pots by the hearth at the Stones of Stenness is the idea of sacrifice. Sacrifice fundamentally implies 'a renunciation which the "I" imposes on itself'.[124] In the sacrifice – gift, offering, purification for intercession, and thanks or atonement – 'religious faith attains its true visible guise'. The formation, elaboration and regulation of the formulae associated with the practice of offerings raises this kind of ritual above the level of the magical world view, for magic demands no sacrifice. Magic is 'wish fulfilment' where an individual believes he can bend the will of the gods, spirits or supernatural powers. In contrast, sacrifices imply a renunciation – privations, or ascetic measures taken – which leads to a sense of the divine being superior to man. By dealing with this in sacrifice, Cassirer says, man withdraws from 'the objects of immediate desire' so characteristic of magic. Objects instead become for him 'a kind of religious means of expression, the instrumentality of a bond which he creates between himself and the divine'.[125] A link between the sacred and the profane is made through the medium of a consecrated thing or space which restores the original common bond of ritual blood made through ancestors descended from the tribal gods. The shift from magic to religion is not only slow but the two will overlap. Just as the process demonstrably comes to a conclusion in developed monotheistic religions such as Christianity with its mass, chalice, altar and church, then logically there must be a point in time when the process begins. The new form of ritual site that is the stone circle – connecting together as it does at Stenness fire, circle, stone, ancestors, earth and sun – would seem to represent exactly such a fundamental shift of world view in a rudimentary first formulation. At the most general level, Burl considers stone circles to represent a change in belief system to one focused on the sun and the moon. The more detailed anthropological analysis of Parker-Pearson and Ramilisonia led them to conclude that there was not 'ancestor worship as such' in the late Neolithic. Rather there was a 'community of ancestors in an incorporeal world ... parallel to the corporeal world inhabited by the living'. From this standpoint they see two intersecting axes: the living to the ancestors; and the people (both living and dead) to the 'object of worship'. We have seen how lines of sight and alignments were made between Maes Howe and the Stones of Stenness that conform to this conceptual framework. Stone circles perhaps emerged from the perception of the roundness of the sun, the moon, the raindrop and the eye, say Parker-Pearson and Ramilisonia, from which 'the architectural concern with precise circularity suggests that this transcendental entity was manifested in the heavenly bodies of the sun and the moon'.[126]

There will always be a mystery attached to stone circles, but with the cautionary words of Jacquetta Hawkes – 'every age gets the Stonehenge it desires' – ringing in our ears, let us conclude this discussion of stone circles. At the Stones of Stenness we see the earlier 'magical' practice focused on the burial cairn transferred to the stone circle and in some way transformed. At the stone circle we see the significant celestial objects of the sun and the moon drawn into its orbit through the medium of burial mound-like hills in the landscape. Perhaps here then we can tentatively say that some kind of religious practice had emerged from the background of magic. Radin went on to say that the obsessive subjectivism of the religious formulator leads ultimately to its 'opposite pole, the conception of a Supreme Deity'.[127] These lines on the landscape drawing circles from the sky and casting them in stone (the sun, blood red and accessible to the eye, and the moon, the first of the dead and white as bone) suggest that here we may have concrete evidence for the emerging appearance of supreme deities in the heavens.

5

MYTHICAL THINKING

Henry Poincare queried with some irony whether 'a naturalist who had studied elephants only under a microscope would think he knew enough about these animals?' The microscope shows the structure and mechanisms of the cells, a structure and mechanism which are the same in all multicellular organisms. But is that all there is to know? At the microscopic level one cannot be certain. At the level of human eyesight, which does at least recognise the elephant as a phenomenon of zoology, all uncertainty departs.[1]

This book began with a quotation describing the Neolithic settlers travelling through Europe and Britain to arrive in Orkney having 'colonised visible horizons'. Without doubt there were pressingly practical reasons for this, but the hypothesis upon which this study is based is that such a mode of moving through the world, circumscribed by the visible horizon, had its counterpart in the settlers' mental activity. They navigated their world of thought by constructing a mental map from a complex network of visual relationships, resemblance, differences, metaphors and other associations.

The introduction outlined the premiss that prehistoric people held a world view markedly different from our own and that if we want to understand their material culture we must make some attempt to grasp the way they thought about their world. Action and practice in a web-like cosmos would have been guided by presumptions very different from those that operate in our universe. In this final chapter I would like to examine this proposition more closely including a consideration of Renfrew's objections to any basic difference between Neolithic thinking and our own. This involves further consideration of Eliade and Levi-Strauss, but in particular a detailed account of Cassirer's conception of mythical thinking. If Thomas' *Rethinking the Neolithic* has led to a position where we might usefully see the Neolithic as a way of thinking rather than purely as an economic model, then this investigation might help clarify the nature of such a world view. Cassirer is particularly important to such an enterprise because he was a philosopher who discovered the concept of mythical thinking during the course of his search for a philosophy of mind. From the vantage point gained by a consideration of this, I will conclude by briefly revisiting the Orkney remains to compare them one with another, and to see whether there are patterns of relationships or transformation that correspond to mythical thinking.

The quotation from Eliade above contrasts the scientific world view – which seeks the causal laws of things in their invisible structure – with the common-sensical understanding based on the eye's ability to make relative judgements. That is, the eye not separated from phenomena by an instrument but immersed in the body from which eye and mind ascribe measure, weight, tactility, etc. Eliade is, of course, making a tacit critique of the scientific world view by phenomenology. Anyone who has been persuaded by the phenomenological description of our being-in-the-world will recognise certain similarities between it and savage thought.

Eliade's quotation comes from his *Patterns in Comparative Religion*. As the title suggests, Eliade identifies common motifs or themes from a wide-ranging survey of the world's religions and myths from which he deduces patterns or a common structure. In this sense his study is empirical although not in a narrowly scientific way. He acknowledges its value in accumulating and organising facts but considers that empirical thinking cannot in itself explain the meaning myths had for their creators and users. It is here that he departs from Renfrew. Reflecting upon his lifetime's work on the world's religions, Eliade makes the point that 'the proper procedure for grasping their meaning is not the naturalist's "objectivity" but the intelligent sympathy of the hermeneut. It was the procedure itself that had to be changed'.[2] He is quite clear about his approach where two systems of thought are at work in his studies and about how the critical faculties of the modern scholar must be distinguished from, yet intertwine with, the primitive mind under study.

In their book *The Ancient Mind*, Renfrew and Zubrow discuss the question of how prehistoric people thought. They review challenges made to the processual approach by post-structuralists and others but remain unconvinced by their methods or claims. They are suspicious of the conceptual leaps that tend to be made by those writers using what they call 'an interpretationist, anti-scientific, literary approach' or a 'hermeneutic, semiotic approach'.[3] Renfrew instead makes the case for what he terms 'cognitive archaeology' or 'cognitive-processual archaeology'. This would be a relatively pragmatic approach continuing to use 'the methods of scientific enquiry'. He outlines the inherent danger of approaches where interpretative leaps tend to overlook the precepts of scientific enquiry, as formulated by Popper, where validation has to rest upon testability and explicit argumentation. '[It] is not the source of the insight which validates the claim, but the explicit nature of the reasoning which sustains it and the means by which the available data can be brought into relationship with it'.[4]

From this Popperian position Renfrew is wary of assuming that prehistoric man's thinking was different from our own. The term 'ancient mind' he uses simply as shorthand for cognitive archaeology; 'it is not meant to imply that there is necessarily something inherently different between the thought processes of yesterday and those of today. No distinction is implied between the ancient mind and the modern mind'.[5]

For Eliade, in contrast, there seem to be at least two essential characteristics that distinguish what he calls 'archaic mentality' from the modern mind. In the preface to *The Myth of the Eternal Return* he discusses one of these by way of comparing titles given to earlier editions of the book. In manuscript form originally called *Cosmos and History*, the book contrasts the attitudes of ancient and modern societies towards events in time. He characterises 'archaic man' as always operating within what he calls the horizon of *Archetypes and Repetition*, the title under which the book was first printed. Out of this grew Eliade's articulation of archaic man's desire to abolish historical time, which he did through rituals that connected his life and culture with nature's cyclical time, something we touched upon when discussing the Stones of Stenness. Myth is very different from history, and the mind shaped by one will operate very differently from the other.

> The chief difference between the man of the archaic and traditional societies and the man of the modern societies with their strong imprint of Judaeo-Christianity lies in the fact that the former feels himself indissolubly connected with the Cosmos and the cosmic rhythms, whereas the latter insists that he is connected only with History.[6]

Eliade goes on to describe how the cosmos might well have its own 'history' for those inhabitants who lived within it, but that this was a 'sacred history', one which could be repeated indefinitely and returned to in ceremonies that reactivated the originating events at the beginning of time. This is what he means by the horizon of archetypes and repetition. He explains that 'myths preserve and transmit the paradigms, exemplary models for all the responsible activities in which men engage. By virtue of these paradigmatic models revealed to men in mythical times, the Cosmos and society are periodically regenerated'.[7]

The second significant characteristic that Eliade sees as distinguishing archaic mentality from its modern successor is in how matter is understood. Shaped by the assumptions of physics, matter for the modern mind is fundamentally dead or inert. It can have no consciousness, purpose or intentions of its own. For archaic man, in contrast, material partakes of a force or forces that pervade the cosmos. Eliade sums up a chapter entitled 'Earth, Woman and Fertility' (from where we drew our comments on midden at Rinyo) in these words: 'the cosmos-repository of sacred forces'.[8] In some places, at some time, and in some materials, this force seemed to manifest itself more strongly, and in this way the fundamental duality of the sacred and the profane emerges as significant for the archaic mentality. We pursued the implications of the idea of a hierophany (where the sacred manifests itself) in the example of stone, which might be both a material object but also a conduit of a force. This provided insights into why Neolithic people might have built stone burial tombs. According to Eliade, the force or forces which ran through material and were a manifestation of a living presence could reside in the substance or the form of things. Hence the significance of certain forms (such as the circle) for archaic man and the constant recourse to ritual, which can be thought of as organising formal patterns out of actions directed towards these supernatural forces. As Eliade says:

> every territory occupied for the purpose of being inhabited ... is first of all transformed from chaos into cosmos; that is, through the effect of ritual it is given a 'form' [that] makes it become real. Evidently, for the archaic mentality, reality manifests itself as a force, effectiveness, and duration.[9]

This question of 'force' in things will be examined shortly from a philosophical point of view rather than from these anthropological parallels. Yet how does Eliade's assertion of the peculiar nature of archaic mentality stand up to Renfrew's scepticism? An important aspect of Renfrew's argument is predicated on a distinction he makes between 'idealist' thinkers and 'materialists'.[10] Within this framework he discusses two particularly important aspects of the ancient mind, meaning and symbolism, in such terms that are open to challenge from the position occupied by Eliade. Renfrew sees the search for meaning as a chimera pursued by the idealists. He considers this approach invalid because their 'primary business is the understanding of "meaning" located within the minds of specifically identifiable historical personages, and for whom historical explanations are to be found in the intentions of individual (or even sometimes collective) actors'.[11] As we have seen, however, for Eliade meaning is not construed in such a way. The archaic mentality sees homologies between things, between man's life and that of the cosmos. Hence meaning is present in things, or perhaps more accurately, in the nexus of relationships between human life, perception, experience and things. We saw this particularly strongly in the relationship between stone and bone, where the hardness of stone and the way it erupts from the earth's surface could be seen as a manifestation of an eternal force that stands outside of the passage of time. Stone was not simply perceived as inert matter but as pervaded by particular forces of the cosmos. Precisely because archaic man believed that 'the cosmos lives' and had been 'created by the gods', then the world, the whole living cosmos 'means something'.[12] Consequently for Eliade the question of meaning becomes a principal concern – indeed something inescapable – if we are to grasp how the archaic or ancient mind worked. His identification of how the primitive saw meaning in material allows us, in drawing upon his work, to avoid the otherwise insuperable problem posed by Renfrew of needing to gain access to the minds of prehistoric individuals or collectives.

Renfrew contrasts the search for meaning with the cognitive-processual approach which aims to 'examine the ways in which symbols were used', a procedure he contrasts with seeking meaning. His approach is rather different from Eliade's, who concludes his *Patterns in Comparative Religion* with an investigation into what he calls 'the structure of symbols'. Renfrew sees symbols operating as fundamentally one thing standing for another – coins for exchange, insignia for rank, etc. – a basically horizontal transferable process. Consequently he tends to see the signifier's relation to that which is signified as conventional, i.e. in the case of coins, in spite of acknowledging the almost universal early use of precious metals, he concludes that 'the very notion of "intrinsic value" for a precious metal is conventional'.[13] Eliade would not accept this. He devoted a whole book, *The Forge and the Crucible*, to myths that accrued to metals and metal-working precisely because of the way people perceived the significance of delving deep into the earth, combined with the intensity of fire required for the transmutation of ore into metal. While he would share Renfrew's view of the symbol as one thing standing for another, for Eliade the symbol allows what might be called a vertical movement from one reality to another. As we saw with the beginning of burial mounds, for example, a shell might be a symbol for fertility or healing but only 'because it was "born of the waters"'.[14] That is, its being concentrates the material out of which creation sprang (also drawing into its watery nature woman and moon), and in the course of time leaves at its death a material with analogous properties to stone and bone, which are everlasting. For Eliade the crucial attributes and role of symbols is that 'symbolic thought makes it possible for man to move freely from one level of reality to another'.[15]

In his exposition of symbolism Renfrew pays insufficient attention to this aspect, and perhaps it is his one-dimensional approach to how symbols operate that leads him to underestimate the possibility of a peculiarly archaic mentality. Ingold has described how a similar difference exists in anthropology between cognitivists and phenomenologists. The cognitivist understands the body 'as a passive instrument ... delivering sensations for processing by the mind', he says, whereas for phenomenologists 'the body is active, intentional rather than instrumental'.[16] Eliade was not a didactic phenomenologist, but from his long study he came to see that ritual activity underlies all religion and myth. Renfrew, in contrast, subscribes to the idea that humans are rational animals, that is, biological material with something added. In presuming a rational and practical engagement with the world, there is clearly an inherent danger of extending our own world view backwards, a problem identified by Vico at the inception of modern historiography. However, Renfrew does recognise the importance of symbolism, citing approvingly a statement that 'all human behaviour is symbolic behaviour'. Elaborating upon this he turns to Cassirer who, he says, defines the human individual as an 'animal symbolicum' and that 'he lives, so to speak, in a new dimension of reality'.[17] Although sceptical of a peculiarly pre-modern mode of thought, in fact Renfrew doesn't entirely rule out 'mythic thought in early societies'. He does not deal explicitly with Cassirer's formulation of this concept that underlies all later related lines of enquiry, including those of Levi-Strauss whom he refers to in this way.

Whether or not this is an entirely appropriate notion of a mode of thought to contrast with our own, it cannot be excluded that concepts and modes of thought may have been employed in earlier times which may not feature prominently in the processes of thought and argumentation of modern societies. Even if we dislike the generalisation implied in the term 'savage mind', this possibility cannot be overlooked.[18]

I will return in a moment to consider Cassirer's mythical thinking in detail, but first of all it might be useful to consider Levi-Strauss' savage mind, for this has had some impact on archaeology as Renfrew's allusion indicates.

As is well known, Levi-Strauss was a structural anthropologist and, while the critique made by post-structuralism has called into question many of the broader claims made by structuralists, his method has continued to provide a framework useful to anthropology. In two or three places he uses the phrase 'mythical thought' or 'mythical thinking', which indicates his familiarity with Cassirer's work. The most significant point Levi-Strauss demonstrates is that savage thought (a more literal translation of the French original) is not fundamentally mystical or irrational, nor is it necessarily inferior to modern scientific thinking. Rather it is a different way of seeing the world and ordering things, a world view that nevertheless has its own form of logic. The primitive's way of thinking stems from what Levi-Strauss describes as 'the intimate contact between man and his environment'.[19] From this comes an extraordinarily detailed knowledge of plants and animals, which has led ethnologists to remark upon their complex taxonomies. Brody's more recent anthropological fieldwork confirms this, as we have seen. Not only did the Inuit, for example, have complex categories with no generic term to describe fish, but they also relied on their knowledge, their dreams and their drums to direct the hunt. An important point for Levi-Strauss, although a contentious one, is 'that animals and plants are not known as a result of their usefulness; they are deemed to be useful or interesting because they are first of all known'. That is, savage thought develops not so much for its practical effect as that it 'meets intellectual requirements'. He says that this 'thirst for objective knowledge is one of the most neglected aspects of the thoughts of people we call primitive'. Moreover 'it implies comparable intellectual application and methods of observation' to that of modern science. Primitive thinking he characterises as 'the science of the concrete'.[20]

The great arts of civilisation bequeathed by the primitives – pottery, weaving, agriculture, the domestication of animals – 'assume centuries of active and methodical observation', all of which, continues Levi-Strauss, implies 'a genuinely scientific attitude, [a] sustained and watchful interest and a desire for knowledge for its own sake'.[21] But this was not scientific in our terms, of course. Rather, he says that there are two distinct modes of scientific thought that operate at two strategic levels: 'one roughly adapted to that of perception and the imagination, the other at a remove from it'. They can be distinguished by the two differing ways they make connections, which are 'arrived at by two different routes, one very close to, and the other more remote from sensible intuition'. In this formulation we find ourselves returned to our point of departure – Eliade's contrast between an understanding made by way of the microscope and that of 'sensible intuition'. This also has echoes of Eliade's view that the symbolic preceded the practical, through which the archaic mentality is able to shift easily up and down between these two different ways of dealing with the world.

Levi-Strauss puts forward an interesting if unlikely example that helps illuminate what he means by savage thought. He compares it to 'bricolage' and contrasts the 'bricoleur' with the engineer. 'Bricoleur' is a term not easily translated into English (the translator discusses how it means something like 'odd-job man' or 'handyman' but without the low standing implied by these names). The 'bricoleur' is someone who can turn his hand to many and diverse tasks, making things and repairing things from materials ready to hand, although not always using them for the purpose originally intended.[22] Hence the bricoleur always remains within the world of familiar things and operations, rearranging them as necessary to make do whenever he encounters a new task. The engineer, in contrast, is able to reach beyond the constraints of his culture by means of calculation. So for Levi-Strauss the essential difference between mythical thought and modern scientific thought is that the former is a kind of 'intellectual bricolage' that always uses a limited, heterogeneous repertoire of connections for making explanations. Making a clay pot in a similar form to a basket and decorating the rim with a pattern reminiscent of basket weave would be an example of this, as would the processes of transformation we saw at work in the resemblance between basket, boat and building at Knap of Howar.

This way of working has its inception in the savage mind noticing resemblance or congruity between things, from which 'some initial order can be introduced into the world by means of these groupings'.[23] He gives an example of this kind of reasoning at work when he describes why the Ojibwa think thunder is a bird. Birds from the south appear in April and stay until October, a period that coincides with the incidence of thunder. (An example of this way of thinking lingers on in our own folklore with the proverb 'one swallow doesn't make a summer'.) From this basic building block of congruity the savage mind develops mental structures that take the form of 'a system of concepts embedded in images'[24] that are derived from the 'primitives' concrete grasp of phenomena. These cultural images – verbal in myths or visual in artefacts – 'facilitate an understanding of the world in as much as they resemble it'. Although he is concerned to show in *The Savage Mind* how the totemic systems common to primitive peoples elaborate this principle of resemblance or congruity, he does point out that they are also organised around differences. In fact, being 'able to oppose terms' is an imperative of savage thought, and such systems 'derive from their formal character'.[25] This formal system of binary opposition he saw as stemming from the 'observed contrasts in the sensory qualities of concrete objects, e.g. the difference between raw and cooked, wet and dry, male and female'.[26] This simple set of oppositions he developed into a linked set or schema:

FOOD	SOCIETY	RELIGION	SOUND
raw/cooked	culture/nature	sacred/profane	silence/noise

It is from this bedrock that Levi-Strauss developed his structural anthropology. As previously mentioned, many of the larger claims made for structuralism have been called into question, but this basic set of binary oppositions identified by Levi-Strauss has remained in currency amongst anthropologists. It is, however, not without its problems. I will return to the question of nature/culture in a moment, for this has become a recurring concern of archaeologists who see it as a modern, western concept imposed upon the past. His sacred/profane dichotomy is important for our understanding of spatial ordering, and this will be discussed when considering nature and culture. Having seen Levi-Strauss outline his concept of savage thought, let us turn finally to Cassirer, for his mythical thinking was almost certainly its inspiration.

Mythical thinking

Cassirer examined what he came to call mythical thinking in the second volume of his major work *The Philosophy of Symbolic Forms*. Although his enterprise began as an enquiry into the concept of culture, it became a vehicle for reflection on philosophy. Cassirer sees culture as having three basic symbolic forms: myth, language, and technical activity. Others such as art, history, science and mathematics were established from these, 'fanning out' rather than developing in any hierarchical way. 'Language, at first completely bound up with myth, becomes the vehicle for logical discourse and this in turn is the basis upon which science evolves'.[27] All symbolic forms, says Cassirer, 'must first be emancipated from the common matrix of myth'.[28]

Cassirer was a philosopher whose insights into mythical thinking arose from a deep study of language. The first volume of *The Philosophy of Symbolic Forms* deals with language from a purely modern and empirical perspective, pursuing the logic of language back to demonstrate how it took shape. This inevitably leads him on to the question of what would have been the characteristics or conditions of thought at an ever earlier stage of development. Cassirer was not interested in the primitive past as such, but only insofar as it had a bearing on the way he tackled the problem of the 'theory of knowledge, or the philosophy of mind'. This early form of thought is what he calls mythical thinking, which he contrasts with contemporary thought and which he variously calls 'empirical-scientific thinking', 'discursive thinking' or ' theoretical thinking'. Modern forms of thought have evolved from (and hence must have some connection to) an earlier, much less differentiated form. All forms of knowledge, argues Cassirer, have become increasingly abstract by processes of qualification and sub-division. What drove him to consider primitive language was the vicious circle that traditional logic found itself in when trying to explain how distinct categories or concept formation emerged; 'logic tells us that the concept arises "through abstraction"'. That is, 'it instructs us to form a concept by comparing similar things or precepts and abstracting their "common characteristics"'.[29] The problem with this is that logic sees concepts or categories arising from 'abstractions' but treats the characteristics of things as already given. It is in this that Cassirer sees an endless circularity, because the characteristics of things are not given so that similar things can be compared and categorised. Rather, the fact that 'the contents of comparison have specific characteristics' implies that some form of judgement has already been made. He summarises this in a short study *Language and Myth*: 'our problem is not the choice of properties already given but the positing of the properties themselves'. This is not unlike the conundrum of the chicken and the egg.

It is this problem that leads him to decide that 'to penetrate to the ultimate source of the concept, our thinking must go back to a deeper stratum, must seek those factors of synthesis and analysis, which are at work in the process of word formation itself'.[30] Thus in a somewhat unexpected way, what began as a modern search for a theory of mind led Cassirer to look at primitive language and myth, for the two are intertwined. Together they deal with a state of mind that can give clues to how the first monuments might have been conceived. Before the world appeared to consciousness as empirical things it was immersed in mythical explanations.[31]

To understand what mythical thinking is, Cassirer first traces the character of modern thought and shows how it became 'emancipated' from earlier forms. The beginning of a more rational world view Cassirer ascribes to some time after Homer. Clear signs of it are present in Pythagoras who, he says, is at the cusp of a shift in world view. Bound up with this transition, 'the mythical concept of fate for the first time passes into the logical capacity of necessity'.[32] From this point, the two opposing paths of *mythos* and *logos* become available. In the work of Socrates, Plato and Aristotle, the primacy of the latter is upheld and with it the course of the West becomes set. Mankind can gain control over his mythical dæmon and fate by a process of will and understanding: 'your genius will not be allotted to you,' wrote Plato, 'but you will choose your genius'.[33] In the words of the title of a book by F.M. Cornford, there is a shift *From Religion to Philosophy*.

Cassirer constantly reminds his reader of the extensive periods of overlap in these changes of world view. In the last chapter, for example, we discussed his thoughts on the emergence of the 'I'. This philosophical conception seemed to have distinct parallels not only with what Radin called the shift from magic to religion but also with anthropological evidence that primitive cultures have little or no sense of individuality. He interprets the myth of Dionysus and its cult that lived on into classical Greece in the light of what he calls the 'Mythical Feeling of Unity and Life'. The god being torn to pieces is a reflection of the Dionysian sense of tragedy at the impending separation of man from the primordial unity. Another response to this sense of change Cassirer sees in a peculiar characteristic of Greek theatre in the person of 'the *coryphaeus* [who] steps out of the chorus as a whole and is set off from the rest as an independent individual'.[34] Notwithstanding the rise of philosophy, a primordial stratum persisted through to Greek tragedy. From Cassirer's analysis we see two distinctive world views each having specific and contrasting characteristics that lend themselves to distinctive modes of thought. On the one hand we have a world saturated in myth, elaborated by cultures whose people have little or no sense of individuality, and in which fate is a dominating force. On the other hand we have a world in which logic and rational thinking come to hold sway, where the idea of the individual emerges, and where the concepts of necessity and determinable cause will eventually overthrow the mythical paradigm of gods and heroes.

For empirical-scientific thinking, truths or laws lie in the abstracted relation between things. Progressive analysis allows the elevated understanding of cause and effect from the particular to the universal as, for example, in the famous case of Newton's apple and the law of gravity. 'This isolating abstraction is alien to mythical thinking',[35] says Cassirer. 'Mythical thinking knows only the principle of equivalence of the parts with the whole'.[36] In this manner of thinking, for example, the whole man is contained 'in his hair, his nail-cuttings, his clothes, his footprints', any trace, even his shadow, could be acted upon by magic to affect the man himself.

In this we begin to see how diametrically opposed our modern framework of thinking is from that of the primitive – how fundamentally different is the way we go about organising our own conceptual framework from the way they did. Empirical-scientific thinking links the essence of any one thing with other things, abstracting from them their phenomenal characteristics so as to fit them into a schema whereby specimens are related to species that are in turn subsumed with a 'higher' genus by an invisible law. We classify an elephant, for example, by the structure and mechanisms of its cells rather than by its size, shape, weight or wrinkliness. There is a particular direction to this process, upwards and outwards; 'a concentric expansion over ever-widening spheres of perception and conception'.[37] Mythical thinking in contrast 'concentrates', it comes under the spell of particular things, it is 'possessed' by them. Where empirical-scientific thinking sees processes in terms of function, series and mathematical law, mythical thinking sees them in material or substantial terms. In what Cassirer calls 'scientific, critical, or analytical' thought, matter is replaced by force and substance is 'liberated' by cause, whereas in mythical '"logic" – the form of its contents – clings to bodies'.[38] In the case of mythical thinking, systems of relationships are made on the basis of specific, concrete points of similarity as we saw in the example of stone and bone. Cassirer explains the process:

> Whereas empirical thinking is essentially directed toward establishing an unequivocal relation between specific 'causes' and specific 'effects', mythical thinking ... has a free selection of causes at its disposal. Anything can come from anything, because anything can stand in temporal or spatial contact with anything. Whereas empirical thinking speaks of 'change' and seeks to understand it on the basis of a universal rule, mythical thinking knows only a simple metamorphosis. [...] When scientific thinking considers the fact of change, it is not essentially concerned with the transformation of a single given thing into another; on the contrary, it regards this transformation as possible and admissible only insofar as a universal law is expressed in it, insofar as it is based on certain functional relations and determinations which can be regarded as valid independently of the mere here and now and of the constellation of things in the here and now. Mythical 'metamorphosis', on the other hand, is always the record of an individual event – a change from one individual and concrete form to another. The cosmos is fished out of the depths of the sea or moulded from a tortoise; the earth is shaped from the body of a great beast or from a lotus blossom floating on the water; the sun is made from a stone, men from rocks or trees. All these heterogeneous mythical explanations, chaotic and lawless as they may seem in their mere content, reveal one and the same approach to the world. Whereas the scientific causal judgement dissects an event into constant elements and seeks to understand it through the complex mingling, interpenetration, and constant conjunction of these elements, mythical thinking clings to the total representation as such and contents itself with picturing the simple course of what happens.[39]

Although we have followed Cassirer some way in describing mythical thinking, we have yet to learn from him how words are actually formed and how distinctions are made if they are not already given in the logical categories of language itself. He broaches this problem by way of an account of the multiplicity of gods that remained present in imperial Rome, accessible to us through history yet, as his example shows, still steeped in myth.

> For all actions and conditions special gods are created and clearly named; and it is not merely the actions and conditions as a whole [that] are deified in this way, but also any segments, acts, or moments of them that are in any way conspicuous ... In the agricultural sacrifice the Flamines had to invoke twelve gods in addition to Tellus and Ceres,

and these twelve corresponded to as many actions of the tiller of the soil: Veruactor for the first breaking of the fallow field (*veruactum*), Reparator for the second ploughing, Imporcitor for the third and final ploughing in which the furrows (*lirae*) were drawn and the ridges (*porcae*) thrown up, Insitor for the sowing, Oberator for the ploughing over after the sowing, Occator for the harrowing, Saritor for the weeding (*sarire*) with the hoe, Subruncinator for the pulling out of weeds, Messor for the reaping, Convector for the transportation of the grain from the fields, Conditor for the garnering, Promitor for the giving out of the grain from granary and barn. [40]

This example in itself reminds us of how wide of the mark we would be if we approached the question of primitive religion from anything like the perspective of more recent monotheism. Cassirer's example shows how the specific nature of the supernatural world continued to remain in the names of the multiple Roman gods which sprang from the concrete objectivisation in mythical thinking – designating differences, fixing them, making them visible in images and words. This corresponds to a similar process Cassirer sees at work 'in primitive languages, which often divide an action into several sub-actions, and instead of comprehending it all under one term denote each part by a separate verb, as though they had to break up the idea into little pieces in order to handle it'.[41] This is, however, a considerable number of steps down the line of mythical thinking where culture gods are replacing nature gods. The cyclical phases associated with farming were responsible for this particular systemisation, says Cassirer, who goes on to say this about the yet deeper layer of nature myths:

> Folk beliefs show that this primordial force of the mythical imagination is still alive and active. In it is rooted the belief in the vast throng of nature demons who dwell in field and meadow, thicket and wood. In the rustling of leaves, the murmuring and roaring of the wind, and the play and sparkle of the sunlight, in a thousand indefinable voices and tones the life of the forest first becomes perceptible to the mythical consciousness as the immediate manifestation of the innumerable elemental spirits who inhabit the woods: the wood sprites and elves, the spirits of tree and wind.
>
> But the development of the wood and field cults show us step by step how myth gradually grows beyond these figures, how without ever abandoning them entirely it adds other spirits arising from different spheres of thought and feeling. The world of the mere elemental spirits gives way to a new world view as the 'I' passes from mere emotional reaction to the stage of action. It comes to see its relation to nature no longer through the medium of mere impression but through the medium of its own action. It is from the rule

of this action, from its cyclical phases, that the reality of nature obtains its true content and fixed formation. The transition to agriculture, to a regulated tilling of the fields, represents a crucial turning point in the development of the vegetation myths and cults. Here again, it is true, man does not at once confront nature as a free subject but feels himself inwardly enmeshed in it, at one with its destinies. Its growth and passing away, its flowering and fading, are intimately bound up with its own living and dying.[42]

Cassirer uses this hazy context of nature gods or demons to make the most important point for his thesis; that we should not conceive these as 'personifications of universal forces or processes of nature but as mythical objectivisations of particular impressions'.[43] Cassirer's main point is that before denoting can take place there must first be a noticing. This is the crucial stage of his investigation. For even if we offered a list of the nature gods, they would already be denoted, whereas Cassirer wants to trace the process of how denoting – naming and distributing into categories – arises from the act of noticing. From anthropology he detects another more primordial level of language, into which he plunges to discover if there is an essential structure that will reveal the process to him.

He refers to an anthropological study that shows 'the root of all Melanesian religion to be the concept of a "super-natural power" which pervades all things and events and may be present now in objects, now in persons, yet is never bound exclusively to any single and individual subject or object as its host, but may be transmitted from place to place, from thing to thing, from person to person. ...In this light the whole existence of things seem to be embedded, so to speak, in a mythical "field of force"'.[44] This concept became designated as 'mana', which Cassirer describes as a universal phenomenon, 'nothing less than a special category of the mythic consciousness'. He quotes an early attempt to clarify the word's ambivalent meaning: 'remarkable, very strong, very great, very old, strong in magic, wise in magic, supernatural, divine – or in a substantive sense as power, magic, sorcery, fortune, success, godhead, delight'.[45]

He cites another example that shows the fluidity of the concept of mana. Using it as a noun, as did many early anthropologists, makes it a kind of substance and hence too similar to our monotheistic notion of spirit. Nevertheless, mythical thinking organises itself into a kind of unity because the phenomena designated all seem to have been noticed as participating in that mythical 'field of force' called 'waka^{n}da' by the Sioux Indians, for example.

Among these tribes the creation and control of the world and the things thereof are ascribed to waka^{n}da, ... just as among the Algonquin tribes omnipotence was ascribed to 'ma-ni-do'; yet inquiry shows that waka^{n}da assumes various forms, and is rather a quality than a definite entity. Thus among many of the tribes the sun is waka^{n}da – not the waka^{n}da or a waka^{n}da, but simply waka^{n}da; and among the same tribes the moon is waka^{n}da, and so is thunder, lightning, the stars, the winds, the cedar and various other things, even a man, especially a shaman might be waka^{n}da.[46]

Cassirer allows this quotation to run on for almost two pages, a longer and longer list of things that partake of waka^{n}da. This culminates in the author's attempt to translate the term, resulting in a string of possible synonyms such as those we saw earlier ascribed to mana. Whittle says that for the Chewong of Malaysia, 'reality is not divisible into material and spiritual, into mind and body, emotion and intellect. Rather it is perceived as being made up of endlessly mutual interacting and fluid beings and qualities'.[47] Cassirer points out that these Sioux examples demonstrate that 'the level of mythic conception on which we find ourselves here corresponds to a level of linguistic conception to which we may not assign offhand our grammatical categories, our neat classifications of sharply distinguished words'.[48] Rather, these mythic conceptions are more like 'interjections' or 'exclamations' indicating 'not so much a certain thing as a certain impression'.

The fact that mana can appear in all kinds of things, animate and inanimate, physical or spiritual, reveals that it is not a particular class of objects but has something to do with the 'character' that makes these objects 'stand forth from the ordinary background of familiar, mundane existence'.[49] It is here that Cassirer finds the solution to the problem of original word formation; the concepts of 'character', 'mythic wonder' and that which 'stands forth' all share in the primacy of being noticed rather than denoted. Certain things, events or phenomena emerge from the generalised background of the world by the fact that they are noticed and, for whatever reason, appear to be significant. Hence a cluster of these things, events or phenomena emerges and they are named and categorised as incorporating mana. It is perhaps best to leave to Cassirer a summary of how he arrives at his goal.

Mana and its several equivalents do not denote a single, definite predicate; but in all of them we find a peculiar and consistent form of predication. This predication may indeed be designated as the primeval mythico-religious predication, since it expresses the spiritual 'crisis' whereby the holy is divided from the profane, and set apart from the sphere of the ordinary, in a religious sense indifferent, reality. By this process of division the object of religious experience may really be said to be brought into existence, and the realm in which it moves to be first established. And herewith we have arrived at the crucial factor for our general problem: for our original aim was to treat both language and myth as spiritual functions which do not take their departure from a world of given objects, divided according to fixed and finished 'attributes', but which actually first produce this organization of reality and make the positing of attributes possible. The concept of mana and the correlative, negative concept of taboo reveal the ways in which this construction is originally effected. From the fact that we are here moving on a level where the mythic and religious world has not yet attained any fixed form, but is presented to us, so to speak, *in statu nascendi*, we may gain insight into the many-coloured, variegated play of meanings in the word – and the concept – of mana.[50]

Although he does not spend much time on the concept of taboo, it is clear that Cassirer finds in these two opposed original realms of feeling, mana and taboo, the fundamental basis for category formation. He sets aside, as we will for the moment, the question of taboo. Yet it is from this fundamental contrasting pair, 'which seem wholly subject to immediate sensory impression and elementary sensory drives, …which disperses the world into a confused multiplicity of demonic forces, [that] we find traits pointing to a kind of articulation, a future "organisation" of these forces'.[51]

At the end of his pursuit of the logical problem of the origin of category formation, Cassirer was led to conclude that 'all sensory intuition and perception rests on an original foundation of feeling'.[52] Harrison succinctly describes a similar process at work in the way Greek drama emerged from a preceding era of *dromenon* – 'the rite done'. 'The genius of the Greek language felt, before it consciously knew the difference. This feeling ahead for distinctions is characteristic of all languages'.[53] The basis of category formation arises when certain things or phenomena become separated from the 'commonplace experience' by being noticed. From this springs the opposition between what we saw Cassirer himself at one point call the sacred and the profane, terms that have become the bedrock for understanding the primitive mind. In being noticed they might be considered 'sacred' and then seem to have one of two fundamental possible meanings for the primitive mind: they seem to occupy either a positive part of a mythical 'field of force' or a negative part and hence are either mana or taboo.

Through his rigorous analysis of language Cassirer not only clarifies the nature of primitive thinking but also the development of belief systems that successively unfold from mana and taboo to the rites of nature cults, animism, the heroes of classical and Celtic mythology, and ultimately to the God of monotheism. Only with the arrival of monotheism, says Brody, do mana and taboo shift from an association with an anonymous force to become ascribed with moral values of good or bad.[54] A man-like God judges and the devil tempts. Cassirer contends that man originally does not make distinctions, rather mythical images make themselves visible to him. This first step in the process of conceptualisation he called 'radical metaphor'. Certain phenomenal entities impressed themselves upon him, such as stone erupting from the earth and manifesting itself as an aspect of eternal force that, as we saw, became linked in the imagination with bone. Material and things became an important medium by which sympathetic relationships to the world of fluid forces became structured and stabilised. Levi-Strauss said that the savage mind builds images of the world that resemble it so as to understand it.[55]

At the beginning of this long process that led from 'magic to religion', then, Cassirer identifies the fundamental opposition between mana and taboo. This came to form the basis of the later structural anthropology of Levi-Strauss who, as we saw, argued that being 'able to oppose terms' was the foundation of savage thought. As mentioned earlier, much of Levi-Strauss' work is now contested, in particular the opposition between nature and culture. Many archaeologists, among others, have come to consider this to be a modern, western construct imposed upon primitive or prehistoric modes of operating. However, this response can be shown to oversimplify Levi-Strauss' views on the question. He interweaves his remarks on the nature/culture opposition, for example, with the statement that 'savage thought stems from the intimate contact between man and his environment'. Although Levi-Strauss' whole system of thought is predicated on the idea of binary oppositions, he points out that it is the frequent role of myth to effect their reconciliation, 'to overcome the opposition between nature and culture and think of them as a whole'.[56] To explain this he describes a myth common to several North American Indian tribes of the marriage between a buffalo and a girl, in which correspondences are made between parts of the beast and cultural artefacts. The outcome of the marriage is the metamorphosis of the buffalo from its original mythical status of 'all bone' to 'all flesh'. The cultural artefacts were collected together in the form of the bride's dowry and this mythical union had a very particular purpose in the context of savage thought, as Levi-Strauss explains:

> The marriage exchange thus functions as a mechanism serving to mediate between nature and culture, which were originally regarded as separate. By substituting a cultural architectonic for a supernatural primitive one (i.e. the set of cultural artefacts for the bones of the first buffalo), the alliance creates a second nature over which man has a hold, that is a mediatised nature.[57]

This is his crucial point, for in it lies the explanation of how magical operations are thought to work by primitive people. Levi-Strauss is not interested in the relative efficacy of modern scientific thought and savage thought. He seeks rather to understand how a practice that, from the modern standpoint, seems fanciful and of dubious practical value to the activity in hand is considered to be essential to the savage mind. It lies in the concrete or apparent link perceived between things made possible by savage thinking's fundamental principle of congruity or reciprocity, and how this can effect bridges between the spheres of culture and nature. Harrison describes how the snake became a fertility dæmon in Ancient Greece, for example, and that it is often depicted with olive branches and ears of corn, the symbol of fertility brought into congruence with the food supply. Culture and nature at first glance can be seen as opposed from within the framework of savage thought, yet the construction of a culture depends upon the manipulation of nature as much as human life itself depends upon mankind taking from nature. It is the desire to assert or acknowledge the differences between the human world of culture and nature that underlies all savage thought and ritual activity, yet at the same time to recognise the correspondences and effect the necessary link between them.

Levi-Strauss draws this conclusion from hunter-gatherer societies. Yet, as Thomas says, the Neolithic would have been a distinctive way of thinking about the world dominated by the habitual practice of farming, a way of life that separated humanity (culture) from nature much more than hunting and gathering. However, the role of rituals and the places that came to house them were designed to reconcile the perceived differences, as we have tried to show. Rites and material artefacts were designed to weave human culture into nature's eternal return. This would take on a distinct form under farming. Cummings has said that 'Neolithic people may not have understood the world as we do' but argues that megalithic monuments were related to potent symbolic places 'as part of a broader process of negotiation between people and ancestral places'. This broad process aimed to overcome the division between nature and culture, which is essentially the aim Levi-Strauss describes. Although farming does involve a process of increasing control over nature, nevertheless it would be a mistake to think of this as the beginnings of a form of 'brutal domination' as suggested by Russell. In actual fact, as Eliade's work shows, until quite recent historical times among peasant societies, the practice of farming was one of developing appropriate and reciprocal relations between nature and culture.

It is from this position that Levi-Strauss is able to assert that, to the savage mind, the difference between practical and 'magical' action is almost the reverse of what we think. Practical actions are subjective as they represent interference in the world, whereas magic seems an addition to the objective order of the world because the aspirations expressed in magic seem to be of the same kind as those occurring in the natural world. Magic is a supplementary link in the natural order. For Levi-Strauss, this procedure, or structure of thought, helps make sense of such extraordinary myths as the marriage of the maiden to the buffalo and the precise terms by which the binary oppositions of culture and nature are linked. 'This reciprocity of perspectives, in which man and the world mirror each other "explains" the properties and capacities of the savage mind'.[58]

The resemblance of mythical thinking to phenomenology's being-in-the-world is easily detected here. A kindred basic concept that has been called 'being-with-others' leads to a point where binary oppositions are considered to form the very foundation of human existence. John Macquarrie introduces this concept in his book *Existentialism* with the purpose of demonstrating that all existence 'is fundamentally communal in character'. Two principal supports for his contention are language and sex: 'it is immediately obvious ... that both sex and language imply that no human individual is complete without others. Sex refers to the fact that although the human body contains several complete 'systems' (nervous, alimentary, respiratory, and so on) it has only half a reproductive system and is thus incomplete without another person of the opposite sex'. [59]

He goes on to say how this is not merely an empirical or biological fact for mankind but is something inescapably noticeable in all animal life: 'the categories of sex, male and female, are cosmic categories, not merely anthropological ones'.[60] Underlying the very basis of existence then are these binary oppositions of male and female. Archaic man lived close to the fundamental conditions of life and death, and, as Eliade shows, he saw the world or cosmos as alive. Given this, it is easy to see why the basic opposition of male and female would be projected upon the phenomenal world to form the kind of pattern of structured oppositions that characterises Levi-Strauss' approach and which Cassirer found organised at bedrock around the polarity of mana and taboo.

A similar misunderstanding about oppositions can often be detected in the use of the concepts sacred and profane. A detailed consideration of these, however, confirms and expands upon what has gone before and will bring us to a concluding consideration of Neolithic Orkney monuments. To the Romans, 'sacrum meant what belonged to the gods or [was] in their power'.[61] This did not necessarily refer to the gods or gods' names as such, but to essential aspects of the cult and rituals associated with them. Specifically it came to be applied to a sacred space or place. '*Profanum* was what was "in front of the temple precinct" (the *fanum*)'. As we have come to see with other oppositions, *sacer* and *profanum* were therefore linked. Originally designations of space or place, the terms have come to be applied to distinctions more generally between the sacred and the profane. Yet as we have seen, anything in the cosmos is potentially sacred. There can, however, be something that is fundamentally sacred or some way of getting closer to the sacred; this was the role of the *sanctum* or sanctuary. For the Romans the sacred was approached through the structured relationship between the *profanum* and the *fanum*. Hence also the important role of the portico in the Greek temple derived from the early form of *megaron* house. Hodder detected something similar in the presence of a large and distinct porch in the LBK longhouses. A variation of his *domus-agrios* concept is what he calls the *domus-fores*, a concept that has bearing on thresholds. 'So again, in the structuring of our language, a set of concepts (the forest, the foreigner, the wild, the public) is defined in terms of the house – in this case its door'.[62] Hence the almost universal significance of thresholds, as both boundary and passage, to the concept of sacred space.

In *The Savage Mind* Levi-Strauss set out to 'explore totemism's positive side'.[63] This is a particular case of the 'positive' links that cultures make with nature, what Cassirer identified as mana, those systems of resemblance and reciprocity that are constructed so as to forge links because a culture wishes to partake of something of value seen in nature. This fundamental attribute of myth has its counterpoint in taboo, touched upon by Cassirer but more central to Levi-Strauss. Taboo is in many respects a more familiar concept, entering the mainstream of modern thought through the writings of Freud. Taboo is generally taken to mean a thing or an activity that is forbidden. It is perhaps more accurate to say that what is taboo is 'interdicted through its relation to the sacred, or its relation to cosmic forces'.[64] That is, in the same way people might contrive to get closer to the sacred – the positive life-force or mana – by incantation, ritual, or spatial manipulation, then equally and oppositely they might try to 'insulate' themselves from the negative forces abroad, all that is taboo.

That such a structure of oppositions emerges in different ways in the work of Levi-Strauss, Cassirer and Eliade, emanating from such diverse disciplines as anthropology, philosophy and the history of religion, indicates its significance and suggests its applicability for prehistory. There are two points worth emphasising as we move towards a conclusion. The first of these is that savage thought or mythical thinking sees everywhere something like a life force that flows through things or is present in phenomena, and that culture is largely dependent upon making the appropriate links to and separations from the things and phenomena, felt to be either desirable or undesirable. The second of these is that the fundamental structure of savage thought is such that it both understands and operates upon this in terms of a binary opposition between mana and taboo, between the positive and the negative. In the confluence of these ideas we find support for the hypothesis of a peculiar pre-modern form of thinking, something Renfrew doesn't really accept but did not entirely rule out. Keeping his caution in mind and utilising no more than the fundamental structures of oppositions that Cassirer traced to be the bedrock of mythical thinking might be the most prudent way to proceed with a concluding review of Neolithic Orkney remains.

The Neolithic on the Atlantic seaboard is neatly framed between the emergence of two types of megalithic monuments that precisely correlate with Cassirer's formulation of mana and taboo. The burial tombs, which open this phase of the Neolithic, insulate the living from the taboo associated with death. The stone circles that mark its close are, in contrast, conductors of positive forces associated with those orchestrators of natural or cosmic rhythms, the sun and the moon. Whittle has said that the idea of 'open' and 'closed' might be usefully applied to archaeology.[65]

Monumental Orkney – open and closed constructs

The most appropriate way to pursue this argument might be to adopt or adapt the processual approach where discernible changes in the archaeological record are used as the basis for speculations about patterns of social change. This was touched upon in discussing Renfrew's work on the Stones of Stenness and Richards' study of the Barnhouse settlement where changes in society were inferred from the built remains. By comparing how artefacts changed over time, archaeologists have been able to make deductions about the kinds of social organisation that produced them. If we follow this approach in reviewing the Orkney built remains, not only noting changes in relation to time but also in the arrangement of space, then this will take up and conclude the examination of the proposition advanced in the introduction.

Chapter by chapter the various types of built structure have been considered – house, tomb, feast hall (as we might designate Barnhouse Structure 8) and stone circle – and interpretations offered that were consistent with the operating mechanisms of savage thought or mythical thinking. This attempted to weave something like the web of concrete relationships that characterise the idea of a cosmos, a primitive or pre-modern world view. The final step in this study will be to consider explicitly the relationships between the various types of built structure. Each chapter pursued leads in search of possible interpretations suggested by the particular details of evidence. This left the investigation deliberately open-ended and allowed all kinds of suggestions to be incorporated from the range of disciplines brought to bear – anthropology, archaeology, mythology, folklore and the history of religion. It is proposed to conclude using the framework of a fundamental structure of binary oppositions that we have just seen to be characteristic of mythical thinking, concentrating only on the qualitative aspects embraced by the concepts of mana and taboo. These will serve as a means to identify certain key characteristics of the various types of built structure and to facilitate the comparison between them.

From the four basic types of building in Neolithic Orkney – the house, the burial tomb, the feast hall and the stone circle – six pairings are possible; house-tomb, feast hall-tomb, house-feast hall, tomb-stone circle, house-stone circle, and feast hall-stone circle. Each of these pairings will be looked at as possible binary oppositions.

In the history and theory of architecture, the mythical primitive hut is seen as the origin of architecture itself. Nevertheless, I have suggested that we might best consider the impulse for architecture to come from something that is, strictly speaking, not necessary from the perspective of our own practical world view. There was no practical need to erect buildings for the dead or for any other ritual purpose. Clearly, therefore, burial cairns were primarily cultural or symbolic constructs. So let us begin this final assessment with those classes of structure, the tomb and the stone circle, that most obviously have no inherent practical value and hence must embody primarily cultural ideas. As well as opening and closing the Neolithic, these also show patterns of evolution or development, an advantage for a processual approach.

Burial tomb and stone circle

Although strictly speaking it cannot be said that the stone circle evolves from the burial cairn, there is some evidence to suggest that they are connected and that the stone circle came to replace the burial cairn as the principal site of ritual. Typologically, one form of Orkney burial cairn seemed to develop to its culmination at Maes Howe where, at the same time, a completely new feature was introduced, the enclosing ring of its low earth bank. This feature links it with the entirely new type of construction, the stone circle, enclosed within its own earth bank and ditch. As we have seen in the last chapter, the so-called 'dolmen' at the Stones of Stenness set up an alignment linking it with Maes Howe. Radiocarbon dating suggests that there was a chronological sequence to the building of Maes Howe and the Stones of Stenness. So a reasonable interpretation of the evidence seems to be that one kind of structure, the stone circle, emerged in some way from another, the burial tomb. However, it must be added that one does not seem to supplant the other, at least not immediately. The circle seems rather to emerge in response to the burial tomb, both as something radically different but also in some way connected. This, of course, is precisely the way Levi-Strauss has explained the operating system of binary opposites, using the example of the 'bricoleur' who could make some new and useful thing out of the substance and form of existing material ready to hand.

If we take the stone circle and the tomb as a developed pair of structures, we find that their built form corresponds precisely to what we would expect from a culture on the one hand seeking an active engagement with mana and on the other separating itself from taboo. The tomb is a closed form, the stone circle is open. The tomb has an enclosing wall and a narrow, low entrance passage; it often has a blocking stone and portal stones marking the threshold; it is covered by a heavy stone vaulted roof; it is dark and all its attributes speak of containment. The earlier burial cairns often had two enclosing walls, the space between filled with stones. Maes Howe itself is constructed of massive recumbent stones. The stone circle is defined by huge vertical stones girdled by a low earth bank and ditch; its boundary is open to the world; its roof is the vault of the sky; it is filled with light. Access to Maes Howe is oriented towards midwinter sunset, the sun at its lowest ebb. In contrast the approach to the Stones of Stenness is due south, towards the sun at its point of maximum power. The tomb is dark, cold and filled with white bones, echoing the whiteness of the moon, 'the first of the dead'. The stone circle is centred on a fire, warm like life and red like blood. The tomb contains death around which gathers all that is most taboo. Its form severely curtails any connection between the world of everyday action, and death is buried, as it were, in stone beneath the earth. The stone circle in contrast opens itself to the heavens and in particular to the principal life force of the world: the sun, blood-red at sunset. The tomb insulates the culture from the polluting taboo of death whereas the stone circle is a conductor for the life-giving force or mana.

Sealing the ground with clay between the cairn at Maes Howe and its unbroken encircling bank symbolically contains the pollution of death, insulating the earth from it just as the stone encased the bones of the dead. The passage to the Stones of Stenness through bank and ditch conducts the life force, symbolised by the sun and fire, into the surrounding earth through which it mysteriously flows. A threshold, as Eliade explains, both separates domains and connects them; here the passage is open but perhaps controlled by the alignment of sun and fire. With these two structures we have perhaps the strongest indication of how the funda-mental act of noticing, posited by Cassirer as the basis of mana and taboo, could develop symbolic cultural forms that embrace and develop the binary polarities Levi-Strauss saw everywhere in savage thought.

House and burial tomb

A comparison was made between the house and the tomb when we looked at the burial cairn and remarked upon the similarity between Knap of Howar and early tripartite chambered cairns such as Bigland Round. From this apparent relationship it seemed not unreasonable to describe cairns as houses for the dead. While there is an obvious formal resemblance between these two types of building, there are distinct differences in points of detail and material which can be interpreted as developing structures of meaning by binary oppositions. The most striking is the cavity of the house being filled with midden – waste and dying organic matter in the process of being transformed into humus or living earth – whereas the burial cairn's cavity is filled with stone, a material associated with death and eternity. Moreover, in the separate discussions on the house and chambered cairn, it proved possible to consider them both in the context of a phenomenology of containment. The plan of the earliest Orkney house could be read as morphologically developed from boat and basket. The appearance of the earliest cairns was like an inverted Unstan ware pot. So it is perhaps in details such as these that we might find a binary opposition between house and tomb.

Another opposition suggests itself in relation to the contrast between midden and stone. The house is sunk into the earth, its form would have been hardly discernible from the outside, its meaning would have been grasped from the occupation of its interior space. The burial cairn in contrast was usually built upon the earth, often high up in extremely visible locations, its meaning imme-diately grasped from the outside from its form. In addition there are aspects of relative openness to the spatial arrangements of the house that strengthen the opposition between house and tomb. In both Neolithic Orkney house types the entrance is quite open, which contrasts with the cairn. Although the difference in the size and depth of entrance between Knap of Howar and Bigland Round is quite small, the development of long narrow passages to the chambered cairn came to emphasise the separation and control of that considered taboo. The

Knap of Howar house also presents a relatively open termination to the axis that runs through the dwelling with its cubicles and shelves, in stark contrast to the great vertical slab of stone that emphatically closes the chamber of its related tripartite cairn.

The Skara Brae-type house also, and most dramatically, presents an open face to the entrance in the form of the lattice stonework of the dresser or altar. In both house types, of course, the thread from entrance to terminus crosses the fire, red and in flux, symbolic of life, at the centre or heart of the house. The tomb had no hearth. The Skara Brae-type house evolved from an arrangement of small cells to a more open plan within a roughly circular perimeter where the beds replace relatively distinct chambers. The type of passage grave associated with this type of dwelling retained the more enclosed multicellular form through to its culmination at Maes Howe. Very small openings between the central chamber and the side chambers reiterate the closed nature of the burial cairn. Just as the Skara Brae-type of house came to develop an open spatial character, so the culmination of its related burial cairn became emphatically closed at Maes Howe, where the side chambers were sealed with blocking stones and the long narrow entrance passage itself had a closing stone.

Yet of course there remains an essential ambiguity in the opposition between the house and tomb because, as has been suggested, the tomb seems to have been conceived as a kind of house itself. The fundamental opposition here seems to lie in the notions of containment on the one hand – which would appear to be deep-rooted, archaic – and openness on the other hand. Although no polarity can be starker than that between life and death, nevertheless we have seen how the notion of containment was perhaps necessary to both. On the one hand it was used to shelter life, as the basket with its open weave collected and contained the stuff of life, and on the other hand it was for encasing the pollution of death in addition to establishing the reciprocity between eternal stone and bone. A binary opposition between house and tomb seems to have been constructed by significant differences of detail and material.

Feast hall and house

The feast hall has been described as an enlarged and elaborated form of the Skara Brae house type. As Richards says: 'Structure 8 is a representation of a house in just the same way that Maes Howe is a representation of a tomb, although neither appears to fulfil its function'.[66] By representation he means that the symbolic role has supplanted that of actual use in these two cases. He uses the term representation in a similar way to how Renfrew describes the working of symbols. In Richards' examples, however, there is not only a horizontal transference of meaning – i.e. insignia for rank – but also a deep resonance with an actual event and a past – as the Christian cross, for example, refers to Christ's crucifixion itself.

Although bones were probably kept at Maes Howe, Richards considers that it had become more mausoleum than a site of ongoing burials. Similarly, Structure 8 shows little evidence of everyday domestic occupation, although one essential function of dwelling – eating – seems to have been more intensely practised. Yet how can two buildings with such formal and functional similarity as house and feast hall be opposed? Significant details are as illuminating in comparing these two buildings as proved to be the case when looking at the relationship between house and house of the dead.

As mentioned, the feast hall appears formally to be an enlarged version of the Skara Brae type of house, more geometrical, having a proportionally larger dresser, and with the addition of a complex porch that thrusts the sign of entrance out into external space. The expansion and elaboration of these two features can be read as reinforcing the open aspect of that complimentary open-closed system we saw in the house. The archaeological evidence of feasting in conjunction with anthropological parallels where 'big men' or chiefs developed social power through this activity, suggests an expansion of openness, thrusting the feast hall out into the social realm. For the house – open to a single family group – becomes, in the feast hall, opened further to the larger social group that could participate in it. The elaboration and projection of the porch could thus be construed as a built detail that reiterates the hypothesis of a social hierarchy emerging that could call upon immense labour to build the adjoining monumental complex. A puzzling feature of the feast hall is that a stone wall surrounds it. The house itself embodied a balance between open and contained, so perhaps the projecting porch created an imbalance. Presenting an unacceptable asymmetry, perhaps the equation open:open–closed needed to be re-balanced, hence the addition of an outer wall to provide appropriate closure. Richards suggests that the enclosing wall marks an increased control of ritual in the late Neolithic where signs of a hierarchy emerge. The foregoing does not necessarily imply a challenge to his interpretation. Rather, it shows how the different approach taken here of exploring how mythical thinking manifests itself in symbolic form tends to confirm the processual-societal approach. Such a multi-layered view of explanations also rests comfortably with how we know the primitive mind operated within the idea of a cosmos.

Tomb and feast hall

Richards' excavations at Barnhouse revealed a specific similarity between the feast hall and Maes Howe. Both had a clay platform between the central structure and a perimeter boundary. Evidence of ritual activity outside some early chambered cairns, in conjunction with the presence of fires in the space between the feast hall and the wall at Barnhouse, led him to propose that these clay covered areas were sites of ritual feasting. This fits with the interpretation of the

Maes Howe – Stenness – Brodgar complex as reflecting the rise of a social hierarchy in late Neolithic Orkney, with which went increasing control over ritual activity. While the size of the burial tomb greatly increased, access to it became more restricted. Yet the surrounding clay platform and perimeter boundary provided an extended place of gathering that allowed the larger population into proximity with the meaning embodied or enacted in the structure at the centre.

The presence of a clay platform at both Maes Howe and the Barnhouse feast hall, in addition to their formal similarity – a central building with encircling boundary – is consistent with the kind of reciprocity we would expect to see in the development of a binary opposition. The fact that both these structures are quite novel in relation to what preceded them in Neolithic Orkney and that they emerged at more or less the same time reinforces the possibility that they were developed with some inter-related aim in view. Nevertheless, as we have seen, both structures acquired their particular characteristics by being transformations of inherited types, a process typical of mythical thinking. Richards described Maes Howe and the Barnhouse feast hall as representations or symbols of tomb and house respectively, as we have seen.

It has been suggested here that the projecting porch at the feast hall might have been introduced to give it a greater sense of openness in relation to the house itself. This elaborated, open, projecting entrance also establishes the most striking polarity with Maes Howe, where the entrance is recessive, unelaborated and sealed with a blocking stone. Richards suggested that the presence of a hearth in the entrance to the feast hall may have been for the purpose of purification. The hearth also brings to the threshold the central feature of the house. At the same time it formalises the placement of fires in the space between building and perimeter wall. As well as a distinct polarity between projecting and recessive entrance then, there is also an associated one that involves meaning embodied in material. Blocking the entrance to the ritual building is fire, symbolic of life's ongoing transformational processes, of warmth and the heart. Blocking the tomb is stone, symbolic of bone and the eternal bodiless cold life in death. Exceptionally long horizontal stones form the entrance passage to Maes Howe, whereas two tall standing stones mark the threshold to the feast hall.

The orientation of the respective openings reinforces this polarity; the passage into Maes Howe receives the midwinter sunset whereas the entrance to the feast hall faces midsummer sunset. One building faces the dying throes of winter, the other is orientated to the earth's most fully alive and abundant point, the year closed and open respectively.

Although what it might signify is less clear, a polarity can also be discerned in the perimeter walls. At Barnhouse the wall is close to the building which it encloses, it was built of stone (as the feast hall) and Richards considers it to have been tall. At Maes Howe, in contrast, a low earth bank surrounding the tumulus at a considerable distance from the enclosure and there is no opening in this perimeter wall whereas there is at Barnhouse. Looking at this polarity suggests yet another, although one more allusive, where the deepest meaning of this particular pair of buildings, developed at the same time and with such novel appearance, might have been put into play. The form of Maes Howe is more earth mound than inverted pot as were the earliest cairns, and its interior symbolised the older form of house. So Maes Howe could be read as an ancestral house in or under the landscape, an appropriate symbol for the place of death in such a culture. The ritual feast hall, in contrast, would have appeared as a house or built construction, which its encircling stone wall would have reiterated. Consequently feasting was made manifest emphatically within the social life world, the built world of the settlement.

Feast hall and stone circle

As Richards says, Barnhouse Structure 8 'is a representation of the house'. To avoid undue repetition, therefore, I will pass over the house – stone circle comparison and conflate it with the comparison between the feast hall and the Stones of Stenness, which becomes our final pairing. Richards has suggested that the former represents a closed site of ritual activity and the latter an open site, responding in different ways to an emerging social hierarchy.[67] From our set of comparisons, however, both these structures have appeared as open; the feast hall in relation to both the house and tomb, the Stones of Stenness in relation to the tomb. If this is so can there be an open–closed polarity of spatial structure between this pair? Is there a structured opposition that would tie in with Richards' suggestion of a polarity of access to ritual? At the level of direct perception there clearly is, in that, as we have seen, the Stones of Stenness present themselves as a structure fundamentally open to view whereas a tall wall apparently enveloped the feast hall. Comparing their boundaries, furthermore, we find a polarity in the details similar to those that marked the difference between house and feast hall.

Both these late Neolithic ritual structures have a complex boundary condition: the feast hall has a double stone wall whereas the Stones of Stenness have an earth bank and ditch. The stone wall and the ditch give the strongest polarity. The stone wall rises from the earth whereas the ditch is cut down into the earth. The stone wall visually and materially connects the ritual building to the everyday world of material culture embodied in the house, whereas the ditch is an entirely new feature which 'cuts off' the stone circle from everything around and about on the land. Encircling the ditch is an earth bank similar to that which surrounds Maes Howe. Yet where that contained an insulating clay platform at the Stones of Stenness the ditch cuts open the site to the earth. As suggested earlier, however, the ditch might have been a way of breaking the continuity of the earth's matrix, hence insulating a particular piece of earth from all that surrounding it. In this way a polarity was established between the sacred and profane through its circular form, by being a place 'cut off', and by a controlled threshold. Emulating the appearance of the sun and moon, the stone circle sets up a structured spatial sequence involving a causeway into the enclosure that allowed people to 'come closer' to the sacred, itself drawn down into the circle at significant times of the year. A line of enigmatic remains from the central hearth to the causeway into the stone circle suggests an attempt at control over the connecting section of earth, the threshold between the inner sanctum and the outer world.

Despite these aspects of polarity, nevertheless stone circle and feast hall share significant points of similarity that confirm their fundamental openness and their active engagement with positive forces at work in the world. Both are centred on a hearth and both have a significant orientation to the sun. The feast hall is aligned with sunset at the midsummer solstice, a time of light and plenty, an orientation consistent with celebration through feasting. The Stones of Stenness on the other hand has a significant orientation to the sunset at midwinter. The feast hall is a relatively simple structure, closing its walls around the social bond of feasting, whereas the Stones of Stenness is a more complex structure perhaps because it is trying to deal with the sun's annual death and the consequences of this for the cosmos. In this perhaps lies an explanation of its complexity, its innovative, emphatically open and upright form, and the connection to other points in the landscape that radiate from it. Owing to the fact that the Stones of Stenness are connected with both that which is most taboo – the death of the sun – as well as celebrating the sun's cycle of life-giving warmth, perhaps it developed its particular characteristic of linking the sun's burial with that of the ancestors. The sun setting into its cairn-shaped mountain is drawn into a relationship with humans in their ancestral house of the dead beneath its mound at Maes Howe by the framing feature of the dolmen. This new form of space, the stone circle, is then linked to the point of the sun's maximum power by a line running through it that embraces fire and offerings to the earth. The Stones of Stenness, with their entrance aligned north to south, mark the climax of this openness to the vital sustaining force of the sun, marking out or even orchestrating the great cyclical drama of its rise and fall across the heavens. Perhaps in this way the Stones of Stenness can be seen as a temple in the established sense – as Lethaby described it, linking microcosm and macrocosm – whereby the forces of mana are brought into the sphere of human action. Through the construction of a sacred space incorporating both an *axis mundi* and this macrocosm/microcosm relationship, some form of control by mediation and offerings may have been sought; the eternal cycles of the sun and moon brought into the human world through the circle of immense standing stones. For the first time in western European culture we see a built construction that established itself as a conductor of positive force or mana.

Conclusion

This study set out to examine Neolithic monuments – the first architecture – from within the perspective of a cosmos. The conception of a cosmos was defined in contrast to our own scientific world view as a complex web of things and phenomena bound together by tangible resemblances and differences. Into this cosmos humans wove their material-culture by reciprocal and metaphorical relationships. The hypothesis of a distinctive form of primitive thought that co-existed with this has been demonstrated through the philosophical investigations of Ernst Cassirer. He traced what he called mythical thinking back to where it rested upon a foundation of feeling, what he described as a primal 'noticing' of the difference between a positive and negative force running through the cosmos, between mana and taboo.

From the idea of a cosmos, then, came the impetus for this study not only to interpret cultural artefacts by embedding them in the complex web of visual and material relationships they had with other things and phenomena, but also a structure of thinking and practice that could be applied to built remains. Orkney was chosen for this investigation because there we are particularly fortunate to have such rich and well-preserved remains that enable us to see how the land was occupied from the pioneer Neolithic settlements to the final flourish of their magnificent stone circles. The immediately preceding analysis took up Whittle's suggestion that the distinction between open and closed constructs might prove useful for archaeologists investigating the Neolithic. This we found to have a correlation with the anthropological concepts of mana and taboo. Focusing our study on built remains in Orkney allowed us to explore in considerable detail the elements that made up a Neolithic culture and cosmos. In addition this concentration allowed us to suggest something of the meaning these cultural forms might have had to the people who built them. Out of this conceptual framework, with its stress on the concrete nature of savage thought and the significant place given to symbolism, has emerged the suggestion that the first architecture developed from simple and closed containers – insulators against taboo – to complex and open 'temples' that developed an active engagement with the cosmos by lines on the landscape that are linked to the heavens – conductors of mana. In the processes of transformation that could be detected in the sequence of basket, boat, building, for example, or in the metaphoric relationship between stone and bone, we saw a Neolithic cultural practice that seemed similar to that of Levi-Strauss' 'bricoleur'. Producing new things out of materials ready-to-hand could be seen as kindred to a paradigm of ideas. Embedded in the very structure of mythical thinking itself could have come the germ of the idea for the 'invention' of the passage grave and the stone circle. Responding to mana or taboo, they brought together habitual practice in the everyday world – weaving baskets and coiling pots – with the broader cosmos – the circles of the sun and moon, the cycle of the seasons.

The emergence of stone circles in Britain is generally considered to mark the evolution of a hierarchical society. Beginning from the premiss that any made thing is a reflection of the mind that makes it, this study has suggested an equally plausible explanation. Stone circles might reflect an evolution in the structure of mythical thinking from magic to religion, from an emphasis on the taboo of death reflected in burial cairns, to an open, more active engagement with the positive forces gathered together under the rubric of mana. If the Neolithic can be thought of as a conceptual framework rather than simply an economic model, then perhaps the fundamental structure of mythical thinking allows us a glimpse of such a world view at work. Two major structuring concepts that coincide with this have been identified in the Neolithic by archaeologists; Hodder's *domus-agrios* 'line' and Bradley's 'circular archetype'. It is interesting that the line appears quite early in the Neolithic associated with a period of relatively prolonged settlement; the LBK longhouses are the first 'monumental' expression of this. Stone circles in Britain and Ireland first appear at the end of the Neolithic after a period of prolonged, circumscribed occupation. The circle, which was first contained in baskets and pots in the depth of the *domus*, became opened up to the sky across which rode the two circular orchestrators of nature's eternal return, the sun and the moon. The first burial cairns were not unlike upside-down pots turned to stone, pressing down upon the earth, containing the dead. The stone circles are like upright coronets of eternal stone open to the ever-returning cycle of the heavens. At the Stones of Stenness we found evidence of a link with Maes Howe and with death. The life force that came to be associated with the sun could be conveyed to the dead in the underworld. The hope for regeneration after death, like plants from seed in the ground, was thus reinforced by a change in belief system as evidenced by the emergence of stone circles as new and principal monuments. The form of explanation offered here and the processual-societal explanation need not be viewed as mutually exclusive. If the evolution of society led inevitably to certain individuals being endowed with or assuming privileged significance, then perhaps the sun and the moon would come to appear as equally and especially significant forms of cosmic force. Given the nature of the primitive mind it is quite likely that these two explanations would appear as inter-linked, as part of those concrete relationships that we have seen to be the basis of mythical thinking. We know from later, historical societies that hierarchies did emerge and that they drew their political legitimacy from celestial comparisons. Along the way we made comparisons with the familiar ritual practices and beliefs of the Christian church to illuminate the dark past of prehistory. Habitual practice not only confirms belief and understanding but can also conceal. At the end of this study into the ultimately unknowable past of prehistory, can we understand the definitive cause for building a stone circle any more than we can a cathedral? Whether the power of the bishop or the faith of the people, whether the emergence of chiefs and astronomer priests or the changing belief of late Neolithic people, this question will always remain.

NOTES

1 Introduction

1. A. Ritchie, *Exploring Scotland's Heritage: Orkney and Shetland*, p.11.
2. C. Levi-Strauss, *The Savage Mind*, p.264. In this and other books, Levi-Strauss did much to show that 'primitive' people are not inferior to us, but rather that they see the world differently. Hence the inverted commas around the word in modern usage. In what follows, the inverted commas disappear, but the use of the word primitive in this work should be read only as implying a different relationship to the world from our own, not an inferior one.
3. H. Brody, *The Other Side of Eden*, pp.197-198.
4. M. Russell, *Monuments of the Neolithic*, p.109.
5. S. Mithen, *The Prehistory of Mind*, pp.222 & p.256.
6. Brody, op. cit., p.220, and Levi-Strauss, op. cit., p.110.
7. W. Lethaby, *Architecture Mysticism and Myth*, p.5.
8. J. Thomas, *Time, Culture and Identity*, p.85.
9. C. Wickham-Jones, *Scotland's First Settlers*, p.65.
10. C Renfrew, *Archaeology & Language*, p.121.
11. Thomas, op. cit., pp.65-66.
12. T. Ingold, *Evolution and Social Life*, pp.298-322.
13. Thomas, op. cit., p.11.
14. *Ibid.*, pp.64-72.
15. R. Bradley, *The Social Foundations of Prehistoric Britain*, p.30.
16. Bradley, *Ibid.*, p.157.
17. Renfrew, op. cit., p.171-172.
18. *Ibid.*, pp.240-242.
19. *Ibid.*, pp.259-260.
20. *Ibid.*,. p.174.
21. Langer, op. cit.,
22. Brody, op. cit., p.152.
23. T. Neat, *The Summer Walkers; Travelling People & Pearl-Fishers in the Highlands of Scotland*, p.202.
24. . *The Encyclopedia of Religion*, vol. 3, p.149. H. Glassie, *Passing the time in Ballymenone*, pp.162-172.
25. J. Campbell, *The Flight of the Wild Gander*, p.21.
26. C. Tilley, *A Phenomenology of Landscape*, p.3.

2 House, form and culture

1. Jamal Ali, *The Encyclopedia of Vernacular Architecture*, vol. 1, p.593.
2. J. Megaw & D. Simpson (eds.), *Introduction to British Prehistory*, p.78.
3. Wickham-Jones, op. cit., pp.70-74.
4. R. Mercer, 'Cumulative Cairn Construction and Cultural Continuity', in N. Sharples & A. Sheridan (eds.), *Vessels for the Ancestors*, pp.49-61.
5. Brody, op. cit., p.305.
6. D. Hunt, *Early Farming Communities in Scotland; Aspects of Economy and Settlement 4500-1250 BC*, p.78.
7. Renfrew, op. cit., pp.128-149.
8. N. Sharples, 'Aspects of Regionalisation in the Scottish Neolithic', in N. Sharples & A. Sheridan (eds) op. cit., pp.327-328.
9. B. Cunliffe, *Facing the Ocean*, p.142.
10. H. Brody, op. cit., pp.158-9, and M. Russell, op. cit., p.170.
11. Renfrew, op. cit., p.149.
12. B. Cunliffe (ed.), *The Oxford Illustrated Prehistory of Europe*, pp.138-142.
13. S. Buteux, 'Settlements at Skaill, Deerness Orkney', *British Archaeological Review No. 260*, pp.10-11.
14. A. Ritchie, 'The First Settlers', in C. Renfrew (ed.), *The Prehistory of Orkney* p.37 & p.53.
15. M. Eliade, *The Sacred and the Profane*, pp.56-57.
16. *Ibid.*, pp.165-169.
17. P. Oliver (ed.), *Encyclopedia of Vernacular Architecture*, vol. 1, p.593.
18. Eliade, op. cit., p.52.
19. *Ibid.*, p.167.
20. A. Ritchie, op. cit., p.42. The following description draws extensively upon this as well as the report of the earlier excavation; W. Trail and W. Kirkness, 'Hower, a prehistoric structure on Papa Westray, Orkney', in *Proceedings of the Society of Antiquaries in Scotland*, vol. 71 (1936-37), pp.309-321.
21. J. Hedges, *The Tomb of the Eagles*, p.230.
22. Ritchie, op. cit., pp.39-41.
23. I. Hodder, *The Domestication of Europe*, pp.114-148.
24. A. Whittle, *Neolithic Europe; a Survey*, p.186. See also A. Whittle, 'Houses in context: Buildings as process', in T. Darvill & J. Thomas (eds), *Neolithic Houses in North-west Europe and Beyond*, p.25. See also J. Last, 'Neolithic Houses; a Central European Perspective' in the same volume, pp.27-40.
25. A. Whittle, 'Houses in Context', op. cit., p.31-33.
26. J. Thomas, 'Neolithic Houses in Mainland Britain & Ireland; a Sceptical View', in Darvill & Thomas, op. cit., pp.2-4.
27. B. Orme, *Anthropology for Archaeologists*, pp.60-68.
28. M. Parker-Pearson & C. Richards (eds), *Architecture and Order*, p.12.
29. Cunliffe, op. cit., pp.137-161.
30. C. Scarre, *Ancient France*, p.227.
31. L. Masters, 'Chambered Tombs and Non-Megalithic Barrows in Britain, in C. Renfrew, *Megalithic Monuments of Western Europe*, p.110.
32. G. Barclay, *Farmers, Tombs and Temples*, p.15.
33. I. Armit, 'The Hebridean Neolithic', in N. Sharples & A. Sheridan (eds), op. cit., p.315.
34. *Ibid.*, p.311.
35. D. Simpson, 'The Ballygalley House, Co. Antrim', in T. Darvill & J. Thomas (eds), op. cit., p.132.
36. E. Grogan, 'Neolithic House in Ireland', in T. Darvill & J. Thomas (eds), op. cit., p.43.
37. *Ibid.*, pp.44-45.
38. T. Darvill, 'Neolithic Buildings in England, Wales and the Isle of Man', in *Ibid.*, p.86.
39. B. Cunliffe, *Facing the Ocean*, pp.65-67.
40. E.G. Bowen, *Britain and the Western Seaways*, pp.36-67.
41. Personal communications from Caroline Wickham-Jones and Nick Card.
42. Bowen, op. cit., p.36.
43. *Ibid.* Scandinavian rock-carvings also support the suggestion of such a boat.
44. Aldo van Eyck, 'The Interior of Time', in G. Baird & C. Jencks (eds), *Meaning in Architecture*, p.183.
45. P. Parin, in *Ibid.*, p.179.
46. See J. Rykwert, 'Semper and the Conception of Style' in his *The Necessity of Artifice*, pp.123-125. See also W. Ungless, 'Theory into Practice', *Architecture Today 123, Nov. 2001*, pp.43-48.
47. G. Bachelard, *The Poetics of Space*, p.xxxiv.
48. Cited in Cunliffe, op. cit., p.68.
49. Bachelard, op. cit., pp.237-238.
50. R. Bradley, *Monuments of the Neolithic*.
51. J. Barber, 'Megalithic Architecture', in N. Sharples & A. Sheridan, (eds) op. cit., pp.24-25 & 29-30.
52. E. Partridge, *Origins: a Short Etymological Dictionary of Modern English*, p.25.
53. A. Ereira, *The Heart of the World*, pp.94-95.
54. *Ibid.*, pp.175-180.
55. *The Encyclopedia of Religion*, vol. 3, p.537.
56. Clarke & Sharples, op. cit., pp.58-60.
57. Sharples, op. cit., pp.324-325.
58. D. Frazer, *Land and Society in Neolithic Orkney*, p.434.
59. A. Whittle, *Neolithic Europe*, p.231.
60. A. Ritchie, *Prehistoric Orkney*, p.37.
61. Clarke & Sharples, op. cit., p.71.
62. Parker-Pearson &. Richards, op. cit., p.40.
63. A. Shepherd, 'Skara Brae; Expressing Identity in a Neolithic Community', in A. Ritchie (ed.), *Neolithic Orkney in its European Context*, pp.146-155.
64. Hedges, op. cit., p.176.
65. *Ibid.*, p.187. He uses the 1992 census for this information.
66. *Ibid.*, p.107.
67. Darvill, op. cit., pp.85-92.
68. P. Oliver (ed.), *The Encyclopedia of Vernacular Architecture*, p.1287.
69. V. Childe & W. Grant, 'Stone Age settlement at the Braes of Rinyo', in *Proceedings of the Society of Antiquaries of Scotland*, vol. 81, 1946/47, p.17.
70. Eliade, op. cit., p.452.
71. M. Eliade, *Patterns in Comparative Religion*, p.242.
72. *Ibid.*, p.254.
73. Parker-Pearson & Richards, op. cit., p.44.
74. *Ibid.*, p.42.
75. Oliver, op. cit., p.602. The tribes referred to are the Massa (Cameroon), the Moba & Koukomba (Togo), the Bisa, the Mossi, the Kasena, the Nakami and the Kasari (Burkina Faso).
76. Thomas, op. cit., p.30.
77. C. Norberg-Schulz, *Existence, Space and Architecture*, pp.37-38.
78. *Ibid.*, p.9.
79. M. Merlau-Ponty, *The Phenomenology of Perception*, pp.98-148.
80. Norberg-Schulz, op. cit.,
81. Hodder, op. cit., p.45 & p.114.
82. Thomas, op. cit., p.181.
83. Oliver, op. cit, p.591.
84. J. Rykwert, *The Idea of a Town*.
85. Oliver, op. cit., p.592. See also J. Summerson, *Heavenly Mansions* for an interpretation of Gothic architecture as a form of 'housing' in the form of repeated *aedicules*.
86. C. Richards, 'The late Neolithic settlement complex at Barnhouse Farm, Stenness', in C. Renfrew (ed.), op. cit., p.306.
87. A. MacSween, 'Orcadian Grooved Ware', in N. Sharples & A. Sheridan, op. cit., pp.262-263.
88. M. Edmonds, 'Their Use is Wholly Unknown', in *Ibid.*, pp.185-191.

89. Thomas, op. cit., p.100.
90. Richards, op. cit., p.308.
91. *Ibid.*
92. *Ibid.*
93. C. Malone, *The Neolithic in Britain and Ireland*, p.61.
94. C. Richards, 'Monumental Choreography' in C. Tilley (ed.) *Interpretative Archaeology*, p.167.
95. J. Richards, 'The late Neolithic settlement at Barnhouse', op. cit., pp.313-314.
96. *Ibid.*, p.314.
97. Sharples, op. cit., p.324-325
98. N. Sharples & A. Sheridan, 'Introduction; the state of Neolithic studies in Scotland', in N. Sharples & A. Sheridan (eds.) op. cit., p.9.

3   A house for the dead

1. A. Henshall, *The Chambered Cairns of Scotland* vol. 1, p.61.
2. *Ibid.*
3. Malone, op. cit., p.104.
4. Scarre, op. cit., p.2.
5. Thomas, op. cit., p.101 and B. Cunliffe, *At the Oceans Edge.*, p.143.
6. Scarre, op. cit., p.71.
7. M. Eliade, *Patterns in Comparative Religion*, p.361.
8. *Ibid.*, p.156.
9. R. Bradley, *The Past in Prehistoric Societies*, pp.28-29.
10. Cunliffe, op. cit., p.151.
11. C. Scarre, *Ancient France*, p.314.
12. Masters, op. cit., p.110.
13. C. Renfrew, *Before Civilisation*, pp.149-159.
14. M. Shanks & C. Tilley 'Ideology, Symbolic Power and Ritual Communication', in I. Hodder (ed.), *Burial, Houses, Women and Men in the European Neolithic*, p.150.
15. M. Bloch and J. Parry, *Death and the Regeneration of Life*, p.12 or p.15.
16. Eliade, op. cit., pp.21-32.
17. M. Eliade, *The Myth of the Eternal Return*, p.4.
18. *Ibid.*, p.12.
19. M. Eliade. *The Sacred and the Profane*, p.11. He explains its etymology as coming from the Greek work meaning 'bring to light, make known' – a hierophant was an official expounder of ancient mysteries or religious ceremonies.
20. C. Kereyni, *The Gods of the Greeks*, pp.226-229.
21. *Ibid.*, p.228.
22. *Ibid.* p.229.
23. Cited, M. Eliade, *Patterns in Comparative Religion*, p.234.
24. J. Harrison, *Themis; a Study in the Social Origins of Greek Religion*, p.295 & p.419.
25. Eliade, op. cit., pp.376-378.
26. *Ibid.*, p.388.
27. M. Eliade, *Shamanism*, p.488-489.

28. M. Eliade, *Patterns in Comparative Religion*, p.217-219.
29. J. Davidson & A. Henshall, *The Chambered Cairns of Orkney*, p 77. Bigland Long itself is an unusual pear-shaped cairn with two chambers, which will be discussed later. All the facts concerning the chambered cairns in the following discussion are drawn from this work.
30. Bloch & Parry, op. cit., p.33.
31. R.C. Jones, 'Life after Death: Material Culture & Social Change in Neolithic Orkney', in A. Ritchie (ed.) *Neolithic Orkney in its European Context*, p.134.
32. D. Fraser, *Land and Society in Neolithic Orkney*, 1983, cited Davidson & Henshall, op. cit., p.85.
33. Cited in *Ibid.*, p.93.
34. M. Eliade, *Patterns in Comparative Religion*, pp.188-189.
35. *Ibid.*, p.212.
36. Davidson & Henshall, op. cit., p.52.
37. Eliade, op. cit, p.205.
38. Hedges, op. cit,. p.47.
39. C. Chaundler, *Everyman's Book of Ancient Customs*, p.166.
40. *Ibid.*, pp.167-168.
41. Eliade, op., cit., pp.78-79.
42. Hedges, op. cit.,
43. H. Ellis Davidson, *The Lost Beliefs of Northern Europe*, p.33.
44. *Ibid.*, pp.33-34
45. J. Hedges, op. cit., p.134.
46. *Ibid.*, p.141-142.
47. Bloch & Parry, op. cit., p.11.
48. *Ibid.*, p.34
49. Shanks & Tilley, op. cit., p.145.
50. M. Eliade, *Shamanism.*, p.159-161. Ezekiel 37:1-8
51. *Ibid.*
52. Ellis Davidson, op. cit., p.194.
53. *Ibid.*, pp.105-108.
54. Eliade, op. cit., p.163.
55. J. Mellaart, *Çatal Hüyük*, pp.166, 188 & 204.
56. M. Green, *The Gods of the Celts*, pp.27-28.
57. A. Ross, *Pagan Celtic Britain*, p.55.
58. *Ibid.*, pp.255-257.
59. *Ibid.*, p.57.
60. *Ibid.*, p.54.
61. Eliade, op. cit., p.98.
62. *The Encyclopedia of Religion*, vol. 2, p.225.
63. Ibid p.276.
64. Eliade, op. cit., p.210.
65. *Ibid.*, p.210-211.
66. M. Eliade, *Patterns in Comparative Religion*, p.171. (see also pp.253-254).
67. Harrison, op. cit., pp.315-316.
68. Eliade, op. cit., p.240.
69. *The Encyclopedia of Religion*, vol. 15, p.182.
70. Eliade, op. cit., p.114.
71. Bigland Round is unusual in that the portal stones that define the entrance to the chamber

coincide with the inner wall, hence its chamber is more off centre than the others.
72. Davidson & Henshall , op. cit., p.77.
73. C. Richards. 'Doorways into Another World,' in N. Sharples and A. Sheridan (eds.), op. cit., pp.71-74.
74. Davidson & Henshall, op. cit., p.85.
75. C. Scarre, *Monuments and Landscape*, p.5.
76. *The Encyclopaedia of Religion*, vol. 3, p.8.
77. Green, op. cit., pp.12-32.
78. A. Burl, *The Stone Circles of Britain*, p.128.
79. J. Frazer, *The Golden Bough*, cited Burl, *Ibid.*
80. Butler, *Lives of the Saints*, p.225. 'Patrick and Brigid – the columns on which all Ireland rested'.
81. A. Ross, *Druids, Gods and Heroes from Celtic Mythology*, 1986, p.99.
82. *Ibid.*, p.358.
83. M. Dames, *Mythic Ireland*, p.247.
84. *Ibid.*, p.209.
85. *Ibid.*, p.247.
86. A. Watts, *Myth and Ritual in Christianity*, p.127.
87. Ellis Davidson, op. cit., p.154.
88. Davidson & Henshall, op. cit., pp.41-43.
89. *Ibid.* pp.112-142.
90. C. Richards, 'Monumental Choreography', in C. Tilley (ed.) op. cit., p.149-150.
91. Renfrew, op. cit., pp.213-218.
92. Hedges, op. cit., p.121.
93. Eliade, *Shamanism*, p.245.
94. *Ibid.*, p.167.
95. C. Renfrew (ed.), *The Prehistory of Orkney*, p.308 and p.253.
96. A. Henshall, 'The Chambered Cairns', in C Renfrew (ed.), *Ibid.*, p.113.
97. G. Eogan, 'Scottish and Irish Passage Tombs; some Comparisons and Contrasts' in Sharples & Sheridan, op. cit., p.122.
98. R. Bradley, *The Significance of Monuments*, p.105
99. M. Eliade, *Images and Symbols*, p.143.
100. Davidson & Henshall, op. cit., p.46-51.
101. Ross, op. cit., p.242.
102. Green, op. cit., pp.33-34.
103. Ross, op. cit., p.233.
104. *Ibid.*, p.41.
105. Dames, op. cit., p.202.
106. Green., op. cit., p.73.
107. Ross, op. cit., p.209.
108. Dames, op. cit., p.237.
109. *Ibid.*, pp.159-162.
110. Cited Dames, *ibid.*, p.11.

4   Lines on the Landscape

1. A. Burl, *The Stone Circles of Britain, Ireland and Brittany*, p.22.
2. A. Scarre, *Monuments and Landscape in Atlantic Europe*, p.6.
3. R. Williams, *The Country and the City*, p.170.
4. B. Bender, *Stonehenge*, p.25.
5. C. Tilley. *A Phenomenology of Landscape*, p.10.
6. A. Burl, *Rites of the Gods*, p.38.
7. Tilley, op. cit., p.24.
8. A. Burl, *The Stone Circles of Britain, Ireland and Brittany*, pp.29-30.
9. *Ibid.*, pp.78-82.
10. *Ibid.*, p.38.
11. *Ibid.*, pp.89-93.
12. *Ibid.*, p.201.
13. Scarre, op. cit., p.7.
14. M. Eliade, *Patterns in Comparative Religion*, p.191.
15. V. Cummings, 'All Cultural Things', in Scarre, op. cit., p.109.
16. Burl, op. cit., p.62.
17. Site information board.
18. Richards, op. cit.,
19. G Ritchie., op. cit., p.130.
20. M. Edmonds, 'Interpreting Causeway Enclosures', in C. Tilley (ed.), op. cit., pp.113-114.
21. Harrison, op. cit., pp.63-64.
22. C. Tilley, op. cit., p.58.
23. Burl, op. cit., pp.50-66.
24. *Ibid.*, pp.32-37.
25. Tilley, op cit., p.204.
26. C. Renfrew, *Investigations in Orkney*, pp.31-38.
27. Thomas, *Rethinking the Neolithic*, p.29.
28. G. Ritchie, op. cit., pp.16-18.
29. *Ibid.*
30. A.Burl, *The Stonehenge People*, p.49.
31. Cited *Ibid.*, p.53.
32. *Ibid.*
33. *Ibid.*, p.65.
34. J.G. Scott,' Mortuary Structures and Megaliths', in N. Sharples & A Sheridan (eds.) op. cit., pp.104-119.
35. *Ibid.*, p.114.
36. M. Parker-Pearson and Ramilisonia, 'Stonehenge for the Ancestors', p.311.
37. G. Ritchie, op. cit., pp.12-13 and p.47
38. G. Ritchie, op. cit.,
39. J. Harrison, *Ancient Art and Ritual*, p.103.
40. Harrison, *Themis*, p.273.
41. C. Richards. This is the subtitle of his essay 'Monuments as Landscape'.
42. R. Bradley, *The Archaeology of Natural Places*, pp.11-12.
43. Cited J. Rykwert, *The Idea of a Town*, p.117.
44. F.M. Cornford, *From Religion to Philosophy*, p.53.
45. Rykwert, op. cit., pp.58-59.
46. *Ibid.*, p.73.
47. Green. op. cit., p.133.
48. Ross, op. cit., p.25.

49. Green, op. cit., p.135.
50. Ibid p.133
51. *Ibid.*, p.9. Born in a manger, the infant Christ was visited and seen first by animals.
52. Rykwert, op. cit., p.214.
53. Plutarch, *Romans Questions*, cited *Ibid.*, p.29.
54. Harrison, *Ancient Art and Ritual*, op. cit., p.1.
55. Rykwert, op. cit., p.214.
56. *Ibid.*
57. Kereyni, op. cit., p.191.
58. W. O'Brien, 'Megaliths in a Mythologised Landscape', in Scarre, op. cit., p.169
59. A. Burl, *The Stone Circles of Britain, Ireland and Brittany*, p.40.
60. M. Eliade, *Patterns in Comparative Religion*, p.150.
61. *Ibid.*, p.125.
62. *Ibid.*, pp.38–40.
63. *Ibid.*
64. *Ibid.*, p.110.
65. Harrison, *Themis*, p.91.
66. *Ibid.*, pp.137-143. Certainly this symbolism did become utilised in Egypt, where the sun god absorbed other sky divinities and with whom the earthly sovereign became identified.In death the pharaoh was guided by Ra to the Field of Offerings or Field of Rest.
67. Kereyni, op. cit., p.191.
68. Eliade, op. cit., p.143.
69. *Ibid.*, p.149.
70. *The Encyclopedia of Religion* vol. 3, p.505.
71. Bradley, op. cit., p.32.
72. Eliade, op. cit., pp.135-138.
73. Harrison, op. cit., pp.33-36.
74. *The Encyclopedia of Religion* vol. 3, p.508.
75. Burl, *Rites of the Gods*, p.110.
76. J. Hawkes, *A Land*, p.101.
77. J. Campbell, *The Way of the Animal Power*, p.211. Citing Thomas Harriot, *A Brief & True Report of the New Found Land of Virginia*.
78. *Ibid.*, p.224-225. Among the strange events represented are a warrior fixed to the tree by thongs and skewers passed through his chest and a horned dancer with four buffalo skulls skewered to his back.
79. *Ibid.* Other Indian dances also depict clearly a sunrise movement; the Last Race of the Mandan Okipa Festival and the Ojibwa (or Chippewa) snowshoe dance of the northern Algonquian tribes.
80. *Ibid.*, p.232.
81. A. Whittle. 'Long conversations; concerning time, descent and place in the world', in C. Scarre, op. cit., p.196.
82. See Marwick in the appendix to G.Ritchie, op. cit.
83. Ellis Davidson, op. cit., p.48 and pp.93-94.

84. Harrison, *Themis*, p.24.
85. Thomas, op. cit., p.184.
86. *The Encyclopedia of Religion* vol. 2, p.122.
87. F. Nietzsche, *The Birth of Tragedy*, p.
88. Green, op. cit., p.70.
89. *The Encyclopedia of Religion* vol. 15, p.386.
90. Bradley, op. cit., p.80.
91. *Ibid.*, p.122.
92. C. Jung, *Archetypes of the Collective Unconscious*, p.5.
93. *Ibid.*, p.10.
94. Burl, *The Stonehenge People*, p.71.
95. Burl, *The Stone Circles of Britain, Ireland and Brittany*, p.203.
96. Eliade. op. cit., p.154.
97. E. Cassirer, *Language and Myth*, p.97.
98. Eliade, op. cit., pp.162-171.
99. *Ibid.*, p.179.
100. Renfrew, *Investigations in Orkney*, pp.39-43.
101. Burl, op. cit., p.211.
102. A. Thom, *Megalithic Lunar Observatories*, p.123.
103. C. Ruggles, *Astronomy in Prehistoric Britain and Ireland*, p.148.
104. Hodder, *The Domestication of Europe*, p.45.
105. *Ibid.*, p.138.
106. *Ibid.*, p.177.
107. *Ibid.*, pp.255-257.
108. R. Bradley, 'The Land, the Sky and Scottish Stone Circles', in Scarre, op. cit., p.137.
109. Thomas, op. cit., p.47.
110. Orme, op. cit., p.254.
111. P. Radin, *Primitive Religion*, p.25.
112. *Ibid.*, p.41.
113. *Ibid.*, p.26.
114. *Ibid.*, p.196.
115. *Ibid.*, p.45, footnote 4.
116. *The Encyclopedia of Religion* vol. 9, p.85.
117. Orme, op. cit., p.218.
118. Radin, op. cit., p.240.
119. *Ibid.*, p.246. It is interesting, although of no supporting value, to recall that Inigo Jones believed that, of all the earlier British settlers, only the Romans could have erected Stonehenge. He went on to say that it was probably a temple dedicated to the god Coelus or Uranus (or Heaven, son or husband of Gaia – Earth – in the early pantheon of Greek gods). Jones said that the Romans 'counted it a heinous matter to see those gods confined under a roof, whose doing good consisted in being abroad'. R. Legg, *Stonehenge Antiquities*, p.65.
120. C. Renfrew. 'The Archaeology of Religion', in C. Renfrew & C. Zubrow, *The Ancient Mind*, p.51-2.
121. E. Cassirer, *The Philosophy of Symbolic Forms* vol. 2, p.155.

122. *Ibid.*, pp.158-160.
123. *Ibid.*, p.221.
124. *Ibid.*, p.223.
125. Parker-Pearson and Ramilisonia, op. cit., p.322.
126. Radin, op. cit., p.65.

5 Mythical thinking

1. Eliade, *Patterns in Comparative Religion*, p.xi.
2. M. Eliade, *No Souvenirs; Journals 1957-1969*, p.xii.
3. Renfrew & Zubrow, op. cit., p.xiii.
4. C. Renfrew, 'Towards a Cognitive Archaeology', in *Ibid.*, pp.4-6.
5. *Ibid.*, p.5.
6. Eliade, *The Myth of the Eternal Return*, pp.xiii-xiv.
7. *Ibid.*, p.xiv.
8. Eliade, *Patterns in Comparative Religion*, p.242.
9. Eliade, *The Myth of the Eternal Return*, p.11.
10. Idealists he mentions include Hegel, Croce, Collingwood, Levi-Strauss, Geerz and Ricouer alongside which, he says, align post-processual archaeologists such as Hodder, Shanks and Tilley. Materialist predecessors to the processual approach he lists as Darwin, Marx, Popper and Gellner. Renefrew & Zubrow op. cit., p.4.
11. *Ibid.*
12. Eliade, *The Sacred and the Profane*, p.165.
13. Renfrew, op. cit., pp.6-7.
14. Eliade, op. cit., p.439.
15. *Ibid.* p.455.
16. T. Ingold, *Companion Encyclopedia of Anthropology*, p.332.
17. Renfrew, op. cit., p.6.
18. *Ibid.*, p.5.
19. Levi-Strauss, *The Savage Mind*, pp.3-9.
20. *Ibid.*, the title of Chapter 1.
21. *Ibid.*, p.14.
22. *Ibid.*, pp.16-18.
23. *Ibid.*, p.9.
24. *Ibid.*, pp.263-264.
25. *Ibid.*, p.75.
26. E. Leach, *Levi Strauss*, p.84.
27. J. Krois, *Cassirer; Symbolic Forms and History*, p.79.
28. Cassirer, *Language and Myth*, p.44.
29. E. Cassirer, *The Philosophy of Symbolic Forms* vol. 1, pp.278-279.
30. *Ibid.*, p.280.
31. Cassirer *The Philosophy of Symbolic Forms* vol. 2, p.1.
32. *Ibid.*, p.130.
33. *Ibid.*, p.172.
34. *Ibid.*, p.197.
35. *Ibid.*, p.45.
36. *Ibid.*, p.64.
37. Cassirer, *Language & Myth*, p.90.

38. Cassirer, *The Philosophy of Symbolic Forms* vol. 2, p.59.
39. *Ibid.*, pp.46-47.
40. *Ibid.*, pp.202-203. He is quoting from H.K. Usener, *Gotternamen*. Eliade, a Romanian, considers that aspects of 'archaic mentality' persisted in the substratum of eastern European peasant cultures beneath the layers of Greek, Roman, Byzantine, and Judeo-Christian beliefs.
41. Cassirer, *Language and Myth*, p.42.
42. Cassirer, *The Philosophy of Symbolic Forms*, vol. 2, p.201.
43. *Ibid.*
44. Cassirer, *Language and Myth*, pp.63-64.
45. *Ibid.*, p.66, Cassirer is citing Söderblow, *Das Werden des Gottesglaubenos Untersuchingen über die Anfänge der Religion*, p.95.
46. *Ibid.*, p.68. Cassirer is citing McGee, *The Siouan Indians, 15th annual report of the Bureau of Ethnology* (Smithsonian Institute).
47. A. Whittle, in Scarre, op. cit., p.195.
48. Cassirer, op. cit., p.71.
49. *Ibid.*, p.65.
50. *Ibid.*, p.66-67.
51. Cassirer, *The Philosophy of Symbolic Forms*, vol. 2, p.62.
52. *Ibid.*, p.95.
53. Harrison, *Ancient Art and Ritual*, p.16.
54. Brody, op. cit., p.247.
55. Levi-Strauss, op. cit., p.263.
56. *Ibid.*, p.127.
57. *Ibid.*, p.128. Although Levi-Strauss does not discuss why the first buffalo were considered to be 'all bone', there would seem to be a strong link to our earlier discussion on stone and bone. If bone was in some way the vehicle for life's essence as it passed from life to death, from present to past, then given the way savage thought can collapse the diachronic process of time into synchrony, it is quite possible that the past could become the present through the agency of bone.
58. *Ibid.*, pp.220-222.
59. J. Macquarrie, *Existentialism*, pp.102-105.
60. N. Berdyaev, *The Meaning of the Creative Act*, cited *Ibid.*, p.106.
61. *The Encyclopedia of Religion* vol. 12, p.511.
62. I. Hodder, op.ii cit., p.130.
63. Levi-Strauss, op. cit., p.xi.
64. *The Encyclopedia of Religion* vol. 14, p.233.
65. Whittle, op. cit., p.196.
66. Richards, 'Monumental Choreography' in C. Tilley, *Interpretative Archaeology*, p.167.
67. *Ibid.*, pp.172-175.

BIBLIOGRAPHY

Armit, I., The Hebridean Neolithic, in Sharples, N., & Sheridan, A., (eds), *Vessels for the Ancestors* 307-321

Armit, I., *Scotland's Hidden History,* Tempus/Historic Scotland, Stroud, 1998.

Baird, G. & Jencks, C. (eds), *Meaning in Architecture,* The Cresset Press, London, 1969.

Barber, J., 'Megalithic Architecture', in Sharples, N., & Sheridan, A., (eds), *Vessels for the Ancestors,* 13-32.

Barclay, G., 'Are the Clava "Passage Graves" Really Passage Graves?', in Sharples, N., & Sheridan, A., (eds), *Vessels for the Ancestors,* 77-82.

Barclay, G., 'Neolithic buildings in Scotland', in Darvill,T ., & Thomas, J., (eds), *Neolithic Houses in Northwest Europe and Beyond,* 61-76.

Barclay, G., *Farmers, Temples and Tombs; Scotland in the Neolithic and Early Bronze Age,* Canongate Books/Historic Scotland, Edinburgh, 1998.

Barrett, J., 'Defining Domestic Space in the Bronze Age of Southern Britain', in Parker Pearson, M., & Richards, C., (eds), *Architecture & Order,* 87-97.

Bender, B., *Stonehenge; making space,* Berg, Oxford, 1998.

Black, G.F., *County Folklore; Orkney & Shetland Islands,* David Nutt, London, 1903.

Bloch, M., & Parry, J., *Death and the regeneration of life,* Cambridge University Press, Cambridge, 1982.

Bourdieu, P., *Outline of a Theory of Pratice,* Cambridge University Press, Cambridge, 1977.

Bowen, E.G., *Britain and the Western Seaways, ,* Thames and Hudson, London, 1972.

Bradley, R., *An Archaeology of Natural Places,* Routledge, London & New York, 2000.

Bradley, R., 'Excavations at Clava'. *Current Archaeology, Vol. Xiii No. 4, June 1996, 148,* 136-142.

Bradley, R., 'The Land, the Sky and the Scottish stone circle', in Scarre, C., *Monuments and Landscape in Atlantic Europe,* 122-138.

Bradley, R., *The Significance of Monuments,* Routledge, London & New York, 1998.

Bradley, R., *The social foundations of prehistoric Britain,* Longman, London & New York, 1984.

Brody, H., *The Other Side of Eden,* Faber and Faber, London, 2001.

Burl, A., By the Light of the Cinerary moon, in Ruggles, C., & Whittle, A., (eds), *Astronomy and Society in Britain during the Period 4000-1500 BC, British Archaeological Reports, British series, 88, 1981.*

Burl, A., *From Carnac to Callanish; The Prehistoric Stone rows and avenues of Britain, Ireland and Brittany,* Yale University Press, New Haven, 1993.

Burl, A., *Prehistoric Ritual and Astronomy,* Shire, Aylesbury, 1983.

Burl, A., *Rites of the Gods,* J.M. Dent & Sons, London, 1981.

Burl, A., *The Stonehenge People,* .M. Dent & Sons, London and Melbourne, 1994.

Burl, A., *The Stone Circles of Britain, Ireland and Brittany,* Yale University Press, New Haven, 2000.

Burl, A., *The Stone Circles of the British Isles,* Yale University Press, New Haven, 1976.

Butler's Lives of the Saints, Burns & Oates, London, 1956.

Campbell, J., *The Flight of the Wild Gander,* Harper Collins. New York, 1990.

Campbell, J., *The Hero with a Thousand Faces,* Princeton University Press, Princeton, 1949.

Campbell, J., *The Masks of God: Primitive Mythology,* Penguin, London, 1976.

Cassirer, E., *An Essay on Man,* Yale University Press, New Haven, 1972.

Cassirer, E., *Language and Myth,* Dover, New York, 1953.

Cassirer, E., *The Philosophy of Symbolic Forms, Vol. 1,* Yale University Press, New Haven, 1953.

Cassirer, E. ,*The Philosophy of Symbolic Forms, Vol. 2,* Yale University Press, New Haven, 1955.

Champion, C., *Prehistoric Europe,* Academic Press, London, 1984.

Childe, V.G., & Grant, W.G., 'Stone-Age Settlement at the Braes of Rinyo, Rousay, Orkney', *Proceedings of the Society of Antiquarians of Scotland, Vol.73, 1938/3,* 6-31.

Childe, V.G., & Grant, W.G., 'Stone-Age Settlement at the Braes of Rinyo, Rousay, Orkney', *Proceedings of the Society of Antiquarians of Scotland, Vol.81, 1947,* 16-42.

Cirlot, J. E., *A Dictionary of Symbols,* Rouledge & Kegan Paul, London, 1962.

Clarke, A., 'Artefacts of Coarse Stone from Neolithic Orkney', in Sharples, N., & Sheridan, A., (eds), *Vessels for the Ancestors,* pp. 244-258.

Clarke, D.V., 'Settlements & Subsistence' in C. Renfrew (ed.) *The Prehistory of Orkney,* pp 54-82.

Colvin, H., *Architecture and the After-Life,* Yale University Press, New Haven, 1991.

Cooney, G., 'Body Politics and Grave Messages: Irish Neolithic Mortuary Practices', in Sharples, N., & Sheridan, A., (eds), *Vessels for the Ancestors,* 128-142.

Cornford, F.M., *From Religion to Philosophy,* Princeton University Press, Princeton, 1991.

Cunliffe, B., *Facing the Ocean; the Atlantic and its People 8000 BC-AD 1500,* Oxford University Press, Oxford, 2001.

Cunliffe, B., (ed.), *The Oxford Illustrated Prehistory of Europe,* Oxford University Press, Oxford, 1994.

Dames, M., *Mythic Ireland,* Thames and Hudson, London, 1992.

Daniel, G., & Renfrew, C., *The Idea of Prehistory,* Edinburgh University Press, Edinburgh, 1988.

Darvill, T., 'Neolithic houses in England, Wales and the Isle of Man', in Darvill,T., & Thomas,J., (eds), *Neolithic Houses in Northwest Europe and Beyond,* 77-112.

Darvill, T., *Prehistoric Britain,* B.T. Batsford, London, 1987.

Darvill, T., & Thomas J., (eds), *Neolithic Houses in Northwest Europe and Beyond,* Oxbow Monographs, Oxford, 1996.

Davidson, DA., & Jones R.L., 'The Environment of Orkney', in Renfrew, C., (ed.), *The Prehistory of Orkney* 10-35.

Davidson, H.R. Ellis, *Gods and Myths of Northern Europe* Penguin, London, 1964.

Davidson, Hilda Ellis, *The Lost Beliefs of Northern Europe,* Routledge, London & New York, 1993.

Davidson, J.L., & Henshall, A.S., *The Chambered Cairns of Caithness,* Edinburgh University Press, Edinburgh, 1991.

Davidson, J.L., & Henshall, A.S., *The Chambered Cairns of Orkney,* Edinburgh University Press, Edinburgh, 1989.

Dennison, W.T., *Orkney Folklore and Sea Legends,* Orkney Press, 1995.

de Santillana, G., & von Dechend, *Hamlet's Mill; an essay on myth and the frame of time,* David R. Godine, Boston, 1977.

Douglas, M., *Natural Symbols; Explorations in Cosmology, ,* Routledge, London & New York, 1996.

Downes,J., & Richards, C., 'Excavating the Neolithic & early Bronze Age of Orkney', in Ritchie, A (ed.), *Neolithic Orkney in its European Context,* 159-168.

Edmonds, M., 'Their use is Wholly Unknown', in Sharples, N., & Sheridan, A., (eds), *Vessels for the Ancestors* 179-193.

Eliade, M., *Autobiography Volume 1; 1907-1937; Journey East, Journey West,* University of Chicago, Press, Chicago, 1981.

Eliade, M., *Autobiography Volume2, 1937-1960; Exile's Odyssey,* University of Chicago Press, Chicago, 1988.

Eliade, M., *A History of Religious Ideas, Volume 1,* University of Chicago Press, Chicago, 1978.

Eliade, M., *Images and Symbols; Studies in Religious Symbolism,* Princeton University Press, Princeton, 1991.

Eliade, M., *Myth and Reality,* Harper Row, New York, 1975.

Eliade, M., *The Myth of the Eternal Return or, Cosmos and History,* Princeton University Press, Princeton, 1971.

Eliade, M., *Occultism, Witchcraft and Cultural Fashions,* University of Chicago Press, Chicago, 1976.

Eliade, M. *Patterns in Comparative Religion,* Sheed and Ward, London, 1958.

Eliade, M., *The Sacred and the Profane,* Harcourt Brace Jovanovich, New York, 1959.

Eliade, M., *Shamanism; Archaic techniques of ecstasy,* Arkana, London, 1989.

Eliade, M., (editor-in-chief) *The Encyclopaedia of Religion*

Eogan, G., *Knowth and the passage-tombs of Ireland,* Thames and Hudson, London, 1986.

Eogan, G., 'Scottish and Irish Passage Tombs: Some comparisons and con- trasts', in Sharples, N., & Sheridan, A., (eds), *Vessels for the Ancestors,* 120- 127.

Ereira, A., *From the Heart of the World,* Cape, London, 1990.

Evans-Pritchard, E.E., *Theories of Primitive Religion,* Oxford University Press, Oxford, 1965.

Foucault, M., *The Order of Things,* Tavistock Press, London, 1974.

Frankl, P., *Archaeology of the Mind,* Open Gate Press. London, 1990.

Fraser, D., *Land and Society in Neolithic Orkney,* British Archaeological Reports, British Series, no.117, Oxford, 1983.

Frazer, J.G., *The Golden Bough,* MacMillan & Co., London & Toronto, 1967.

Glassie, H., *Passing the Time in Balleymenone,* Indiana University Press, Bloomington, 1995.

Gould, S.J., *Times Arrow, Times Cycle,* Penguin, London, 1988.

Green, M., *The Gods of the Celts,* Alan Sutton, Gloucester, 1986.

Grogan, E., 'Neolithic Houses in Ireland', in Darvill,T., & Thomas,J., (eds), *Neolithic Houses in Northwest Europe and Beyond,* 41-60.

Hadingham, E., *Early Man and the Cosmos,* Heineman, London, 1983.

Harrison, J., *Ancient Art and Ritual,* Moonraker Press, Bradford-on –Avon, 1978.

Harrison, J., *Themis; A Study in the Social Origins of Greek Religion,* Merlin Press, London, 1963.

Hawkes, J., *Dawn of the Gods,* Sphere Books, London, 1972.

Hawkes, J., *A Land,* The Cresset Press, London, 1951.

Hawkes,J., *Man and the Sun,* , The Cresset Press, London, 1962.

Hawkes, J., *Man on Earth,* The Cresset Press, London, 1962.

Hedges, J.W., *Tomb of the Eagles,* John Murray, London, 1984

Heidegger, M., 'Building dwelling thinking', in *Poetry, Language, Thought,* Harper Row, New York, 1975.

Henshall, A., 'The Chambered Cairns', in Renfrew, C., (ed.), *The Prehistory of Orkney* 83-117.

Henshall, A., *The Chambered Tombs of Scotland,* (2 volumes), Edinburgh University Press, Edinburgh, 1963 and 1972.

.Hodder, I., 'Burial, houses, women and men in the European Neolithic', in Miller, D. & Tilley, C. (eds)., *Ideology,Power and Prehistory,* Cambridge University Press, Cambridge, 1984. 52-65.

Hodder, I., 'Archaeology and Meaning; the example of Neolithic Houses and Tombs', in Parker Pearson, M., & Richards C., (eds), *Architecture and Order,* 73-86.

Hodder, I., *The Domestication of Europe,* Blackwell, Oxford, 1990.

Hodder, I., *Reading the Past,* Cambridge University Press, Cambridge, 1986.

Hodder, I., *Symbolic and Structural Archaeology,* , Cambridge University Press, Cambridge, 1982.

Hood, S., *The Home of the Heroes,* Thames and Hudson, London, 1967.

Hugh-Jones, C., Houses in the Neolithic imagination, in Darvill, T., & Thomas, J., (eds), *Neolithic Houses in Northwest Europe and Beyond,* 185- 194.

Hunt, D., *Early Farming Communities in Scotland; Aspects of Economy and Settlement 4500-1250BC,* , British Archaeological Reports, British Series, no.159, Oxford, 1989.

Hunter, J.R., 'Pool, Sanday & a Sequence for the Orcadian Neolithic', in Ritchie, A.(ed.), *Neolithic Orkney in its European Context,* 117-126.

Hutton, R., *The Pagan Religions of the Ancient British Isles,* BCA, London, 1981.

Hutton, R., *The Stations of the Sun; A History of the Ritual Year in Britain,* Oxford University Press, Oxford, 1996.

Jones, A., Life after Death: Monuments, Material Culture & Social Change in Neolithic Orkney, in Ritchie, A.(ed.), *Neolithic Orkney in its European Context,* 127-138.

Jones, A., 'Where Eagles dare; landscape, animals and the Neoilthic of Orkney', in *Journal of Material Culture, 3 (3),* 301-324.

Jones, R.E. & Brown, B., 'Neolithic Pattern-making in Orkney: A New Look', in Ritchie, A.(ed.), *Neolithic Orkney in its European Context,* 169- 184.

Jones, S., & Richards, C., 'Neolithic Cultures in Orkney: Classification and Interpretation', in Ritchie, A.(ed.), *Neolithic Orkney in its European Context,* 101-106.

Joussaume, R., *Dolmens for the Dead; Megalith-Building throughout the World,* Guild Publishing, London, 1987.

Jung, C., *Man and his Symbols,* Aldus Books, London, 1964.

Jung, C., & Kereyni, C., *Science of Mythology,* Routledge, Kegan Paul, London, 1985.

Kereyni, C., *The Gods of the Greeks,* Thames and Hudson, London, 1974.

Kereyni, C., *The Heroes of the Greeks,* Thames and Hudson, London, 1959.

Kinnes, I., 'Balnagowan and After: The Context of Non-Megalithic mor- tuary Sites in Scotland', in Sharples, N., & Sheridan, A., (eds), *Vessels for the Ancestors,* 83-103.

Kirk, G.S., *The Nature of Greek Myths,* Penguin, London, 1974.

Krois, J.M., *Cassirer; Symbolic Forms and History,* Yale University Press, New Haven, 1987.

La Barre, W., *The Ghost Dance; Origins of Religion,* George Allen & Unwin, London, 1970.

Laporte, L., Joussaume, R., & Scarre, C., 'The Perception of Space & geometry: Megalithic Monuments of west-central France in their rela- tionship to the Landscape', in Scarre, C., *Monuments and Landscape in Atlantic Europe,* 73-100.

Last, J., 'Neolithic houses – a central European perspective', in Darvill,T., & Thomas,J., (eds), *Neolithic Houses in Northwest Europe and Beyond,* 27-40.

Leach, E., *Levi-Strauss,* Fontana, London, 1970.

Lethaby, W., *Architecture, Mysticism and Myth,* Solos Press, Dorset, 1994.

Levi-Strauss, C., *The Jealous Potter,* University of Chicago Press, Chicago, 1988.

Levi-Strauss, C., *The Savage Mind,* Oxford University Press, Oxford, 1972.

MacSween, A., 'Orcadian Grooved Ware', in Sharples, N., & Sheridan, A., (eds), *Vessels for the Ancestors* 259-271.

Malone, C., *Neolithic Britain and Ireland,* Tempus, Stroud, 2001.

Macquarrie, J., *Existentialism,* , Penguin, London, 1973.

Marwick, E., *The Folklore of Orkney and Shetland,* Berlinn/Canongate, Edinburgh, 2000.

Megaw, J.V.S., & Simpson, D.D.A., (eds), *Introduction to British Prehistory,* Leicester University Press, Leicester, 1979.

Mellaart, J., *Catal Huyuk,* Thames and Hudson, London, 1967.

Mellaart, J., *Earliest Civilisations of the Near East,* , Thames and Hudson, London, 1965.

Mercer, R., 'Cumulative Cairn Construction and Cultural Continuity in Caithness and Orkney', in Sharples, N., & Sheridan, A., (eds), *Vessels for the Ancestors,* 49-61.

Merlau-Ponty, M., *The Phenomenology of Perception,* Routledge, Kegan Paul, London, 1962.

Middleton, J., (ed.), *Gods and Rituals; Readings in Religious Beliefs and Practices,* The Natural History Press, New York, 1967.

Mithen, S., *The Prehistory of Mind,* Thames and Hudson, London, 1996.

Murray, O., *Early Greece,* Fontana Press, London, 1993.

Neat, T., *The Summer Walkers; Travelling People and Pearl-Fishers in the Highlands of Scotland,* Canongate, Edinburgh, 1996.

Nietzsche, F., *The Birth of Tragedy,* Dover, New York, 1995.

Norberg-Schulz, C., *Existence, Space and Architecture,* Studio Vista, London, 1971.

Norberg-Schulz, C., *Genius Loci; Towards a phenomenology of Architecture,* Academy Editions, London, 1980.

O'Brien, W., 'Megaliths in a Mythologised Landscape', in Scarre, C., *Monuments and Landscape in Atlantic Europe,* 155-174.

Oelschlaeger, M., *The Idea of Wilderness; From Prehistory to the Age of Ecology,* Yale University Press, New Haven, 1991.

O'Kelly, M.J., *Newgrange; Archaeology, Art and Legend,* Thames and Hudson, London, 1982.

Orme, B., *Anthropology for Archaeologists: an introduction,* Duckworth, London, 1981.

Ovid, *Metamorphoses,* Oxford University Press, Oxford, 1987.

Paget, R.F., *In the Footsteps of Orpheus; the discovery of the Ancient Greek Underworld,* Robert Hale, London, 1967.

Parker, H.W., *Greek Oracles,* Hutchinson University Library, London, 1967.

Parker Pearson, M., & Ramilisonina, 'Stonehenge for the Ancestors; the stones pass on the message', *Antiquity 72 (1998),* 308-326.

Parker Pearson, M., & Richards, C., (eds.), *Architecture and Order,* Routledge, London, 1994.

Radin. P., *Primitive Religion,* Dover, New York, 1957.

Radin, P., *The World of Primitive Man,* Abelard Schuman, London & New York, 1953.

Redfield, R., *the Primitive World and its Transformation,* Penguin, London, 1968.

Reid, M.L., *Prehistoric Houses in Britain,* Shire, Aylesbury, 1993.

Renfrew, C., *Archaeology and Language; the puzzle of Indo-European Origins,* Jonathan Cape, London, 1987.

Renfrew, C., 'The Auld Hoose Spaeks: Society and Life in Stone Age Orkney', in Ritchie, A.(ed.), *Neolithic Orkney in its European Context,* 1-22.

Renfrew, C., *Before Civilisation,* Penguin, London, 1978.

Renfrew, C., *Investigations in Orkney,* The Society of Antiquaries/Thames and Hudson, London, 1979.

Renfrew, C., (ed.), *The Megalithic Monuments of Western Europe,* Thames and Hudson, London, 1981.

Renfrew, C., (ed.), *The Prehistory of Orkney,* Edinburgh University Press, Edinburgh, 1990.

Renfrew, C., & Zubrow, E., *The Ancient Mind,* Cambridge University Press, Cambridge,

Richards, C., *A Choreography of Construction,* Forthcoming.

Richards, C., 'Doorways into Another World; the Orkney-Cromarty Chambered Cairns', in Sharples, N., & Sheridan, A., (eds), *Vessels for the Ancestors,* 62-76.

Richards, C., 'The late Neolithic settlement complex at Barnhouse Farm', in C. Renfrew (ed.) *The Prehistory of Orkney,* 305-316.

Richards, C., 'Monumental Choreography; Architecture and Spatial Representation in Late Neolithic Orkney', in Tilley, C., (ed.), *Interpretative Archaeology* 143-178.

Ritchi, A., 'Excavation of a Neolithic farmstead at Knap of Howar, Papa Westray, Orkney', *Proceedings of the Society of Antiquarians of Scotland, Vol13,* 40-121.

Ritchie, A.(ed.), *Neolithic Orkney in its European Context,* MacDonald Institute Monograph, Cambridge University Press, Cambridge, 2000.

Ritchie, A., *Prehistoric Orkney,* B.T. Batsford/Historic Scotland, London, 1995.

Ritchie, A., & Ritchie, G., *The Ancient Monuments of Orkney,* HMSO, Edinburgh, 1995.

Ritchie, G., 'Ritual Monuments, in Renfrew', C., (ed.), *The Prehistory of Orkney 118-130.*

Ritchie, G., 'The Stones of Stenness, Orkney', *Proceedings of the Society of Antiquarians of Scotland, Vol.107, 1976,* 1-60.

Ross, A., *Pagan Celtic Britain,* Routledge & Kegan Paul, Columbia Univ. Press, New York, 1967.

Russell, M., *Monuments of the British Neolithic; the Roots of Architecture,* Tempus, Stroud, 2002.

Rykwert, J., *The Necessity of Artifice,* Academy Editions, London, 1982.

Rykwert, J., *The Idea of a Town; the anthropology of Urban Form in Rome, Italy & the Ancient World,* Faber, London, 1976.

Sahlins, M., *Culture and Practical Reason,* University of Chicago Press, Chicago, 1976.

Saville, A., 'Orkney and Scotland Before the Neolithic Period', in Ritchie, A., *Neolithic Orkney in its European Context,* 91-100.

Scarre, C., *Ancient France; Neolithic Societies and their Landscapes 6000-2000 BC,* Edinburgh University Press, Edinburgh, 1983.

Scarre, C., *Exploring Prehistoric Europe,* Oxford University Press, Oxford, 1998.

Scarre, C., *Monuments and Landscape in Atlantic Europe,* Routledge, London & New York, 2002.

Scott, J.G., 'Mortuary Structures and Megaliths', in Sharples, N., & Sheridan, A., (eds), *Vessels for the Ancestors* 104-119.

Scully, V., *The Earth, the Temple and the Gods,* Yale University Press, London & New Haven, 1962.

Shanks, M., & Tilley, C., 'Ideology, Symbolic power and virtual communication; an interpretation of Neolithic Mortuary Practice', in Hodder, I., *Symbolic and Structural Archaeology 129-154.*

Sharples, N., 'Antlers and Orcadian Rituals: an Ambiguous Role for Red Deer in the Neolithic', in Ritchie, A.(ed.), *Neolithic Orkney in its European Context,* 107-116.

Sharples, N., 'Aspects of Regionalisation in the Scottish Neolithic', in Sharples, N., & Sheridan, A., (eds), *Vessels for the Ancestors,* 322-331.

Sharples, N., 'Excavations at Pierowall Quarry, Westray, Orkney', *Proceedings of the Society of Antiquarians of Scotland, Vol. 114 (1984),* 75-125

Sharples, N., 'Individual and Community: The changing Role of Megaliths in the Orcadian Neolithic', *Proceedings of the Society of Antiquarians of Scotland, Vol. 51, 1985,* 59-74.

Sharples, N., & Sheridan, A., (eds.), *Vessels for the Ancestors,* Edinburgh University Press, Edinburgh, 1992.

Shepherd, A., 'Skara Brae: Expressing Identity in a Neolithic Community', in Ritchie, A.(ed.), *Neolithic Orkney in its European Context,* 139-158.

Simpson, D., 'Ballygalley houses, Co. Antrim, Ireland', in Darvill, T., & Thomas, J., (eds), *Neolithic Houses in Northwest Europe and Beyond,* 123-132.

Simpson, D., & Ransom, R., 'Maceheads and the Orcadian Neolithic', in Sharples, N., & Sheridan, A., (eds), *Vessels for the Ancestors,* 221-243.

Swanson, G.E., *The Birth of the Gods; The Origin of Primitive Belief,* University of Michigan Press, Michigan, 1960.

Tambiah, S.J., *Magic, Science, Religion and the Scope of rationality,* Cambridge University Press, Cambridge, 1990.

Thom, A., *Megalithic Lunar Observatories,* Clarendon Press, Oxford,1971.

Thom, A., & Thom, A.S., *Megalithic remains in Britain and Brittanny,* Oxford University Press, Oxford, 1978.

Thomas, J., 'Monuments, Movement, and the context of Megalithic Art', in Sharples, N., & Sheridan, A., (eds), *Vessels for the Ancestors,* 143-158.

Thomas, J., Neolithic houses in mainland britain & Ireland – A sceptical view, in Darvill, T., & Thomas, J., (eds), *Neolithic Houses in Northwest Europe and Beyond* 1-12.

Thomas, J., R*ethinking the Neolithic,* Cambridge University Press, Cambridge, 1991.

Thomas, J., *Time, Culture & Identity; an interpretive archaeology,* Routledge, London, 1996.

Tilley, C., (ed.), *Interpretative Archaeology,* Berg, Oxford, 1993.

Tilley, C., *A Phenomenology of Landscape,* Berg, Oxford, 1994.

Traill, W. & Kirkness, W., Hower, 'A prehistoric structure on Papa Westray, Orkney', *Proceedings of the Society of Antiquarians of Scotland, Vol. 71, 1936/37,* 309-21.

Tilley, C., *A Phenomenology of Landscape,* Berg, Oxford, 1994.

Van Eyck, A., *The Interior of Time,* in Baird, G. & Jencks, C. (eds.), *Meaning in Architecture,* 170-212.

Von Franz, M-L., *Time, Rhythm and Repose,* Thames and Hudson, London, 1978..

Watts, A.W., *Myth and Ritual in Christianity,* Thames and Hudson, London, 1954.

Whittle, A., *Europe in the Neolithic,* Cambridge University Press, Cambridge, 1996.

Whittle, A., 'Houses in context: Buildings as process', in Darvill, T., & Thomas, J., (eds), *Neolithic Houses in Northwest Europe and Beyond ,* 13-26.

Whittle, 'Long Conversations: concerning time, descent & place in the world', in Scarre, C., *Monuments and Landscape in Atlantic Europe,* 192-200.

Wickham-Jones, C., *Scotland's First Settlers,* Batsford, London, 1994.

Young, D., *Origins of the Sacred,* Little, Brown & Co., London, 1991.

INDEX